# SHOE

# SHOE

## Jonathan Guinness

**HUTCHINSON**
London Sydney Auckland Johannesburg

This edition was first published in 1989 by Hutchinson Ltd,
an imprint of Century Hutchinson Ltd
Brookmount House, 62–65 Chandos Place, London WC2N 4NW

Century Hutchinson Australia (Pty) Ltd
88–91 Albion Street, Surry Hills, NSW 2010

Century Hutchinson New Zealand Limited
PO Box 40-086, 191 Archers Road, Glenfield, Auckland 10

Century Hutchinson South Africa (Pty) Ltd
PO Box 337, Bergvlei 2012, South Africa

British Library Cataloguing in Publication Data
Guinness, Jonathan, *1930–*
Shoe
1. England. Shoe
I. Title
942.085′092′4

ISBN 0 09 173857 1

Typeset in Monophoto Baskerville by
Vision Typesetting, Manchester

Printed and bound in Great Britain by
Mackays of Chatham

# Contents

# Foreword

Many people in the Costa Brava village of Cadaques remember Shoe. She was a 'hippy', one of a group of them who lived there most of the year. Cadaques is surrounded by Pyrenean foothills, terraced in bygone centuries for a cultivation that is now hardly practised. There are caves here and there, and mysterious shelters made of dry stone with domed roofs; Shoe was known to live a lot in the hills, sleeping in these places. However, when she was in town she was unmistakable. She was good-looking, for one thing, with her high cheekbones, balanced features and bold brown-eyed gaze. She strode like an athlete. Her erect posture made her seem tall, though she is not much over medium height. She looked wild, but only up to a point, because she was in fact quite tidy; her gipsy appearance owed more to the casting department than to the caravan site. Her red-brown hair was never stringy or matted, her shawls and big skirts, her corduroy trousers and rope-soled boots, were clean and of good quality. In the summer evenings she would occasionally put on a simple white dress and look really rather stunning. For gainful employment, she did a variety of things. Massage was what she was mainly known for; she had a number of devoted clients, often women of a certain age, as well as the occasional tourist. Sometimes she sang in a café. Sometimes she made and sold lavender bags. One year there was a puppet show that used to play in the central avenue or Rambla; it was advertised and accompanied by a tumbler in a green leotard, made up as a clown. The tumbler was Shoe, walking on her hands, doing cartwheels and crabs, shaking a tambourine, holding out the bowl for contributions. Salvador Dali was the local celebrity, and he would sometimes invite her, with her friends, to entertain at his parties.

On the other hand, one used to hear strange stories of Shoe scavenging, begging for leftovers from restaurants, retrieving bruised fruit from the rubbish dump. Was she destitute? At times, as I now know, she was, but she never looked it. Among the women hippies, she always stood out. She surveyed the world as if she owned it, whereas the others often appeared fey or absent, their gaze downcast or focused on nothing. Not for years afterwards did I know that all this time she was ravaged with bulimia; the addiction to gorging and vomiting. She despised herself, she struggled vainly to get free, often she despaired. Her stomach lining was being destroyed, she was increasingly often in pain. Even her close friends did not know the full extent of her trouble.

Cadaques, for those who do not know it, is one of rather few villages on the Costa Brava which still looks fairly (not entirely) like it did in the old days. Dali has a house nearby, with big white eggs showing above the garden wall and a brick-built pond modelled on the masculine genitalia; his father was the village notary. I have another, a former hermitage with a peasant-baroque chapel dedicated to St Sebastian near the top of the Pani, the 1800 foot mountain to the south-west of the village. I go there from time to time, in season and out; it is a good place to write in. The mountains around are glorious for walking.

Over the years, I became aware of Shoe. For a long time I didn't even know her nationality; she didn't seem Spanish, but 'Shoe', for all I knew, could have been or Chou or Schuh, or Xu in Catalan. In due course I began to pass the time of day with her, upon which it was obvious that she was English, and from the north, but it was still some time before I found someone who knew her real name.

Our first proper meeting was in an art gallery; I fancy we had exchanged words before, though as will be seen in Chapter 22 she disagrees. At all events I found her riveting. She had studied under a Japanese Zen master, she had sat at the feet of gurus in India and Sri Lanka, she had ridden an elephant in a circus, she had been in prison, in Holloway. My mother had been in Holloway during the war, I was able to inform her; for three and a half years, as a political prisoner. This was a convenient way of attracting her interest, but it was also a kind of test. Shoe's whole charm, for me, depended on her being non-political. I should have been disappointed if she had been shocked, or even (much less likely) delighted, by the fact that my mother was the wife of the Fascist leader, Sir Oswald Mosley. There was no reaction; she didn't even know that Britain does not suppose itself to go in for political prisoners. I liked this.

'I'll send you my mother's book,' I said. 'You can see if Holloway has changed between her day and yours.'

When I got back to England I sent it; she replied, I wrote back, and a correspondence started. 'Dear ear,' she used to write; I was the confidant, like the reeds to which the barber whispered King Midas's secrets. To me, Shoe's letters conveyed the quiet crisp atmosphere of Cadaques out of season, the pale sky, the sharp shadows of the whitewashed houses on the cobbles. They conveyed Shoe. I looked forward to them, wrote so as to get them. It was all very Victorian, but in due course it led to other things.

Ten years on, Shoe and I have three children together; the existence of one of them was unearthed by the *Sunday Express* in August 1986. The newspapers ran the story for a day or two, the greatest shock being expressed by one of the ones which displays models with bare breasts. It was this episode that freed me to write this book, in the sense that one might as well be hanged for a sheep as for a lamb. Anyway I always knew I should write about Shoe one day. She is a treasure-trove of stories, almost on the lines of Ray Bradbury's *Illustrated Man*; but I also see her life as a single story, something with unity, with a certain shape and progression. Possibly I could have turned it into a novel; but the point of it is that it is true. This was the existence that presented itself to a particular girl coming to adulthood in the Sixties in provincial England, these were the opportunities, these the temptations, these the dangers. This was what she felt, this was how she coped, this was how she survived – in real life. To pretend that Shoe had been imagined by me would be to diminish her.

But how to convey the flavour of Shoe's life as I have heard it from her? The idea I have hit on may seem strange; I am going to *impersonate* her. Gertrude Stein did this in her *Autobiography of Alice B. Toklas*. But Stein's idea was to present a picture of herself as she supposed someone else saw her; mine is pretty nearly the opposite. I want, quite simply, to tell Shoe's story in the way Shoe might tell it if she could write.

So from now on, I am Susan Mary Taylor, born in Oldham, Lancashire, on 26 July, 1944.

# 1

# Clogs and Scissors

My father, Ronald Taylor, used to give all four of us children our bath together, until we got too big to fit in. So there we were, sister Wynson aged seven, myself aged five, brother Robert aged three and baby Dorothy, fidgeting and squealing as we waited to be doused down with warm water and Rinso; for it was easier, Ronnie found, to scatter a packet of soap powder over his family than to grope after slippery bars that escaped into the sudsy water. The bathroom was the biggest room in the house. It was our playroom, and also featured a big marble slab where the knives were kept: boners, steak knives, stewers. Sometimes I would push these knives aside and range all my dolls on the slab. I had fifty of them; Dutch dolls, rag dolls, china dolls, Scottish and Welsh dolls, baby dolls that blinked their eyes and squawked. Several had lost a limb. I was their nurse, the marble slab their grossly overcrowded hospital ward. I would be a nurse when I grew up.

The knives were there because my father was a butcher; we lived over his shop in Oldham, corner of Egerton Street and Beaver Street. He was then tall and rangy, with bright blue eyes, at once twinkling and commanding. He did well, partly because he and my mother worked like slaves, partly because he was good at mental arithmetic. This also helped him in the illegal bookmaking that he went in for at one time, attracting to the side door strange lean men in Humphrey Bogart hats with dog-ends clamped to their lips. Ronnie has natural authority and charm; people have always wanted to please him. His wife, his children, those who worked for him in the shop and in due course the slaughterhouse, all were under his spell. The farmers liked his gossip and salty masculine banter. At the markets he had the knowing, rather piratical manner typical of those who deal in animals. The wink was his trademark; to this day he winks a lot. Even the animals who came to be killed seemed to see him as friend and master. As to the customers, in

1

early days when food was still short after the war, everyone knew that
Ronnie Taylor would see you all right for meat. More than once my
mother had to sleep with the forequarters of a steer under her bed, in
case the Meat Inspector called.

My mother, born Anne Windle, had dark hair and eyes and a
rounded figure; she had been a hairdresser. She would stand no
nonsense, even from my father; but her manner was gentle, she spoke
almost in a whisper, and she devoted her whole being to her husband
and children. To free her for the shop, she employed daily women who
cleaned the house and looked after us. I remember two of these, Auntie
Aggie and Auntie Maggie. But it was to my mother I clung with a need
that was a sort of tyranny, especially when she went out at night. She
only did this about twice a year, before she put on a black dress and went
to the butchers' dinners. When I saw this dress and the glass of eggnog
she took to fortify herself for the occasion, I made a scene.

'You're staying here,' I shouted, running up and seizing her by the
dress, 'and you're not to drink that stuff either.'

'And why ever not, miss?'

'Because I'm not having you getting drunk.'

'Drunk! What ideas you do get!'

'And you're staying here.'

Gently, my mother unclasped my hands from her dress. 'Now you just
run along to bed, and if you need anything Auntie Aggie's downstairs.'

'I don't want Auntie Aggie,' I whined, 'I want you. And don't drink
that stuff. You'll be a *fallen woman*.'

This was too much for my father who growled, 'Now, young Susan,
that's enough of that. You get straight up to bed or I'll punch you up
them dancers.' He meant chase me up the stairs. But of course my
mother had to take me up herself and tuck me in, still whimpering. My
worry about her getting drunk was because I knew, from observing my
father, that drink changed people. He was never violent or even
unpleasant when under the influence, but he was different. I could
permit this in him, but the idea that my mother could ever be different
gave me a fit of the horrors.

I wore real Lancashire clogs as a child, though these were by then not
so common as in the old days. All the other children were given ordinary
shoes, but I banged about a lot; clogs were the only footwear that stood
up to my treatment. Once my mother got the doctor in case I had St
Vitus's Dance. All the same, my turbulence alternated with daydreaming. I remember loafing around the little yard behind the house,
imagining myself dancing to a rapt audience in a spangled dress and

tights. But it was Saturday morning, and Saturdays had their own routine which did not allow for daydreaming; so as my performance reached its climax my father called me back to the world of clogs.

'Susan! Our Susan! This dripping wants rendering. Get down to it, gal.'

He said 'gal' rather than the Lancashire 'lass' because he was on an American cowboy kick at the time and liked Country and Western singers. I packed the theatre away in my mind and went into the garage where great slabs of fat from the butchered beasts were waiting for me to hump them into the rendering vessel for boiling. In due course the fat was clear fluid with the rubbish at the bottom. I'd turn the tap and carefully fill the two-pound dripping packets, each with a cow's head on it, and stack them neatly. Some of the fat would spill and make a smooth surface on the floor; sometimes I took a break and slid about on this, a skating star. At the end, of course, I had to clean it up. There was a pungent, sickly smell, which at the time didn't worry me but which now I should find revolting.

'Don't forget the maggots,' said my father when I was done. As if I should forget the maggots. There were these great dustbins for the bones and discarded offal, and the fat that was not even fit for rendering. The hide skin and fat merchant had already taken this away to be made into cosmetics for society ladies and *Vogue* models; I know where the shine on their lips comes from. I poured a bucket of boiling water into each bin, then emptied it down the storm-drain with dozens of dead maggots. As a last gesture to my mother I mopped the step to the yard to make it clean for Sunday, then stoned it with a brown donkey-stone. A voluntary Cinderella, when the mood took me I would slave to earn love. This was not as necessary as I thought, for my parents loved me anyway. Perhaps they did not always understand me, but then I did odd and awful things. At the early age of five I got into trouble for assaulting a neighbour's little girl with an oven-bottom muffin. Once I held a knife at Dorothy's throat to make her say 'bloody' and 'bugger'. There was usually some reason for wanting to work myself back into favour.

For from almost as far back as I can remember I felt a dissatisfaction that at first I could not have put into words. I hankered after beauty; the dinginess of our daily life in the back streets depressed me. Often I would try to look beyond what I was seeing; the patches of damp in my bedroom could be made into rabbits or clouds or trees. I also knew that Oldham would not be for ever, that in later years I should break away.

Most of the beauty I did experience was through St Stephen's Church. We went every Sunday, and Wynson and I sang in the choir. It gave me pleasure to put on the red silken cassock, the spotless white surplice and the little square silken cap for choirgirls. I loved the bible stories, the hymns and their splendid tunes, the dignified interior of the church with its shadows where God dwelt. I was a fervent believer; the beauty of religion reinforced my feeling that it was true. As with everything really beautiful, religion contained terror and sadness; I suffered for Our Lord every Good Friday. I have never quite lost my faith, though I have now seen other paths to the Infinite besides Christianity.

Another worry I had, kept to myself and at first quite inarticulate, was about the butcher's trade. Instinctively I felt that living things should be nurtured, not destroyed. This didn't make me any less energetic or efficient in helping my father, in fact everyone would have been most surprised to know I felt like this.

It has to be said that our family did well from the trade. My father bought up the whole row of houses, and set up a slaughterhouse down the street in a group of stables and workshops with a cobbled yard which we called Cobblestone Farm. It really was a farm, except that it had no grass. We fattened chickens and turkeys there, and there was a pony of Wynson's that she sometimes rode to shows, and a trap for it to pull which we used to bedeck with ribbons for gala days.

In the slaughterhouse I sometimes acted as 'rops boy'. The slaughterer shot the beast in the head, then put a stick in the hole and riddled its brains; then he slit its throat and gallons of blood gushed out. A boy played a hosepipe on the flowing blood to keep it thin; without this it would form great clots and block the drain. The slaughterer slit the carcase down the middle, and pushed the steaming insides or rops over towards me. My job was to pick them up, pull each part away from the slime which holds it together and put it in the rops bucket, separating the large intestine from the small, the stomachs from the throttle (oesophagus). Lights and liver and kidneys stayed in the beast; the rops went to the hide skin and fat man.

We went away every summer for two or three weeks' holiday; in my early childhood to Butlin's camps, then to the Cornish coast. Apart from these trips, our entire time as children was spent in just one section of Oldham: Egerton Street and the streets off it. Egerton Street slanted down the side of a hill towards the centre of Oldham; our shop was fairly near the top, the Castle School where we all went was opposite. Nearby was the cake shop where one or other of us would be sent with the order for Eccles cakes, cream horns and the delicious ginger cake we called parkin. St Stephen's Church was lower down. Off Egerton Street were the steep cobbled 'brews'; I imagine the word is the same as the Scottish 'brae'. As soon as I was old enough I was sent out delivering meat on the black bicycle with its big basket, singing on my way between customers. Going up the brews was hard work, but I didn't often have to dismount, for I was strong. Ronnie used to test my biceps and say approvingly: 'You've a good muscle on you', tipping me a twelve-sided threepenny piece with daisies on the back.

At this time I forgot about being a nurse and decided to be an actress. I was going to go to RADA, following which I should succeed immediately as a brilliant unknown. This idea was quite encouraged by my mother who had, deep down, a theatrical streak. She would practise dance steps and even handstands in the kitchen, giving herself a rest from making her delicious beef puddings cooked in muslin or her apple dumplings. When I was a small child and we went to Butlin's camps, my mother used to dress me up as Marie Lloyd and put me in for children's song competitions. 'My old man said, Follow the van', I sang, carrying a birdcage for the old cock linnet. Sometimes I won a prize. But although the Theatre Royal, Oldham, was just down the road, we never actually went there. We were too busy making sausages. When we did have an evening off my father would take over the kitchen, pretend to be the television cook Philip Harben and create enormous meat meals, bacon ribs with cabbage as often as not. Apart from Butlin's it was to the church that I owed my experience of the footlights. Our Sunday School put on a children's pantomime every year at Christmas time. I graduated from the chorus and the bit parts to be Principal Boy, two years running; once as Dick Whittington, once as Prince Charming.

We had maypole dancing in Oldham every May Day. Most people seem to think that this only happens on village greens, but we had maypoles on the street corners. Guy Fawkes Day with its fireworks and bonfires was another annual celebration. Then there was Christmas of course, with carols and candles and a crib in the church. But perhaps the greatest occasion was Whit Sunday, when the town put on the procession with floats known as the Whit Walk. The Church of England, the Methodists, the Baptists and others as well: each denomination had its own float with a Rose Queen and attendants throwing petals. I was never Rose Queen, but I did do some petal throwing.

The Castle School was a fine old building in black brick and stone with a sense of the past to it; we hung up our coats in the 'dungeons', though the building was not really old enough for them to have been used as such. My father supplied the school with meat. Every morning in the school break I would run across the road to get the bottom muffins with pork filling for the teachers' snack. This made me a bit special; I became a licensed eccentric. The place where I did most daydreaming was in class where my father couldn't interrupt me to give me a job. What we were being taught didn't interest me much; information coming through words alone seemed thin and meaningless. My attention sometimes wandered to the vaulted ceiling, or was caught by the motes of dust that shimmered in a slanting sunbeam. But these meditations could not satisfy my more active moods, when sitting in class was almost a torture. I used to persuade or bribe my neighbour to stroke me on the arm; this soothed me. I determined when I grew up to hire someone to stroke my arm for hours on end. I never wanted stroking during maths, though. It would have distracted me from the worship of the Norse god, Mr Travis. He had fair hair, fine eyes and a beautifully modelled face with an alluring dimple on the chin. I blame his blond beauty for my inability to do sums.

Once, the evening before an exam, I decided to take it seriously. I shut myself away and revised for half the night. I was irritated by the way my family, as well as my teachers, had come to assume that I was touched in the head. I felt they also considered me thick, but this seems not to have been so; I looked again at my school reports the other day and they are not as bad as I remembered. All the same it surprised people when I passed near the top of the class in English and Divinity. I then retuned to my usual ways.

I enjoyed games at school, and was rather good at them: hockey in the winter and athletics in the summer. I used often to win at the long jump, also with the javelin and discus. Unlike most people who are good at games, though, I have never been much interested in how other people do at them; watching or following sport does not appeal to me. When playing a game one must want to win, which means being absolutely serious about it while the game is in progress, but once it's over it's over.

Whenever I had any spare time I was always rushing about, alone or with others, and getting filthy. There were plenty of ways of doing this in the back streets of Oldham. We played hide and seek, tig on high where you couldn't be caught if your feet were off the ground, and of course marbles, which we called 'merps'. 'Farmer, Farmer' was a game with two teams called families and one middleman, the farmer, who determined whether the families could cross his 'field' of cobblestones to take their father's dinner to the mill. This depended on whether they more something green or black, whether they had a pencil or a piece of chewing gum. Without whatever was required, they had to hop across the field before the farmer caught them. Hopscotch was another favourite; I was later to introduce this to some friends in Lebanon. In the summer I collected caterpillars and put them in matchboxes. For there is quite a bit of wild life in these back streets. Down the little lanes we called 'ginnels' there were weeds in the pavement cracks, and on the tops of the walls the decaying cement would sprout elder bushes or buddleia or ragwort. There was waste ground with tufted grass and newts in the stagnant pools. I could never keep a ribbon on my plaits. My mother lost patience when I came home for the fifth time with my long hair plastered in mud; she cut it off and chamfered it, giving me short back and sides and a 'Brylcreem front' like boys had in those days. I suppose I was about eleven at the time. This change made me uncertain of my own image. I kept looking at myself in the glass, finally getting on my mother's nerves so much that she covered every mirror in the house with paper.

This worry about how I looked shows that, though a tomboy, I had my feminine side. I used to play 'ladies' with my friend Elaine Fell who lived across Beaver Street from us. We sat under the drop-leaf table in their sitting-room, pretending that it was a coach and that a prince would come for us. Sometimes we dressed as grownups and stuffed our bosoms with paper. It was terrible to be caught doing this. Elaine's father once saw me with a 38-inch bust; I blushed crimson with shame, and avoided their house for several weeks. It would have been better if he had laughed at me, for I must have looked funny; but all he did was stare in surprise, which I read as disapproval.

Elaine's father taught the piano at the grammar school, her mother was a secretary. Their house was neat and spotless, everything folded and in its place. We, as a family, were not tidy. Coming in from a winter outing, we used simply to dump our coats and scarves in a heap on the two safes under the stairs. I remember my father, happening to need some money from one of these safes, simply pushing the whole pile to the floor; the disorder didn't worry him. My mother kept the kitchen and the shop organized, and Auntie Aggie and Auntie Maggie tidied up after us a bit, but we children were allowed to be fairly chaotic. Elaine was not. Her life and mine have continued as they began, for she is now a headmistress, whereas I . . .

For tea, Elaine's mother provided all sorts of lovely things that we never had at home: crumpets, for instance, and pikelets, and above all sardines. My mother never had a tin of sardines in the house, so to me they were the last word in deliciousness. There were also little touches of daintiness which appealed to me. The milk jug was covered by a piece of muslin with beads round the edge, and there was a special little butter knife on a special little butter plate with a neat pat, not an ordinary knife on an ordinary plate beside a half-pound lump. Their house was decorated with old-world charm, the walls covered with sepia pictures of ponies and girls in Edwardian clothes.

I did pick up one bad habit from the Fell family. In their bathroom was a tin of Andrews Liver Salts. Elaine and I had a glass each, and I found it irresistible with its powerful fizz and clean alkaline taste.

'My dad takes it regularly,' said Elaine.

'What for?'

'Oh, it's good for you, it cleans you out.'

And indeed there on the tin was the slogan 'For Inner Cleanliness'. I still think the insides should be kept clean, though I now know that this is best achieved by vegetable fibre in the diet and colonic irrigation, rather than by laxatives. Not that I, or probably Elaine either, thought of Andrews as having anything to do with constipation; this was dealt with at home by syrup of figs. Often this was needed, for we got a lot of meat, but not enough fibre. Inner cleanliness came over to me as a higher and more metaphysical concept than mere regularity. At any rate I soon acquired my own tin of Andrews, and became what modern health writers describe as a laxative abuser.

When I was twelve, I went to stay with my father's mother, Mary Taylor, in her house on the outskirts of Shaw. This was surrounded by fields, many now built on, which sloped up to the hills behind the town. Opportunities for tadpoling were limitless. She also had a barn, bigger than the house, where one could attach ropes to the beams and perform daredevil circus acts. I stayed longer than had been planned; my parents came every weekend to fetch me, but I refused to leave. They did not really mind, for they saw that my grandmother and I were happy in each other's company, and perhaps felt that she could handle me better than they could. In the end I was with her for about six months, going to school on the bus. Her maiden name was Shoesmith, and it was in her memory that I later called myself Shoe. In her prime she was tall, erect and fierce; she once put two burglars to flight with a rolling-pin, smashing the fingers of one of them. She loved her family in her way, but never showed anything that could be called tenderness. I adored her and would do anything she said. Every morning I lit the fire and gave her breakfast in bed; in the evening we would talk before going to sleep in the bedroom which we shared.

She told me about her life. My grandfather had been a haulage contractor, and a prominent man in local politics. She had six children with him, exactly the number she had always wanted. When she learned that a seventh was on the way she went straight to a dentist and made him remove all her teeth, which were perfectly healthy. She had heard that this would bring on a miscarriage, and this was right, because it did. Suddenly, one disastrous day when they were both already quite old, my grandfather had a stroke at the races and was brought home helpless, like a small child. I remember him from when I was little myself, sitting under the table with his long beard, beaming with happiness but completely out of touch. His death was strange and cruel; he wandered out by himself and some boys threw stones at him. He used to put out his tongue at people and make long ears at them; probably he had done this to the boys, and they had taken offence. In any case he was brought home unconscious, and later died. Until this happened my grandmother had looked after him as well as carrying on his haulage business, making out the schedules for the drivers and keeping them in line as effectively as any man. She had two grown-up sons to help her, but was definitely the boss. She had long since retired by the time I went to stay with her.

Years before, her husband had wanted my father to join him, but he refused. Still in his teens, he became apprenticed to a butcher. Among his customers were my mother's family, the Windles. As a girl my mother used to play the piano, and one St Valentine's day she lifted its lid to practise and found on the keys a saucer with a raw sheep's heart transfixed by a skewer. It was my father's way of declaring his love, and after that they started going out together. However, he wanted to see the world. One day he went to Liverpool docks with his brothers, who were collecting the weekly load of shoddy for the cotton mills. Instead of meeting them as arranged to go home, he got on a boat to Australia to work before the mast, sending a postcard to his parents: 'By the time you get this I shall already be on the high seas . . .' He saw the world for a year or two, including New Zealand and the United States. The thought of Anne Windle drew him back; he returned and set up his own business, at first selling meat from a barrow.

I left school at the proverbial age of fourteen, though only just short of my fifteenth birthday. At the same time we moved house. Mary Taylor at last admitted she was too old to live by herself at Shaw, so my father bought her house and our family moved in. She stayed with us till the end of her life, alert to the last. For a year or so after this I worked for my father in the shop. By then he had gone into the wholesale trade and bought another slaughterhouse, on a grander scale than the one in Cobblestone Farm.

When I was sixteen, I went back to the idea of becoming a nurse. My essay got me through the entrance exam, despite bad spelling; so I was accepted as a 'cadet'. It was not a success. My uniform was too big, my shoes pinched. I was set to work on filing and accounts under a pedantic boss with a clipped voice. It seemed so like school that on the first day I actually put up my hand and asked permission to go to the toilet. Everyone tittered; I was hideously mortified. Asked to count the pages in a book, I got a different answer every time. It was exactly the wrong job for me; emptying bedpans would have been better. I soon gave a month's notice, and was back with my father. He made me learn to drive; soon after I was seventeen I got my licence and was in charge of the delivery van.

Then I went into hairdressing, as my mother had done before me. I was taken on as apprentice at Alice and Ann, a ladies' hairdressing shop owned by a mother and daughter. Alice was the mother; not that she was ever Alice to me, I'd never have dared call her anything but Mrs Satterthwaite. She was a first-class hairdresser but a sour, unbending boss. I'm thankful to her for my thorough grounding in the trade, but she put no joy into it. She put me first to cleaning out the shop, then to shampooing the customers, then dyeing and curling; finally I was allowed to use the scissors. Any mistake earned harsh criticism, but when I did anything right all I got was silence and a pursed mouth. The nearest she ever came to a compliment was 'It'll do'. Ann, the daughter, was different; she became a friend. She was about ten years older than me; good at her job but not too proud to pass the time of day when business was slack.

'You mustn't let mother worry you,' she said to me one day. 'It's just her way. Matter of fact, I think you're picking it up quite well considering you've only been with us a couple of months.'

'Thanks,' I said. 'I'm doing my best.' I was, too, and it certainly beat working in the hospital office. At least I was doing things with my hands. Given time, this was a job I knew I could master.

'Tell you what,' said Ann. 'What say we go dancing tonight, in Manchester? I'm meeting my boyfriend at the Student Union disco, they're a good bunch there. I'll pick you up in the car.'

From then on I often went dancing; the Student Union disco, 'Guys and Dolls' it was called, became my constant haunt. For the Sixties were now under way, the time when, as in the Beatles film *Yellow Submarine*, colour and movement were poured into the frozen lives of ordinary people. That really was how it felt, especially to me with my childhood yearnings for a more beautiful world. I took to sporting weird hairstyles. At one time I had a black beehive three feet high, like a Guardsman's bearskin, which I wore with white winkle-pickers and black stockings; at another my hair was red and bouffant, like a chrysanthemum. I jived like a demon to Little Richard, and revered Elvis Presley of whom I can still do an impression when the mood takes me. Now the pop scene became my scene. I took to South American dancing, flung myself into rock and roll, twisted the night away. The Student Union discotheque was my favourite; I met there people of all nationalities, and told my mother nothing of what went on. Not that a great deal did usually go on. I drank no alcohol, for these discotheques were unlicensed, and no-one had yet heard of cannabis; my boyfriends were friends rather than lovers. I would simply wear out one dancing partner after another until at last the whole group of us came out into the night, grateful for the fresh cold air, happy and tired. My ears were ringing with the music, my body at last satiated with the movement it loved and craved. Probably we'd all go round to someone's digs for a late coffee, then I made my way home and quietly let myself into the house. My parents must not wake to find it was half-past four, for my father, not having been born yesterday, would never believe I had only been dancing; so I was silent as a cat as I slipped upstairs.

After a bit I did acquire one proper boyfriend, a Jewish boy called Walter whose main attraction, at first, was the way he danced. His mother came from South America, and he particularly loved the bamba. He was a designer and photographer in his early twenties. Through him I came to know a number of other Jewish people. In their honour I adopted for a time a hairstyle like Jean Seberg's, cropped short like a helmet and dyed jet black; I even sported a Star of David pendant. Walter's own family lived abroad in retirement, but his friends asked me to their houses and fed me with matzos and pretzels and bagels and gefillter fish. When he came to us the first thing my father did was to offer him a slice of my mother's pork pie, which he ate quite happily, not being orthodox. Walter was the first cultured person I ever knew, and he made me love classical music. I would listen with him to records of Bizet's *Carmen*, or Puccini's *La Boheme*. These operas, and other popular classics such as Ravel's *Bolero*, excited me in a way I had never known before. They brought me in later years to the works of greater masters. Walter was quite bossy; he insisted that when I sat down I should do it gently, like a young lady, with my knees together. Before knowing him I used to plonk myself down yokel-fashion, legs apart, equally careless of the chair's springs and my own modesty. We won many dancing competitions together. There is a photograph of us practising, reproduced here, in which his face shows some of the effort involved in throwing a ten-stone girl around, but mine looks completely still and relaxed. It brings back to me the peace that I found in the middle of strenuous activity.

My apprenticeship with Alice and Ann was supposed to last three years, but after about two years of it I got fed up with Alice's incessant carping and simply walked out, without giving notice. This was wrong of me and caused them inconvenience, but I knew I had not only learnt the trade but become quite good at it. My mother ticked me off, as I deserved, but she admitted that I was ready to set up on my own; so my father bought me the goodwill of a shop in Royton, a couple of miles from Shaw. I was nineteen, and the year was 1963. The shop did well; during the two years I had it, I took the profits from £45 a week to £250, and at the end was employing three other girls. My mother kept the accounts. I found I had Ronnie's gift of making people enjoy working for me; I had a way with the customers as well. Over the next year or two I saved quite a lot of money. It was the only period in my life when, for any length of time, I earned more than I spent; and it was lucky I did, because my nest-egg later saved my life. At the time, though, I was also quite a big spender; a happy little animal, buying Jaeger woollens, Mary Quant dresses and the smartest Italian shoes, and running a battered Morris van with Mickey Mouse on it.

Walter and I started quarrelling; I became less submissive and he, I think, resented the fact that I was better off than he was. I wanted to use my money on him, to smarten up the way he dressed; he was sarcastic about my taste, often hurting my feelings. Partly because of this estrangement, I became restless. Oh, it was a good time for me, and I knew it; but the more I prospered, the more I felt that prosperity was not enough. This was a time not only of affluence, but for some of us also of yearning, we didn't quite know what for. We were, I suppose, a bit spoilt. Byron knew the syndrome; his Childe Harold got bored with the easy life and went travelling. But in Byron's day this discontent was for the upper class. The speciality of the sixties was that it reached ordinary people like me. I began daydreaming as I had in childhood; I even wrote poetry. I still did my job well; not only the haircutting itself and the tinting and waving and shampooing, but also the sympathetic talk with the customers that is the real secret of a hairdresser's success. I could ask each one after her husband or boyfriend, how her child was doing at school or whether her beloved pussycat was on the mend. The money was rolling in. All the same, it gradually became clear to me that I must give it all up and go away. My father too had in his day left Oldham for travel and adventure. Was it the times that set me wandering, or Ronnie's genes, handed down from some forgotten and restless Viking?

And remember Christian of *The Pilgrim's Progress*. He was doing all right in the City of Destruction; when he took off on his pilgrimage, his family thought him cruel and his neighbours thought him mad.

My mother and I went to the cinema and saw *The Sound of Music*. As we walked home, she suddenly said:

'You know, Susan, you're the image of Julie Andrews.'

'Do you think so?' I said, delighted.

'Yes, you've got her face a bit, you've got her walk as well.'

The fact is that I was already identifying with her. I liked the way she strode around the Alpine meadows in flowing nun's robes, full of religion and good intentions, energetic, innocently mischievous and, of course, most fetching to look at. It became quite obvious to me that I must leave home and go to Austria. I knew nobody there, I had not a word of German or any other foreign language, but I felt I should get by. My father tried to stop me, of course. 'You're throwing away a goldmine,' he said; yet his case was weakened by his own record. My mother was more worried, as soon as she realized that my idea was serious and not just another of my fantasies; she needed a lot of reassurance, and no doubt wished she had bitten off her tongue rather than make that comparison between me and Julie Andrews.

# 2

# The Sound of Music

So I turned up one January evening at my sister Wynson's flat in London, planning to fly to Vienna next day. Wynson was living with a boyfriend called Roger and selling cosmetics; I was pleased to be able to spend my last night in England with her, especially as I had never been to London in my life before. My outward resources were my passport, my air ticket and a little money; but inside I had my wild excitement at the adventure, my dreams for a whole future life, vague but intoxicating.

Wynson and Roger greeted me at the door. She looked me up and down. 'So, little Susan.' I am several inches taller, but I was still little to her. 'So you really are going through with it.'

'Certainly I am. When you're young's the time to see a bit of the world.'

'You're mad,' she said, resigned not cross, 'you're stark staring raving bloody mad, you know that.'

'Ronnie thinks that as well.'

'Of course he does, so would anybody with a bit of sense. Taking off into the wide blue yonder. What's to become of you, if I may ask?'

'I'll be fine. Anyway it's my life.'

'Austria my foot,' she went on. 'You're not fit to be let out. You've no plans, you don't know anybody, you can't speak the language.'

'Come in anyway and have a drink,' put in Roger, evidently feeling that Wynson might just as well have been talking to a brick wall. But I wasn't so much a brick wall as a tidal wave, as they were both to learn before they were much older.

We made ourselves some supper, but I was too excited to eat much. Fairly soon after that Roger went to bed, but Wynson and I sat up talking – talking of the past and Lancashire, talking of the future, of Austria, of the wide world. I explained that I was going to the well-known ski resort of Katzenbrunn; it was the winter season, there was sure to be work there. Wynson began to see more point in the adventure; it began to infect her, to fill her consciousness as it was filling mine. Finally it swept her away. At about two-thirty in the morning she suddenly said, 'Sue! Give me a shampoo and set; I'm coming with you.'

This really did come as a surprise. 'You're never!'

'I am, though.'

'But what about Roger? What about your job?'

'Roger can take care of himself, I've had selling lipstick, and anyway I'm not letting you go out there on your own.'

So I washed and styled her hair, she wrote a 'Dear John' letter to Roger for him to find when he woke up, we got a couple of hours sleep. Then we set out for Heathrow at 5.00 am, reaching Katzenbrunn that afternoon. Probably Roger blamed me for taking Wynson away, but it really wasn't my fault. This thing, as the films say, was bigger than both of us.

Our lodgings for the first night were nasty as well as cheap, but we didn't care. Next morning, there were the splendid Alps, not on the cinema screen but in solid reality, and the crisp air made one feel that anything was possible. The first thing we did was to go shopping. We bought frilled blouses, patterned skirts with aprons, white stockings, little embroidered waistcoats. We found work easily enough; washers-up and chambermaids are always in demand in the season. The money wasn't good, but we weren't expecting much. After a few days we found some better lodgings with nice motherly Frau Schell. Then one day I walked into the Elizabeth Arden salon, told them I was a trained hairdresser, and asked if they could use me. Yes; they needed a shampooer. It was a bit of a comedown for someone who had had her own shop to be a shampooer, but certainly a great deal better than washing up, so I took the job. Poor Wynson was less well-placed; her work experience had been as bank clerk and saleswoman, and there was no way of putting these skills to work with no connections and no knowledge of German. In due course she went home.

I was learning German all the time, with the help of a phrase-book and by constant practice; I was quite methodical about it. The language has some tricky grammar, but some of its rhythms and sounds recall my Lancashire speech. It is the only foreign language I have really learnt, and I've since forgotten a lot of it. It is strange how well I have got by without languages. True, a lot of people all over the world know some English, but even so I have often had to make myself clear to people who knew none; in France, Italy, Turkey, North Africa, Lebanon, Greece and so on. Spanish I really ought to have learnt, having lived in Spain for years on and off; I can understand it but not speak it. Japan was the most difficult place for communication, yet even there I managed. One does it by gestures, by pointing, by smiles, by picking up one or two key words. I never had to go as far as the Spanish lady who finally scored some eggs from an English grocer by clucking like a hen and pretending to lay one.

It was in Katzenbrunn that I first suffered from my digestion, paying the price for my laxative binges when I was growing up. Frau Schell used to give me a lot of dumplings: Knoedel. They were cheap and, I must say, delicious. She didn't provide a midday meal, so for this I usually had Semmel mit Leberkaese, rolls with liver pâté. The trouble was that both Knoedel and Semmel were extremely binding; I became so badly constipated that on one occassion I had to call the doctor in the middle of the night.

But my diet was about to change for the better. One good-looking blonde I shampooed turned out to be a princess, who lived in a *Schloss* up the hill with her brother. She must have been smitten with my shampooing, because soon a handsome uniformed chauffeur turned up.

'Have I the honour of speaking with Fräulein Susan Taylor?' He asked.

'Yes,' I said, wondering what on earth was coming next.

'I am employed by the princess, who has detailed me to ask you whether you would consider coming to work at the *Schloss* as a maid.'

'I might be interested,' I said. 'Could you tell me more?'

It turned out to be an offer I couldn't refuse. The wage was hardly more than they paid me at the salon, but board and lodging would be provided, so I should be much better off. The living conditions, too, sounded good; I would have a little room to myself, and even the use of a car when the employers were not needing it. When I learned that apart from all this the job included the use of day and evening dirndl costumes, the hills were again alive with the sound of music, and Baron von Trapp seemed just over the horizon. The evening costume was a particularly fetching number in gold brocade with patent-leather shoes sporting silver buckles.

The *Schloss* itself had been built around 1900, so was not old; but it had plenty of antique furniture and stags' heads to give it atmosphere, not to mention zebra skins and other trophies of big game hunting. The staff included Frau Anna the cook, Frau Julie the housekeeper, Frau Schmitz who did nothing but washing, Frau Huber who ironed all day. There were also Helmut the chauffeur and Fritz the gardener. Now and then there was another semi-permanent maid taken on like myself, and extra people were hired when there were big dinner parties, as happened quite often. On the whole the work was manageable, for I never minded hard physical labour; the late hours were the worst part. I remember nursing my feet, swollen with all that standing, in a tub of warm water before going to bed well after midnight. My main shortcoming was in washing up the princely glasses; these were priceless, monogrammed, and unfortunately thin as test tubes, so one or two came to pieces in my hands before I learned how to treat them. Also, never having been out of Oldham and Shaw, there were aspects of the high life I did not know about – fingerbowls, for instance. At my first dinner party I was told to put rose petals in these glass bowls and take them round. What nobody thought to tell me was that besides rose petals the bowls were supposed to contain water. So as the barons and counts and their ladies absentmindedly dipped their fingers in the bowls, they found them dry. But I was considered a good sort on the whole, if a bit scatterbrained, and the princess told me I looked well in the costume.

For a month in the spring, the princess and her brother let the *Schloss* to a grandee of the London catering trade for a houseparty of tall and titled English people, whom he entertained at a standard of luxury such as I have never seen before or since; far higher than that of the princess. He brought over the chef from his establishment in London, an elegant cockney called Vincent who when off duty wore the same sort of tweeds as the men guests. Nearly all the food was flown in, because neither Vincent nor his employer would trust any dealers but those they knew in London. The host was pernickety; anything that fell below perfection went straight back to the kitchen. His eye had that dead look I later associated with certain prison wardresses of whom I used to wonder, as they railed at me for some minor fault, just what it might be like to be someone to whom such trivial things meant so much. Coffee that was less than scalding drove my temporary employer mad; I remember one lot coming back that on reaching the kitchen was still far too hot for me to drink. Vincent was accustomed to being scolded for trivial shortcomings; he was too good at his job, I think, ever to be guilty of serious ones. Far from minding this treatment, he really rather liked it because it showed that his work was noticed, therefore valued. Vincent's attitude spread to the rest of us; we all took more trouble than usual, and enjoyed doing so. I was in rather a special position, interpreting between Vincent and the rest of the staff and sometimes called in by the boss, or one of his guests, so as to make themselves understood. Once some of them went to an old fortune-teller in the town, and took me along to translate what she predicted about their lives and loves. Vincent got the idea that one particular guest, staying without his wife, had taken a shine to me. He apparently owned one of Britain's most famous businesses. I did quite like him. He was not as tall as the others; he had jug ears, a funny hangdog expression, green eyes like grapes, and a mouth that you would call mobile if you were kind or slack if you weren't. He was said to be a good skier. He chatted with me in the corridors, intrigued to find that this maid in a dirndl costume, working in an Austrian Schloss, turned out to be English. Vincent became impressed with me because of this imaginary conquest.

'You could do what you like with him, honest. Trust old Vincent, I've got eyes in my head.'

'Nonsense,' I said. 'Anyway he's too old, must be thirty-five if he's a day.'

'Bless you! That's not old. Fact is, he's spotted that you've got class. It takes one to know one.'

'Class? Me? Don't talk so daft.'

'Yes, you've got class all right. I know what I'm talking about; I've seen more society women than you've had hot dinners. You need a Pygmalion.'

'A pyg-what?'

'A Professor Higgins, someone to dress you properly and cure that accent. You could hang out with the highest in the land.'

Well, I enjoy a compliment as well as the next girl, but this was never quite my sort of daydreaming.

I stayed a whole year in the *Schloss*, seeing all the seasons. The high summer was when the meadows were full of flowers; it was also when the *Herrschaften* had their breakfast by the swimming pool below the *Schloss*, and I had to carry down the heavy trays. On my days off there were tea-dances, skating and evenings in one or other of the *Bierstuben* which are the Austrian equivalent of pubs. I went home for a week or two at Christmas. When I came back I met my man: not Baron von Trapp or Professor Higgins, no such luck. I shall call him Rob Roy.

He came into a *Bierstube* where I was with some friends on my night out, and caught my eye at once because he wore an antique red officer's jacket. Old army uniforms were fashionable at that time on the King's Road. Victorian damsels used to go for a uniform; it had the same effect on me, especially as I had come straight from Lancashire to Austria so hadn't seen anyone else dressed like that. But it was Rob Roy himself who kept my attention, once attracted. His dark hair set off his pale, lean, handsome face under its wide forehead; his body was obviously athletic, and there was a power in his hazel eyes. I was later to discover the strength of his peasant's hands, his practical and mechanical skills; also to find out about his old Scottish family, his good education.

I watched him as he sat down with his group at the next table. The rest of them seemed to be a lot of scruffs; when one looked closely at that uniform, so was he. But there was something about the practised way he rolled his large brandy round in the glass, warming it in his hands and savouring it, which made him stand out from the others. Then I caught his eye, and we talked across the space between our tables.

'You're English,' he said.

'English as roast beef,' I confirmed.

'English, dressed as an Austrian, speaking German. How's that?'

'I work in the *Schloss* up the hill.'

His party and mine joined up, bought each other drinks, talked in English and German; but he and I sat next to each other and soon started a conversation apart from the others. He had just hitch-hiked from India, and he spoke of the gentle Hindu religion, the teachers and devotees, of his own seeking for the special states of mind that might bring enlightenment. We danced together.

Quite soon he became the centre of my world. We made no date that first evening – one didn't make dates with Rob Roy – but I went to Haus Loeffler, the run-down lodging house where he and his friends were staying, and he showed me some of the things he had bought in India: fabrics, carvings and pots. I had never seen anything like them. We talked till about three in the morning. He said, 'You'll write a book one day.'

'Me? But I can't spell, can't write at all.'

'Yes you will,' he said. 'I can see it, it will be all about Lancashire and your life.'

We did not make love that time, but as I walked home through the snow the cold air and the white night sent my consciousness soaring like a firework.

Haus Loeffler, some way out of town, was the classic cheap Austrian pension for ski-bums. Frau Loeffler, the landlady, was about as different from Frau Schell as can be imagined. Semi-detached from her doctor husband, she had long red hair and a face that was still attractive; she drove around in a Porsche convertible. No questions were asked at Haus Loeffler, and anything went. The ski instructors came for wild and lecherous parties with the tourists. Sometimes the guests were packed in four to a room; one of the nice things about Frau Loeffler was that she never turned anyone away. I began spending too much time there, neglecting my duties. I got to know Rob's friends. There was Ben the Wino, who got through a gallon of wine every other day and knocked himself out for twenty-four hours; then a day of skiing prepared him for the next binge. There was a melancholy Canadian, the Alan-a-Dale of the group, who strummed the guitar and sang folk songs or Bob Dylan numbers. There was Fiona with the posh voice; nowadays one would call her a Sloane, but she was rather a good sort. She had this class affinity with Rob, although neither fancied the other; it gave him away as surely as his skill with a brandy glass.

Rob was the catalyst, the vortex of the scene; where he was, everything bubbled. Haus Loeffler steadily filled with more of his friends and hangers-on. He introduced me and some of the others to drugs. What a bald, brutal statement! It is true, but put like that it is very misleading. He was quite innocent; he would not have known a pusher from a stocking salesman. What he really introduced us to was something called Romilar, a cough mixture which contained morphine. One needed a whole bottle to get high on, but one certainly got high, and the rest of the mixture never seemed to do any harm. It was all part of this confused idea he had, and passed on to me, that one should seek enlightenment through altering the consciousness. Dr Timothy Leary's doctrine, though I don't recall anyone at Haus Loeffler mentioning the name. It was an idea that was around.

The first time Rob fed me a bottle of Romilar I returned to the *Schloss* completely spaced out. Frau Julie set me to scrub the hall floor, something I usually did in twenty minutes or so; and was astonished to come back after an hour and find me carefully concentrating on three particular tiles, having ignored all the rest. Once I stayed out all night, for which I was quite naturally told off. But life at the *Schloss* had become irrelevant; I gave a week's notice. My colleagues were sorry to see me go, for I was a good pair of hands; the princess was openly horrified. She shrewdly suspected the sort of company I was keeping and was aware of what it might lead to. A kind employer, she had come to like me, but she knew that I could not be saved from myself.

I took up residence in Haus Loeffler: entirely at my own initiative. If I'd waited for Rob Roy to invite me, I'd still be waiting. Soon I was sharing his bed, though his main interest in me was as a companion in drug taking. We did sometimes make love, but often we were either on a high, when sex seems unnecessary, or on a low, when one doesn't feel like it. I was deeply in love with him, the first time I have ever been in that state. I loved his marble, hairless body, his sculptured legs which tapered down to thoroughbred ankles; I loved his great size twelve feet and his big hands. I also loved his generosity, his charm, his Pied Piper attraction for others.

Rob Roy was the opposite of the Professor Higgins that Vincent had advised me to find. He made me unlearn a lot of the refinement I had picked up from Walter. He taught me to blow my nose without a handkerchief, how a sharp flip rids one's hand of the snot – the North Indian method, as I was later to discover. I also copied his bohemian attire, or at least adapted my style to his. I had a pair of grey and white pinstripe trousers made with bell-bottoms to go with the British Navy surplus trousers he wore. I swapped some of my 'straight' clothes with Frau Loeffler for a blue cape; I had my hair frosted and streaked with white, and got some dark granny glasses with small round lenses and silver frames. In this outfit I came across the princess.

'Susie!' she cried. 'I hardly recognize you. *Was ist mit dir?*'

'I'm fine,' I said. 'I hope all's well at the *Schloss?*'

We chatted pleasantly, but I could see she was worried about me. As a matter of fact I was on my way to the chemist to buy a dozen bottles of Romilar; this was one of my regular errands for Rob Roy. I think the lady in the shop assumed I worked in the local hospital, at all events she never asked questions. Rob would then distribute the bottles to all of us, one complete one each; he himself would sometimes take two.

Getting high is an experience that, these days, I would just as soon not have had; no-one ought to run the risk of deadly addiction. We were, I now realize, silly young idiots. All the same it was at times rather marvellous, especially as I was doing it with someone I loved to the point of obsession. It took about forty-five minutes to go under, then the visions came. Once Rob Roy turned into a waterfall. Another time we were walking in thick, palpable fog, reminiscent of the nightmare when one can't walk quickly enough, except that it was somehow comforting and sustaining. Then I remember everything changing colour, becoming drained of colour, pale pastel. After some hours in this space one would begin to come down, shivering and shaking. This was horrible. When Rob Roy did it I used to say he was 'catharting'; he would look crazy, shake his head violently, writhe around the floor. Taking drugs wasn't all we did; Rob and most of the others went skiing during the day, and we did a lot of dancing, especially at the tea-dance place which opened at 5.00 pm. Rob enjoyed my dancing, which made up to him for what he thought of as my paranoid shyness.

One day Rob ran out of money. 'I need someone to come with me to London,' he said.

'I'll come, if you want.'

'We'll have to hitch, of course. Ever done that?' he asked.

'Never in my life,' I said, 'but I'll learn. What's the idea?'

'Well, I need to see my trustees to get some money from them.'

'Oh yes, the Trustee Savings Bank. I've got an account there too.'

'No,' he said, 'nothing to do with that. Trustees are people appointed by the family to look after my money. It's better to get there and see them myself, rather than beg money from here.'

'So they'll think you're more in control, I suppose.'

'Just that. Then I'll buy a lorry and we'll drive to India in it.' I'm certain he said *we* would drive to India.

We got to London without trouble. The technique of course was that I thumbed the lift, seeming to be a young girl on her own, then when the car or lorry had stopped Rob would appear from behind a hedge. Our only expense was the Channel steamer. When we arrived, Rob went to a call box and rang his chief trustee, and we both got on the Underground and went to the City. He didn't change his clothes or wash, but went in just as he was, looking like a tramp in his great broken boots with their soles flapping. We went to a bank, not one I'd heard of but it looked impressive. The uniformed doorman was too well-trained to show surprise at how we looked, but showed me into a waiting room where I stayed for a bit, not reading the *Investors Chronicle*. Then Rob came in looking pleased; he was rich again. I too got some money, by selling one or two things such as a mink tie my father had given me, and drawing the interest that had accrued in the Trustee Savings Bank; the capital was for emergencies only. Rob then took me to a place where they disposed of old army lorries; he really wanted a Red Cross one, but there was none available, so he settled for an ordinary khaki ten-tonner. He parked it in Cheyne Walk; this would not now be possible. We lived in that parked lorry for the next five days and spent money in the King's Road. We splashed out on clothes and bought records, including everything the Beatles had produced – Penny Lane, Strawberry Fields Forever – so as to renew the repertoire at Haus Loeffler. One day we did something stupid. Rob Roy had heard that the cold cure Contak contained something that would get one high; this turned out to be untrue. What is more, Contak releases its contents into the body over a period. So when we each took a whole packet of twenty, we were sick not just once; we faced two days of hideous nausea and vomiting. After spewing in the street we would huddle together in the lorry, moaning like little wounded animals. When we were well again we started back for Katzenbrunn, taking turns at the wheel; we were there in two days. We all danced to our new records, and Rob gave away his London purchases, a king distributing largesse.

Then late one night, at a crowded party, he came up behind me and said he was leaving, getting a bus in ten minutes. Spring had arrived, he explained, and the snow was thinning; he had outgrown this scene. No talk of taking me; he was headed for London and then for India. It was a shock, all the worse for being completely unexpected; but I knew better than to complain. I carried on inertly at Haus Loeffler without him, getting more and more hard up; Frau Loeffler let me stay on free for a time, in exchange for scrubbing her floors. I did get a letter from Rob saying he was with a friend in Ladbroke Grove, giving an address there. Clearly it was time to move. I wanted to get to the East. I packed my huge sailor's kitbag and started hitching; first to Vienna, then through Yugoslavia and Greece. I was rarely alone, for in those days there were plenty of people on the hitching circuit to team up with. In Yugoslavia I travelled in a sheep lorry full of droppings; it was divided into caged layers, so that it was impossible to sit upright. Then, early one golden morning, from the cab of another lorry, I saw the dome of the Blue Mosque. I was at Istanbul.

# 3

# President Bourguiba's Guest

At the doss-house I was shown into a room with eight beds, most of them, at ten in the morning, still occupied. One tall fellow was sitting on his, rolling queer greenish stuff into a thin cigarette. He got up to greet the newcomer.

'Hi,' he said, and he was American. 'I'm Hank. Where you from?'

'I'm Sue,' I said, 'from England.'

'England. Yeah, well, great to know you, Susie. This is Chuck and this is Sam, you'll meet the rest of the guys when they wake up. Some of us are on sabbaticals, some of us like dropped out, I guess. Chuck and I are from Harvard. Sam's from Yale.'

'What's it like here?'

'Gee, like wild, man. Istanbul's just great.'

He had got his cigarette alight by now, after several false starts, and took a long, slow drag at it with his eyes closed. Sighing, he handed it to me. Obviously I was supposed to do the same, so I did. The taste was surprising: herbal, something like the smoke from a spring bonfire with a lot of fresh weeds on it, or silage before fermentation, but actually like nothing else.

'Hey,' I said, 'what is this? It's not like tobacco.'

'Why, this your first joint? This is best quality Acapulco gold marawanna. Yes, ma'am. Hand it on to Chuck.'

It was pleasant, and I took several more drags before the group of us wandered on down to the pudding shop for breakfast, yoghourt and dates and pitta bread. I was not much affected by that first smoke; perhaps it heightened my sense of well-being in the cheerful sunny streets of unpretentious yellow old houses.

My new American friends were fairly weird; they all seemed hypnotized in some way. Every one of them was on his way to somewhere else; from time to time one would leave, his place to be taken

24

by someone quite similar. They were permanently stoned; and soon I became like them, though less passive than most. I saw the sights of Istanbul, which none of the others seemed to bother with; the Blue Mosque, Santa Sophia, the harbour on the Bosphorus with its bedraggled pelicans. At one time I became paranoid, thought that everyone was looking at me. Then I got the urge to draw; I bought a large supply of white paper and drew with coloured crayons. Shapes and patterns and swirls and swelling life in abstract maelstroms. Eyes. I drew and drew and drew. I felt that cannabis made me creative, that if everybody took it, they would be creative too; I became an enthusiast. One day outside the pudding shop I was approached by a Turk who drew from his robes a fat packet.

'Hey, this best Lebanese hash, you want to buy? I sell for £15.'

I felt it; it was lovely and heavy. Why, it would supply me for a year! I made a quick calculation; I could just about manage it.

'I'll have it. Wait here till I get the money.'

When I got back to the dormitory with my purchase, I opened it. The packet was full of powdered cement. It may be that God was warning me. If so, unfortunately I paid no attention, for a day or two later I bought 55 grammes of the genuine stuff for a couple of pounds, and put it in a small black vanity case, embroidered in petit point, that Ronnie had given me.

Soon after this I left Istanbul, planning to go to Beirut. I took to the highway, stuck out my thumb, and the luck of the Gods was with me. A blue Mercedes drew up, inside which was a kindly German couple headed for Beirut, and they took me and my sailor's kitbag all the way, taking two days. They even paid my hotel bill for the night of the journey.

I was not long in Beirut. I checked in at a cheap hotel near the harbour, and got talking to people, and it turned out that a ship on which one could travel, deck class, for almost nothing was leaving next day for Tunis. The ship was crowded, dirty and insanitary; the lavatories were awash with urine, and the only way I could stand them was with the aid of a joint. After a couple of days of this we reached Tunis. I smartened myself up as best I could and walked off the ship looking quite fresh in my Marks and Spencer shirt and blue jeans. It may have been my wholesome look that made the customs man single me out; I certainly had the impression that he liked the look of me, for he smiled happily. He went straight for my handbag.

'You open,' he said, and I did so, but he looked at me more than at its contents. Then he found the vanity case.

'You open,' he said again, still smiling. I had a surge of fear, but could only comply. Naturally, being a Middle Easterner, he knew at once what he had found.

'Hashish, missy,' he said.

I nodded. We stood for a few seconds looking at each other; I too was foolishly smiling. Then he beckoned, and a number of police came up. Before I knew it I was in handcuffs. They marched me to the police cells on the docks, and soon I was alone in a cell with my luggage. They kept me there two days; it was a hot June, and the flies were annoying. I spoke to no-one; there was no-one to speak to. Twice a day a man in uniform appeared with a meal of bread, water and fruit.

Then I was taken in a car to the big prison on the outskirts of Tunis. I caught a glimpse of barbed wire entanglements on high walls, and towers like minarets with armed sentries. I was measured all over, quite impersonally, by strange brown men. I was escorted into a vast dim dungeon with narrow windows high up, and shown the hessian floor-mat that would be my bed. There were about fifty women there. Soon after I settled down I began to itch, first in one place, then in more, then all over. I began scratching. Itch, itch, scratch, scratch. All the time I stayed in that place I was itching; that and the fierce June heat dominate my recollection of it. There were fleas, bugs, lice, mosquitoes; each made its characteristic bite.

After my first orgy of scratching I could look round and study my fellow inmates. They were of all ages; little old ladies, young girls, women of every age in between. They were also of all shades of colour from Tunisian beige to Senegalese ebony, for as I later learned this was the women's prison that still served most of what had been French North Africa. Quite a few had babies with them. I was the only European, and as such a matter of curiosity; they seemed to think of me as the Great White Wonder, and though I spoke no language that they could understand, many of them were very kind to me. We were let out daily into the yard for about ten minutes for exercise, and to wash our things. I liked to use this time for sunbathing, and when they realized this, some of my kind friends would do my washing for me, absolutely 'for love' as there was nothing I could give in return. They thought sunbathing rather mad; the sun, to them, was something from which one should be protected with yashmaks and veils and flowing robes. Perhaps they were humouring me.

Meals were always the same. Twice a day we queued with our bowls to have them filled with watery soup containing a few mutton bones and olives and some potato, and were also given a piece of pitta bread hard as a weapon which was inedible until soaked for a while in the soup. After my first supper, I was about to throw away my olive stones. My neighbour gestured to me, pointing to the stones; if I didn't want them, could she have them? I gave her them, she put them with a little pile she had. Later I saw her rubbing these stones against the floor; others did this too. It was a favourite prison occupation. If one rubs an olive stone long enough, a soft core appears which is easily removed, leaving a hole, and the stone becomes a smooth polished bead ready for stringing. It is a long, laborious task, but in prison there is plenty of time, so my neighbour and the others made worry beads to sell when they got out. I came to like this neighbour of mine, though she did foam at the mouth from time to time.

Sanitary arrangements centred on the open drain that ran along one side of the room. We defecated in the righthand corner and put the bones from our soup in the lefthand one. Menstrual pads were piled in the centre, popular with the flies and giving off a faint smell of coagulated blood. Every day we were awakened at 5.00 am and each of us grabbed a wet sack to wash her own floor space. Then we shook out our straw mattresses. There was a good spirit of helpfulness in these tasks; the strong helped the weak, the competent helped the incompetent. Finally we took it in turns to mop the whole place with a filthy brown towel that two of us would pull along the floor, running backwards without stopping.

There was one enormous black woman, pig-ugly, with great long arms that hung almost to the floor. In my mind I christened her Queen Leer because of her expression, or the Orang-Outang because of her shape, though her colour made her really more like a gorilla. She was what in English prisons would be called a trusty, or in concentration camps a *Kapo*; expected to keep order in return for privileges. Her diet was quite different from ours. At each mealtime a wardress would serve her a four-course repast, which she never shared with anyone but ate with much slurping and grunting. She used to swagger around, swinging a leather belt with which she would sometimes lash out accurately at someone who had annoyed her, or administer a flogging. She would break up a riot by seizing someone by the hair, or sometimes even two of them, one in each of her huge hands; she would pick them up and swing them round, to the accompaniment of bloodcurdling screams, after which she would wade in with her belt. She was brutal, but some arrangement to keep order was required; fifty women in a confined space will quarrel, have hysterics, sometimes come to blows. She never touched me, though she sometimes came and stared. I can still hear in my mind her shout of '*Yezi!*' when some of the women started caterwauling. I suppose it meant 'silence', at any rate it usually shut them up; and when it failed she would use her belt.

There was one group in the room which never gave trouble: five black-robed bedouin women who crouched all day round a carpet they were making. I would sometimes watch them, fascinated by their quiet skill. What could have made anyone lock them up? Come to that, what were any of the women in for? Without a common language they could not tell me their stories, but we did talk by signs. A number of them opened their mouths and pointed into their throats, conveying that at least part of their trouble had been drink. As for me, the only French phrase I knew was *par avion*, so I would say this and pretend to fly, meaning that I would soon be going home in an aircraft.

The wardresses wore smart blue uniforms and masses of gold jewellery; one particular woman had a heavy ring on every finger of both hands. They were showing off their femininity and flaunting their status, the difference between themselves and the prisoners, who were allowed no jewellery with them. This was just as well; if there had been jewellery to pilfer and fight over, there would have been more trouble. This happened often enough as it was, especially during the early evening bartering session when we swapped items from our bundles of possessions. Veils, bedouin cloaks, even saris would be brought out and exchanged, resulting in some noisy quarrels.

The days dragged on. I wrote poems on a toilet roll to pass the time. Every now and then some of the women did a dance of the seven veils. They did not strip, but put on a few extra wraps and disposed of them while doing a sinuous dance. Somebody would sing a wailing air, the rest of us would beat time by tapping on our upturned soup-bowls. This started my interest in playing drums and tambourines, which I have often done since. There was nothing sexual about the dance of the veils; it was the traditional local dance. If the dancers had been Scottish, they would have been doing reels. Now I come to think of it, there was no lesbianism in that place at all; English prisons, as I was to learn, are full of it.

From time to time I was called out to be interviewed, either by one of several police officers or by a man in Western civilian clothes who I suppose was the examining magistrate; there was also an interpreter. I looked forward to these interviews as they broke the monotony. It emerged that I was thought to be part of an important drug-smuggling ring run by the Mafia. I think half the trouble was that I was too tidy when I got off the boat from Beirut. I didn't look like their idea of a drugs user, so I must be a courier. When this pattern emerged I began arguing with them in favour of the marijuana habit, so as to establish that my interest was in smoking it, not selling it. One policeman made me show him how to roll a joint, so as to prove that I was myself a consumer. Another official was older and clearly of higher rank, for he had rather a large office. There was a whisky bottle on a shelf, under the photograph of President Bourguiba with his full-jowled face and expression of a man of destiny. I had brought with me some drawings I had done in Istanbul, and I spread them on the official's desk.

'This is what I do on marijuana,' I cried. 'It makes me create things like this.' I pointed to the whisky. 'What does that stuff do for you? What did it ever help you create?' But I am not sure the drawings particularly appealed to him.

Then at last the British consul came. This was a real pleasure. For one thing he was on my side, more or less; for another, he was someone I could talk to and know that my exact meaning would be understood.

'Are you Miss Susan Mary Taylor?' he asked.

I nodded.

'You are accused of smuggling drugs.'

'Don't I know it?' I said. 'But it's silly really, I only had a small amount for my own use.'

'It's a very serious offence, you're in bad trouble. But a good defence lawyer would help, if you can pay him. Can you get any money?'

This, clearly, was going to be the time to use my nest-egg. 'I have got some money in England, yes. How much is needed?'

'I'm afraid it will be about two thousand dollars.'

'What's that in pounds?'

He told me, and I thought, damn it, that's going to take well over half.

'I can manage that,' I said.

He told me what needed to be done, we made the arrangements, and a day or two later he came back. My money had reached him and he had hired a good lawyer, Major Benhattan. My case would come up in about a fortnight. He added: 'I thought you might like these,' and handed me some English women's magazines and a tin of condensed milk, the gooey kind. I was really grateful to him; I suppose experience had taught him what prisoners need. The magazines fascinated my friends in the dungeon, and it tickled me when they pointed to a photograph of the Queen and to me, making it clear that they thought I was the person in the picture. All Europeans must have looked the same to them; Sophia Loren's picture was also supposed to be of me. I ate about a quarter of the condensed milk and it was delicious, but not wanting to make myself sick I gave the rest away to some of the girls with children.

On my way to court I managed to pick a flower; I clutched it for luck throughout the hearing, which lasted all day. I felt my life was on the line, that any long sentence in that prison would finish me off. I had survived six weeks, but wasn't at all confident I could take any more. Eventually the verdict and sentence were pronounced. Major Benhattan translated for me. I was guilty of possession and sentenced to two years' prison – suspended. I was to stay two weeks in a hotel to be named by the authorities, then be deported. I shook hands with Major Benhattan and thanked him. But as soon as his back was turned the guards came up to me and put the handcuffs back on. They had heard 'two years' and ignored the fact that the sentence was suspended. It was a typical Third World muddle.

'Didn't you hear?' I was screaming at them. *'It's suspended!'*

But they didn't understand a word, and anyway they were accustomed to prisoners making a fuss. I was driven back to prison in a police van, measured all over again, and returned to Queen Leer's cave, to my mat and the stench and the sad women. I sat down, dazed and dulled with despair. Some of the women came up and jeered at me: I didn't understand what they were saying, but it was clearly on the lines of 'So you thought you'd get off, did you?' Defiantly I shouted: 'It's a mistake, you'll see! *Par avion!*' – and did my flying act. But suddenly it was too much. I returned to my mat, broke down and sobbed. I had never done this before. Perhaps it startled them, perhaps they felt sorry for me. At any rate they let me alone.

Next day the consul came; he was horrified at the mistake and said he would see that I was released at once. I was taken before an official who did, I must say, have the grace to apologize. Then I was driven with my kitbag to the designated hotel. As soon as I was by myself in my room, I looked in the mirror. I was thinner, of course; but the main change was the spots. They were all over. 'Spotted Dick,' I said to myself. I think I counted six kinds: one for each type of insect, and a couple of others. It hardly mattered, for I was free. I dressed again and went out; my first stop was a chemist to get something for the spots and, more important, to see if I could get a bottle of Romilar. I found one easily enough, and swallowed the contents. This was my last Romilar trip, and perhaps my most excusable. If I'd been a whisky drinker I should certainly have had a few doubles.

During the fortnight before deportation I had nothing to do; unusually for me, I found this soothing. A lot of the time I sat around the Café de Paris and similar places, watching life go by. By the third day, I noticed that a particular fat young Tunisian was always to be seen, a few tables away. Might he be following me? Without really believing this but just for something to do, I settled up and went to another café, to see if he would turn up there as well. He not only turned up, he sat right down at my table, grinned complacently, and took from his pocket a card with his photograph on it.

'This will show you who I am,' he said, in passable English. 'Here, have a look.'

It meant nothing to me. 'What is it? Who are you, anyway? Are you following me?'

'Yes. This is my pass. I am a registered private detective, and I am supposed to keep a check on your movements.'

'That's all right by me,' I said.

'Good; so I thought it would be more interesting if we got to know each other.'

Suddenly it seemed clear why the authorities had ordered this strange fortnight's delay before deporting me. Obviously they thought that, if I was after all connected with the Mafia, my employers might contact me during this time, and they had put this bungler on to keep a check on me. Well, perhaps he was not such a bungler; three days of following me must have shown him pretty conclusively that there was no more in me than met the eye, in which case it would obviously be less boring if he could make friends. He turned out to be quite a nice boy, gallant in an old-fashioned way; he presented me with tuberoses and even took me round his father's factory, where they made photographic films under licence. Finally the fourteen days came to an end, and I was flown back to Heathrow. I telephoned the Ladbroke Grove address that was on Rob's letter, and there he was.

# 4

# The Scene

The summer of 1967 was the time of London's flower power; for hippies, the age of innocence. 'Bliss was it in that dawn to be alive, and to be young was very Heaven.' Wordsworth wrote that of 1789; it is how many of us feel about 1967. It was the year before politics crept in, the year when it really seemed as if we were making a new and more loving world. Wordsworth changed his mind when the French Revolution turned ugly and for us, too, the scene that looked rosy in the dawn became drab in the stark daylight. But that was later, and nothing to do with me.

For the first few days after I came back I was with Rob Roy in Ladbroke Grove, then he moved into his new flat in Cadogan Square while I went to my parents' for a day or two. They were pleased to see me, but luckily asked me few questions. The purpose of my visit was to collect my possessions with a view to moving in on Rob Roy, which I did; terrifying him, no doubt, though he never said so. Life was a transfigured version of Haus Loeffler. There we had been just an isolated group of heads and ski-bums. In London we were part of a great movement, sharing our feelings with thousands of others. We felt a togetherness, a mass fellowship. We really did love one another, mostly as friends; straight people used to suspect us of sexual orgies, but they were generally wrong. If some of us slept around, so do a lot of straights. For myself, I wanted nobody but Rob Roy. We dressed as gipsies or as Middle Easterners or Indians or even in medieval costume; kaftans for both sexes, frilled shirts and tunics and tights for men, flowered dresses and floppy hats for the girls – though the boundaries between the sexes in dress were pretty flexible. Embroidered Rajasthani shirts and Kashmiri shawls were also popular. There were a lot of headbands and beads and bells; hair was worn lank and straight. We wandered round with smouldering joss-sticks, sharing joints and exchanging flowers.

One of the chief places we frequented was the UFO Club in Tottenham Court Road, where we would sway in the rhythms of Procol Harum or Jefferson Airplane, bathed in the ever-changing colours of psychedelic light-effects, deeply united in the brotherhood attained on hash or LSD. We had our so-called 'underground press', based on the American equivalent. There was the black and white International Times (IT) which was produced in the UFO club building; both club and paper were co-founded by our friend John Hopkins ('Hoppy'). Then there was Oz, whose news stories were printed in varying colours across pictures, making it sometimes quite hard to read.

Rob Roy had developed a growing interest in macrobiotics (Greek makros = long, bios = life), the Oriental science of healthy eating developed by Dr George Ohsawa. He was giving thought to what one should eat and where and when, to the correct balance between yin and yang; he was also moving towards vegetarianism. Together we discovered the delights of bancha twig tea, three-year mu tea, brown rice and tofu. There was something called Diet No 7 which was supposed to heighten consciousness. The main ingredients were brown rice and mu tea.

It might seem odd to risk our health with drugs while trying to improve it with diets, but this is outsider's logic. The way we saw it was that drugs were something new to try, so we tried them; macrobiotics was another new idea, so we tried that too. We were, though, less silly than this makes us sound. We took drugs not only for kicks; we did really think that the states of consciousness we reached with them were an aid to spiritual growth. As to macrobiotics, it seemed clear that people ate and drank the wrong things and failed to maintain their bodies as they ought. We also noticed what was being done to the environment, and were among the first 'greens'. People of the future may see this as the most important lasting influence we shall have had.

Many of us were religious, but we mostly went outside Christianity and looked towards the East. People who were into reading read Hermann Hesse's *Siddhartha*, the Sufi Messages, the Essene Gospel, the *I Ching*. The Beatles took up with the Maharishi Mahesh Yogi, the Hare Krishna group paraded down Oxford Street with their bells and shaved heads. Those of us who did not go for these essentially Hindu sects often took to the various forms of Buddhism. We tended to pick and choose rather than go exclusively for one thing; I myself was later to follow, in turn, two utterly different men, the gentle Mahatma Charanand and the austere Zen master, Masahiri Oki Sensei. I had the privilege of introducing these two masters to each other. Later still I was to receive powerful grace from the charismatic Boston priest, Father Vanzetti. All of these I revere, for there are many ways to God.

Then again, a number of us were interested in alchemy and in magic; in the magical history of Britain where the central figure is King Arthur rather than William the Conqueror, the important places are Glastonbury and Stonehenge rather than London. This went with the invented worlds of certain fantasy writers: Tolkien notably, but also others like Lord Dunsany and John Cowper Powys. We spent hours looking at Aubrey Beardsley's drawings, we admired Dali and the Surrealists as well as their predecessor, the amazing Hieronymus Bosch. Other worlds became as real to us as this one, and we felt that drugs, particularly LSD, could help us to know them. We subjected ourselves to new experiences, many of which were bad for us, or against the law, or both. Well, some of us suffered for this, and not all of us survived. Laboratory animals do not live long either, but at least we were our own guinea-pigs.

Rob Roy was on LSD. He and I both took a generous dose just before joining the great Legalize Pot Rally organized by SOMA (the Society of Mental Awareness) and Steve Abrams, an American PhD student at Oxford whom Rob Roy and I knew. The rally followed prison sentences on drugs charges that had been imposed on Mick Jagger and Keith Richard; the sentences were later cancelled on appeal, but the case had made us all angry with the 'Establishment'. Our campaign included an advertisement in *The Times* of 24 July signed by sixty-four well-known people. The Beatles signed, so did George Melly, David Hockney, Kenneth Tynan. Psychology was represented by R.D. Laing, publishing by Tom Maschler and Anthony Blond, television by David Dimbleby. These were mostly showy people rather than solid ones, and there was a shortage of politicians. Jonathan Aitken, the budding Tory, and Tom Driberg, the superannuated socialist, were not quite enough. The advertisement was paid for by one of the Beatles and masterminded by Steve Abrams. It called for the use of cannabis to be allowed in private, and for research into its effects. Four days afterwards, on 28 July, there was a debate in Parliament which led nowhere. Looking back I think the campaign annoyed straight society without converting it.

As to me, I have never liked politics or demonstrations; I suppose my feeling was, and still is, that the way to live and to help others is to make your own space within society rather than to try to manipulate it. All the same, I enjoyed going on the Legalize Pot Rally, especially because it was also my first LSD trip. My memory of it is rather vague, because the LSD began to take hold as we trailed with the crowd through the streets of London. The police were there with their dogs; one of them nipped me on the calf, and Rob Roy took me off to a police station to make a complaint. I remember sitting there in a dusty room lit by naked bulbs; the LSD gave the scene significance and a weird kind of beauty. I made some sort of statement, but the blood on my surface wound, so intensely red, interested me more. We found the march again and continued till dawn, ending at the flat. On the bed, Rob Roy turned into a great grey cat, staring at me with cat's eyes that were also his eyes, alight with an impersonal and godlike power. Then he levitated off the bed and floated to the floor, becoming an ancient Indian sage.

The dawn became a fine summer's day, and I went out by myself into the bright streets. After a bit I was walking eastwards along the King's Road. The colours were gay and sharp in the sunshine. Everyone seemed part of a whole, engaged in one enormous film. There were gentle hippies and extravagant freaks, the smartly dressed and the down at heel, a couple of old Chelsea Pensioners in their everyday blue uniforms; the usual varied pedestrians. I went into Peter Jones and wandered to the pottery department. Instantly I knew that a whole section of this pottery was my creation; my name was on every piece. I stood there in the middle of my handiwork, delighted with myself and feeling I could do anything. I didn't need to draw attention to myself; the shop assistants and customers knew perfectly well who I was, so with a modest nod and smile I passed out into Sloane Square and into the Underground station. I forget where I thought I was heading, but I got on a train. More and more I felt I was the centre of everything around me. Everyone was aware of me, was concentrating on me, but this was not sinister as it had been in Istanbul, it was beautiful and rather touching. In this film for which all London was the set I was playing the lead. The bit part players around me were all, of course, aware of me, but the director – subtle man! – had obviously told some of them not to look at me. I missed my connection, forgot where I was going; did it actually matter where I had been going? The colours around me, the advertisements, the women's frocks, were so fascinating. Everyone loved me as well as admiring me. Modestly, I accosted no-one. Where and when I left the Underground I do not know. I must have taken a taxi, because I spent the night on a camp-bed in the garage of a friendly driver in Windsor.

In the morning I wandered out; the effect of the drug had still not worn off. I found myself in the middle of a street market, idly fingering some garments, and then something really peculiar happened. Everything changed, the colours became sepia and brown as in an old photograph. The man behind the nearest stall now wore braces over his shirt, and he was selling white underclothes instead of coloured tee-shirts. The cars disappeared and there were horses and carts and cabs. The people were dressed differently, the men in old-fashioned suits, bowlers and cloth caps, the women in long dresses; some in shawls, some with great hats like overgrown birds' nests. It was as if I had been suddenly transported back to the beginning of this century. There was more; I had changed as well, I felt like an old woman, that I had been to Windsor before and was familiar with it. I was chilled, melancholic, nostalgic for I knew not what. The effect lasted for less than a minute; the modern world returned and I was cheerful again.

I went into a little café for a cup of tea; there were many people there including one or two of African and Asian origin. I was suddenly full of the feeling Schiller put into his *Ode to Joy*. '*Seid umschlungen, ihr Millionen!*' (Be embraced, ye millions!) Schiller may well have been on a trip when he wrote this; he was an O-head or opium user. His poem seems rather windy and overblown to normal consciousness, but it recalls the feeling of oneness, of love for all conscious beings, which can sometimes be reached under drugs.

Suddenly, on the dirty floor, a beautiful little Indian baby appeared in a white loincloth, and I realized that this was the moment when I had to give my message to the world. My scene, my cue! I jumped on to the table.

'Listen to this,' I said. 'It is the most important thing in the world.'

The dumpy shirtsleeved Italian behind the counter turned from his espresso machine, his wife paused at the till, the customers looked at me. I had my audience.

'We are all human beings! There are no races! We must all love each other, for love is in us, in all of us, and everywhere! Black and white, brown and yellow, we are all people and God wants us to be one people.

'Look at him!' I pointed to the baby on the floor, and he smiled, but I don't think anyone saw him except me. 'There is the sign. You must all love him as he loves you. A little innocent baby . . .'

But he wasn't a baby any more, he was a radiantly beautiful boy in a white turban with a glittering jewel for a clasp. As I became aware of this a policewoman appeared, with two policemen behind. What a brilliant piece of casting, I thought; they looked so exactly right, every detail of their uniforms correct. They also appeared exactly on cue, and the whole thing was so beautifully organized that it gave me an access of pure delight.

'Now then, dear,' said the policewoman.

'Dear!' I exclaimed. 'You are my dear as well, and all these people are my dears, and we must all love one another.'

'Yes, dear, that's quite correct,' she said, 'but now you must come along with us.'

She was right, of course; it was in the script. I got down from the table.

'I've got to go with these people,' I said. 'They are in uniform, but don't worry, they are people just like us. And remember my words.'

They took me to the Windsor Royal Infirmary where someone must have given me a shot of something. I woke up in a hospital bed; there was Rob Roy's impish face smiling down at me.

'So what have you been up to?' he said. The sight of him put me back into a state of bliss, though my perceptions were now back to normal. The police had found his address in my bag. I expect they looked for other things too, but there was nothing. Did anyone test my blood? If so the result was probably negative, for it had been two days since I took the LSD. In any case I heard no more. Rob and I sped off in his open-top sports car back to London.

He was getting the Cadogan Square flat decorated. Soon it was hung with silk drapes; one room was made to look like the inside of an Arabian tent. People came and went; I particularly remember the two girl ballet students, Mimi and Mouse. Mimi would never have been accepted for classical ballet in the old days, for she was a graceful, slim six-footer; Mouse was 4 foot 11. They used to practise in an empty room for a double act they performed at the Arts Club in Drury Lane. Rob Roy and I smoked joints, tripped on LSD, went to be-ins and love-ins. Much of this went on in the parks; Hyde Park in particular was full of people like us in ornate dress, dancing or swaying or just holding hands.

Then when autumn came, Rob Roy decided to make another journey to the East. It was a Tuesday when he mentioned this; that Friday we were on a fast train to Dover with nothing more than rucksacks, bound for Katzenbrunn to pick up our ten-ton lorry in which we would drive to India, picking up other travellers on the way. When we got to the lorry and tried it out, we saw that we should require a lot of luck if we were to get anywhere near India; however, we set out, and soon had all the passengers we could take. Rob had a thousand tabs of best LSD in his pack; he distributed some to our new friends so that they could while away the journey. One cold Sunday we reached Zagreb. I took some LSD, and had a drab trip. The drug enhanced the gloom of the place, the queer supermarkets like warehouses with few goods and no advertising, the people dressed in black and grey. The only shops with any colour were the butchers; the meat, what there was of it, was red and white like other meat. All other displays were some shade or other of dun. Then we fell in with a ballet group from New York, and I cheered up. They were a colourful lot, and no doubt they cheered up the Yugoslavs as well. When the time came to leave and Rob started up the lorry there was an explosion, and the engine went dead. We wrote it off, giving it to a bunch of young guys who were not in a hurry and felt they could make it roadworthy again. We ourselves returned to hitchhiking, reaching Athens after some days of living rough.

While in Athens I made a mistake. Rob decided we needed sandals for India, and took me to a shop to buy some for both of us. For himself he bought some sensible monks' cloister-creepers with tough leather straps well fixed to stout soles. But my mood underwent a reaction against the time we had spent tramping on the road. Suddenly my feminine, dress-conscious side surfaced and I chose a pair of fashion sandals with thin silver straplets, fit only for a catwalk. When Rob and I went for a hike in the Greek hills, these wretched things broke, disgracing me and making Rob think, quite wrongly as it happens, that I was no good at hill-walking.

We then took a train to Istanbul. I was pleased to be back there, to be able to have another look at the marvellous Blue Mosque. But I had to put up with a lot of bottom-pinching from Turkish men. This is said to be an Italian habit, but in my experience the Turks are worse. I noticed the nuisance more this time than when I was in Istanbul before because I was less stoned. I would dodge about as one does to avoid naughty children or animals. They seemed to award themselves points: three if they actually reached the bottom, two for the leg, one for the upper arm which was a kind of consolation prize. My style was not in any way come-hither; I was dressed in blue sailor trousers, woolly pullover and grandma's blue brogues. Round my body was a belt containing passport and cash, and in my backpack among other necessaries was my trusty blue cloak for when it got cold.

Rob Roy introduced the Turks to LSD, giving it to people he met. It was his way of promoting the brotherhood of man. Sometimes they would be soldiers on duty; a night sentry would often be glad to share a joint with us to pass the time, and Rob would give him a tab of LSD to put on his tongue. It didn't occur to him or me that if he had been caught doing this we might have been jailed for life; what happened to me in Tunisia ought to have made us more careful. Anyway we never were caught. We were once or twice chased by packs of night prowlers, and although we always outran them, Rob perhaps began to think that it was better to travel without a female companion. Certainly, too, he had not forgotten the fiasco of the Athenian sandals. One day he said:

'There's a steamship leaving for Bombay this morning. I think I'll take it.'

That 'I' sounded sinister. 'Do you want me to come?'

'Not this trip, Susie,' he said, and it would have been no use complaining, even if my pride had allowed me to do so.

We went together to the harbour on the Bosphorus and, as the boat pulled out, my disappointment did not dominate my thoughts enough to mask the beauty and queerness of the scene, the pelicans perched on the houseboats and the strange dwarfish people who lived in them. All the same I felt my lifeline thinning out, my willpower subdued under that tremendous azure sky. I was passive at that moment; nothing more than an observer. My private sun had gone behind a cloud, perhaps for ever, while the real sun still shone exactly as before. So my feelings had no effect on the world outside, and I might as well relax and respond to what would happen.

Obviously I had to get back to England, and since I had almost no money this meant taking to the road. I got a lift to Athens, which was very crowded, at least as regards anything I could afford. Eventually the receptionist at a small hotel took pity on me, and let me stay in the only place he had available, though it wasn't quite what I first expected.

'I have one bath,' he said, and named a price that was incredibly cheap. With bathroom included!

'That will do fine,' I said.

'You come, I show you.' He led me to the top of the house, then out on to the roof. There, sure enough, was an outsize bathtub, without taps; one could sleep in it, just about.

'OK,' I said, 'I'll take it.'

He fetched a duvet and a pillow, and I settled down, hoping that it would not rain. It didn't and I stayed there a day or two, wandering up to the Acropolis, which I found breathtaking. On a postcard the Parthenon looks elegant. When you get up close its elegance is swallowed up by its sheer power; it is enormous, and you suddenly feel the pull of a dead religion which once embodied for people the whole power of the Unseen. The rocky ground adds to the effect; it is rough and uneven but polished by the thousands and thousands of worshippers and soldiers and sightseers over twenty-five centuries. I then took a boat to Palermo, found somewhere cheap and stayed a couple of days, making friends with an American girl. We went together to the Golden Gate disco. On leaving, we had not gone far up the street when there was a sharp crack and something whizzed by me. I whipped round; a man in a hat, pressed against the wall, had fired a shot, and his gun was still pointing more or less at me. Then a couple of shots came from the other end of the street; my friend and I got down on the pavement and stayed there till the shoot-out was over. I took the first ferry to the mainland next morning.

Over the next few days I hitched through Italy and France and reached Paris flat broke, my only resource a good watch my father had given me. That night I slept under one of the Seine bridges, wrapped in my cloak against the autumn. We were a mixed bunch; there were one or two young travellers like myself, a couple of meths drinkers, some old-fashioned tramps. My companions were sad, many of them, and a bit smelly, but there is a gentleness about the true down-and-out, and I felt quite safe with them though my lack of French prevented conversation. The permanent residents slept wrapped in newspapers on flattened cardboard boxes; this made them look odd and pathetic, but kept them snug. The cold woke me early, and I walked around the city till the shops opened, spending almost my last coin on a *baguette* of bread. Gnawing on this, I continued walking till I found a shop where I could sell the watch. I expect I was given a bad price, but it was enough for the boat train to get me back to London where I was by now not short of friends to live, eat and smoke with, and had access to what was left of my nest-egg; little enough by now.

I found a room in a flat in Beaufort Street, Chelsea. There was Sam, a student from Thailand; an English family of two sisters and a brother, others who came and went, like myself. There always seemed to be a spare room. We all lived independently, sharing the kitchen. Everyone made his own room very individual; Sam's was the best, resplendent in red and gold. We painted, played drums or flutes, listened to records, smoked joints. I hopped from scene to scene, in the flat and elsewhere; I took dancing lessons in a studio in Floral Street, where Lindsay Kemp was later to teach.

It was quite a happy time, but I had this feeling that my journey to the East was uncompleted, that I had to be on my travels again. Also, London felt terribly flat without Rob Roy, for so many places and people there reminded me of him. One day in the *International Times* I saw an advertisement; £11 for a one-way trip to Marrakesh. It seemed an opportunity not to miss, so I answered it. People told me that living was cheap in Morocco, cheaper than London, and that it was full of nice people. It turned out that there were also some very nasty ones, but I wasn't to know that. So I packed my things, and a red van turned up in Beaufort Street. I piled in with six others. The journey took several days, but they went quickly; we spent the nights in sleeping bags. Eventually I said goodbye to my companions on the central square of Marrakesh in the warm November sunshine; I never saw any of them again. I went to the nearest café, and found three blond young men at a table; two Germans and a Swede. In due course they shepherded me to the hotel where they lived.

# 5

# Disaster in Morocco

The Hotel Atlantis was a four-storey building round a tiny patio; all the rooms had French windows and balconies that opened on to it. I shared with four others, paying about 50p a night. All the residents were foreigners, I think; there were people from Clapham Common, Derbyshire and Inverness, there were Germans and Scandinavians. A lot of them were artists who sat around the town sketching, or painted the walls of their rooms with garish abstract designs inspired, as often as not, by amphetamines. The management didn't seem to mind this treatment of their property. People played a bit of music, too; pipes, drums, guitars. Then there were those who studied, perhaps wrote. Everyone was on hashish, or rather *kif*, a milder form of it which came in three-cornered packets, nice and cheap, and was usually smoked in a little pipe called a *seepsie*. People did a bit of this, a bit of that; nothing that had anything much to do with Morocco, but it was all pleasant in a low-key sort of way.

I bought an orange jellaba; this, with my sailor trousers, a cashmere V-necked sweater and Granny's faithful blue brogues with the wedge heels, became my uniform. A little later I acquired a small white lamb skin and lined the hood of the jellaba with it, to make it a bit smarter. Thus attired, I would be off to the square every morning to buy dates and bread, then back to my room where I would paint, or play my drums, and light up my *seepsie*.

At first I made no particular friend, but then Jean-François arrived, a young Parisian. He was very tall and thin, with a big beaky nose like De Gaulle; he wore a black jellaba and skullcap and kept his hair very short. He was bespectacled and scholarly, learned in Eastern religions. He read the Bhagavad-Gita and the Tibetan Book of the Dead, and was on a serious spiritual search. Although I was not a reader, I think he recognized that in my own way I was seeking some of the same things. In fact we came to appreciate each other a lot, and usually went about together. For me it was helpful to have someone who knew his way around and spoke French. We had no love affair; I was still keen on Rob Roy, and I don't think Jean-François was particularly interested in sex with anyone. All the same we became quite close, playing gin rummy or knockout whist and telling each other about our lives. I told him about my marvellous man now in India. At last he said:

'I feel I know your Rob Roy.'

'I'm sure you would like each other, though you're very different.'

'Bring him to see me in Paris.'

'Mind you, he hasn't read as much as you have. You're a real reader, aren't you?'

'It's in the family; my mother is a bookseller in Paris.'

'Well, my father's a butcher, but I don't eat much meat; it's too expensive.'

He looked at me. 'You do very well without meat. One day I expect you'll give it up altogether and embrace non-violence.'

In due course Jean-François said he must go home because he was getting short of cash; the same thing was happening to me, and he suggested we travel together. We set off a day or two after Christmas, arriving at Rabat late in the afternoon of 31 December, 1967. We found a really cheap pension that made the Atlantis seem like the Ritz; I can't imagine when they had last changed the sheets. I slept in my jellaba with the hood up.

Next morning Jean-François and I found we had run out of *kif*, so we went to buy a packet each. Jean-François was approached by a youth of eighteen or so, dressed in sharp European clothes, who said he could lead us to a seller; so we went along with him. He took us to a very old man whom we found seated cross-legged in an open-fronted shop, cutting up tobacco and hashish which he would put into separate piles, then run through his fingers and mix together. Occasionally he would take a sip of mint tea from a glass. In a leisurely, friendly way, Jean-François negotiated with him as he continued his mixing. Eventually the bargain was struck, a modest sum for a couple of packets that would last us some time. We were each given a glass of mint tea and sat there cross-legged, the old man, the young man who had introduced us, and ourselves. After a while we left the shop; the boy came along with us and casually said something to Jean-François, who turned to me.

'He's inviting us to meet his mother for an end of Ramadan party. He says she makes good hash cakes.'

'That's very friendly of him,' I said.

'Oh yes,' said Jean-François, 'the real Arabs, the simple people, are very hospitable. You'll see.'

All the time I had been in Morocco I had never been inside a mosque or seen any sights, let alone a private house, so I wanted to accept; yet I remember saying to Jean-François, 'All right, but let's not stay more than an hour.' My time in the Hotel Atlantis had in a way institutionalized me; I looked forward to going back to our room in the sleazy pension to smoke and paint.

It was about half past six in the evening, not quite dark, and I remember that as the youth led us he paused in front of an open-fronted shop which sold cakes and sweets. A Rolling Stones record was being loudly played, and the shop was decorated with pictures of the Stones. There were a number of men inside it, hanging around. Thinking about it afterwards, I have often wondered if the youth was showing us off to these men? Showing off his wares, as it were, for anyone who might fancy them?

We were led down an alley, then another, then another. We came to a great wooden door, on the latch, which the youth opened, letting us all through. We found ourselves in a yard with many staircases. Our guide took us up one of these, to a door which he opened with an enormous iron key, and we entered a large room in what seemed an ordinary family house; that is, it matched my idea of how such a house would be furnished. There were pictures of people round the walls, photographs of relatives and drawings of Muslim saints, a big low table in brass, cushions to sit on and on one side an enormous bed. It was not completely tidy – I noticed a couple of empty wine bottles – but it wasn't especially disordered. We sat there for some time, talking French. Eventually a man came in wearing a striped jellaba; our guide introduced him as his brother. A few more minutes, and another 'brother' arrived, then a 'cousin'. There was a bit of desultory chat which I could not understand.

I began to get rather impatient; if this was all that was going to happen there was not much point in staying. I said to Jean-François:

'Where's his mother, do you think? We must get this going.'

'He says she won't be long.'

Then a fifth man arrived, a black African, taller and older than the four Arabs. He was dressed in European clothes with shirt and tie, a navy blue mackintosh, black winkle-picker shoes. Under his arms he carried half a dozen bottles of red wine. I still thought the mother was on her way.

Then the little character who had brought us beckoned me over; his mother had arrived, he said, and he led me to a side room. He suddenly put his arm round my neck. I elbowed him away hard so that he stumbled, and strode back into the other room.

'Let's get out of here,' I said, affronted; 'that guy's just tried to make it with me.' The North Country lass was having no messing.

But from then on the gloves were off. Jean-François got up and came towards me; the black man went to the door, turned the great key twice, removed it from the lock and held it in his hand. It was a moment of total terror. A minute ago I had been mildly bored; then I had felt annoyed because this little jerk had put his arm round me; now I was in terror, looking at that dark old key.

The 'brothers' and the 'cousin' took off their jellabas, our guide stripped himself of his European clothes, and there were all four of them in their boxer shorts, flexing their muscles, each with a vile grin on his face showing no teeth. The black man stayed dressed. They were like a pack of jackals looking at a captive deer.

Jean-François said: 'No, please have some respect, can't you see we are a married couple?'

We might have been one; I had a number of rings on, he had one or two as well.

Our guide muttered something back, and Jean-François said to me, 'They want to have you, or . . .' and he drew his finger over his throat.

One of them pushed me to the floor; I stood up again. Then he banged me hard on the forehead with his fist, hoping to stun me I suppose; then made as if to strangle me. I broke away and ran to Jean-François. Then someone slashed Jean-François' nose with a sharp knife; I stayed next to him with the blood dripping on my jellaba, staining the lambskin lining of the hood. At the same time, one of the others smashed an empty wine bottle, brandishing the jagged edge, while another got a bicycle chain out of his clothes and wrapped it round his brown knuckles. All the time they were grinning that animal grin.

I was thinking very, very fast, as one does when the adrenals are spurting. It was aparent that I was with a person who could not have swatted a fly; an aspiring Buddhist, a believer in *ahimsa* or non-injury. Jean-François would be no help in handling this pack of five men. I might have floored two of the little Arabs, they weren't impressive specimens; in other circumstances I should have found their muscle-flexing funny. Still, this would have left two more and the big negro. Also they had weapons: a knife, a bottle, a chain. It was a moment of choice; my body, or the lives of both of us. Twenty years in advance of Germaine Greer it occurred to me that a penis does less damage than a

knife in the guts. I never thought of publishing this brilliant insight in the
*Sunday Telegraph*, but it did save my life and my friend's.

The trouble is, my feelings rebel, to this day. I was telling my story
quite recently to help a rape victim, and suddenly, to my own horror, I
broke down and wept uncontrollably: from shame. For something in me
still feels that it would have been better if I had allowed Jean-François
and myself to be slaughtered, that I am *dishonoured*. The idea that rape is
a fate worse than death lies deep in the psyche, in mine anyway. Dr
Greer will think this most unreasonable, but there are situations where
reason does not rule.

I said to Jean-François, 'All right, they can have me,' and made a
gesture of surrender.

They took him into another room. I undressed and lay on the bed.
Then the first one came down on me. He felt for the place, then just
shoved himself in. It hurt like hell, and his squirming body felt vile, but I
managed to shut myself off in my own space. The George Harrison
number 'Hare Krishna' came into my mind, and I turned my head from
side to side, at first to avoid his stale breath, then falling into a rhythm,
chanting 'Hare Krishna, Hare Rama, Hare Krishna . . .' Then came
number two, number three, number four; they were all the same, brutal
but with a saving impersonality. 'Hare Krishna, Hare Rama.' Head left,
head right, head left. My lower half was no longer human or even
animal; it was just a spittoon, a receptacle for slime. But my mind
fastened on this Hare Krishna mantra, though at that time I didn't even
know what a mantra was. I had a vision, gold orange and red. It was
beautiful and calm. One end of me was being degraded, the other was
elevated.

As the fourth Arab was grinding away, I heard an appalling scream. I
thought, they are killing Jean-François. Then the black man arrived; he
pounced on me fully clothed except for his winkle-pickers, satisfying
himself rather quickly. I thought, that's it then, but before I could move
the first one was back for a second helping, followed by the three other
Arabs. I expected the black to follow as well, but he didn't. He really
preferred men, I think; I later learned that he had tried to bugger Jean-
François, hence the scream, but was unable to penetrate. Presumably he
took me as consolation prize, or to show he was one of the boys.

When not raping me they had been drinking the wine; all six bottles
were now empty. This, possibly, saved our lives, because the four Arabs
were all rather drunk as well as exhausted from screwing me; they were
lying about like spent dogs. Even so I was well aware that we were quite
likely to be killed. I sat up, dressed myself mechanically, prepared for

death if that was what was coming. I felt a great stillness.

Jean-François came in from the other room with the black man and said, 'Susie, I've told this man that our passports and papers are back at the Grand Hotel, and if they don't let us out now there are going to be police all over Rabat by tomorrow looking for us.'

As a matter of fact, the papers were in the white leather pouch that Jean-François wore on a string round his neck. But he had not been stripped; not knowing about the bag, they fell for his story.

Perhaps because he had only had one go with me, the black man was the one with the most strength left, and he was the one who now seemed to take charge. He produced the big key, put it in the door, and turned it once. But one of the others said to me, 'Hey, you've got blood on you! Better clean it up.' Or words to that effect. So he got hot water, a brush, a towel and wiped off the blood; tidying me up gently, rather fussily, almost as if he had been the mythical mother with the hash cakes. While this was going on I had to hold on to my stillness, and so did Jean-François. Any show of hostility, any hint of fear, and we were both done for; I felt this instinctively. When the Arab had wiped to his satisfaction, the black man gave the key one more turn and began to open the door.

As soon as I saw light through it I switched from stillness to lightning speed. Like a panther I shot through it, threw myself down the staircase, darted across the cobbled yard, saw the other door, lifted the latch, out into the street. I heard Jean-François shout 'Susie!' but I was no longer with him, no longer with anyone; I was a panther in the night, free and running. I looked back an instant; Jean-François was behind me, behind him was the black man chasing us; luckily as I looked he tripped and fell, having forgotten to lace his winkle-pickers. But he still came after us until we got to a group of men in white jellabas. Jean-François panted, 'Help! We've been attacked!'

At that point the African faded away. I still ask myself what he thought he was doing, running after us. Perhaps he changed his mind about letting us go; perhaps he hadn't meant to let us go at all, but take us round the back to a waiting car to be disposed of somewhere more convenient, and was taken by surprise when we suddenly ran for it. We continued, running and walking as fast as our panting lungs would allow us, till we got to the main street. There we found a good-class hotel, where we checked in. The clock above the desk told us it was 2.00 am. We were given a big room with bath; a bath was what I was longing for most of all. There were clean towels and the water ran beautifully hot; but when I looked round for the soap there was none. Just when I needed to wash more than ever in my life. Even so, to soak in hot water was a comfort.

Jean-François rang the police. They arrived at eight in the morning; we told our story, not holding back the fact that we had been smoking *kif* in our *seepsies* but insisting that we were in no way stoned or high. The police accepted this; *kif* was against the law but part of their culture, so they knew the score in a way that British police might not. In any case they were friendly and helpful. Later we repeated it all to an inspector at the police station.

'There's been a lot of this lately,' he said. 'As a matter of fact you are lucky to be alive; usually they kill them afterwards. We have found two bodies in the last month, separate incidents, both European women, gang-raped and their throats slit.' He turned to Jean-François. 'You did well to say what you did about your papers.'

'What will happen now?' Jean-François asked.

'Well, we should like you to press charges. Then we could probably get these people. But I must be frank with you; the case won't come up for at least two months.'

'Does that mean we should have to stay here till then?'

'Yes.'

'Impossible!' I said when Jean-François had translated. 'I couldn't stay here for two months except under total protection, and I haven't enough money anyway and nor have you.'

There were more reasons than that why I couldn't go through with it. The whole country now seemed menacing. I felt paranoid there; every Moroccan face reminded me of *their* faces. I had to force myself to stand seeing people on the streets, even in broad daylight. As for the five rapists, I had a terror of seeing them again, even in a police line-up or in court. I felt sick at heart and in need of being looked after; not a normal state for me. Jean-François and I left Rabat at once.

He was very good to me. He didn't say much, but I could see that he was devastated; he felt he had been useless. We didn't talk much about it, but I tried to tell him that he had done well, better than if he had fought. I still think this. We had walked a tightrope; either a show of aggression or a show of fear would have been the end of us, and his bluff about the papers was a masterstroke. However, his shame at not protecting me by force mirrored my own shame at surrendering; neither of us could be reasoned out of these feelings.

I felt wrecked in body and mind. I was in pain, all the worse because I had been celibate for all the months since parting from Rob Roy. Probably my desperate sprint had added to the damage; it was only the flow of adrenalin that made this possible at all after what I had undergone, and now I was paying for it, limping a fair amount. I was also haunted by a fear of having caught venereal disease. Logically I should have been worried about pregnancy, but I don't remember this even crossing my mind, oddly enough. If I had turned out to be with child, this would have come as an appalling and unexpected shock. I suppose I should have coped with it, but I am glad I didn't have to.

We went to Tangier, and Jean-François found a clinic where we were both examined. It was pretty primitive, rather like being in a meat shop. They examined me internally and swabbed me down a bit, pronouncing me all right, but I was in the dark as to whether they were competent or doing the right things. It had to be paid for, too; Jean-François managed this somehow.

In Tangier we went to see an acquaintance of Jean-François called Ahmed, a small man in a colourful coat and a fez who had a wonderful shop, better than anything on the King's Road. He was mad about the London pop scene and had clothes of all sorts including one or two of the Beatles' 'Sergeant Pepper' uniforms. He knew many pop stars as well as the smart foreigners who frequented Tangier. We sat with him and had a smoke. Hearing our story he was sorry for me and gave me a lovely present; an enormous fur coat that, he said, Brian Jones had given him. I felt comforted and protected in its caring folds.

We took a train to Madrid, where Jean-François had friends American sculptors. We went to their studio flat to refresh ourselves and spend the night, and they turned out to be a wonderful group of people. Of course they turned on a bit; we all turned on at this time just as straight people have their scotch or beer. Actually, although I have not now smoked hash for more than fifteen years and don't intend to start, I do think that at that time it was helpful. It kept me cool, helped me hold myself in, perhaps stopped me breaking up.

Our hosts were aghast to hear what we had been through, and kept us there a few days. Then I began losing my appetite. I was not visibly freaking out, but becoming more and more listless, almost autistic. Somebody gave me a small piece of cannabis; I accepted it mechanically and put it in my overcoat pocket, obeying a squirrel instinct. It was about the size of a pistachio nut.

One night a girl said:

'You know, you're ill; you ought to go home and be looked after.'

'I suppose I'd better.'

'If we sent for the British consul and told him everything, he could probably arrange to repatriate you by air.'

The consul came and saw me; after checking my story with the Moroccans he arranged for me to be repatriated as a British subject in

distress. This meant handing my passport in to the British Embassy for
forwarding to the Foreign Office in London; they would hold it until I
refunded the cost of the fare. So, since I was passportless, a man from the
Embassy had to come along to see me on to the plane. At Heathrow I
was taken off before the other passengers and shown into a different
entrance with a customs officer all to myself, a Lancashire man by his
speech. He ordered a strip search; this was done by a woman officer who
took me behind a screen, while he went through my rucksack and
greatcoat. Of course he found that piece of hash in the pocket. It was
Tunis all over again. Again I was grinning defencelessly at a customs
man who had caught me redhanded, only this time I was ill and broke.

'Usual address?' he asked, ballpoint poised over the form he was
filling in.

This was a poser. I couldn't possibly give him the Beaufort Street
address; the flat might be searched, then everyone would be in trouble.
For other reasons, I couldn't give Ronnie's address. I said:

'My family live in Shaw, that's all I'm telling you. No way I want my
parents involved.'

The customs man suddenly changed his tone, becoming much more
friendly. 'Shaw?' he said. 'I've got a brother-in-law plays cricket in
Shaw. Are you anywhere near the cricket field?'

'About a field away.'

'Heard of Dougie Ashworth?'

'Used to be one of my father's foremen,' I said.

'So you're Ronnie Taylor's daughter,' he said. 'A fine man.'

It turned out that we knew several people in common. We both
looked at the little bit of hash, and I could feel him thinking, it's a very
small piece, perhaps we can just forget it; but he decided otherwise.

If I had contacted my father I expect he would have bailed me out,
but that was just what I felt unable to do. I had to face this on my own. It
was partly pride, but mainly dread of telling my parents what I had
been through and seeing the unimaginable pain it would give them; or of
not telling them, of talking to them of other things while my appalling
story was ticking away inside me like a time-bomb. It was silly of me, of
course. I ought to have known that my parents were going to find out
anyway, sooner rather than later. But I was not thinking straight. I
refused to give my parents' address and had myself put down as destitute.

I was taken to a police cell in London Airport where I spent the night.
Next morning I was taken before a magistrate, remanded in custody,
and driven to Holloway Prison.

# 6

# The Kingdom of Noise

Arriving in Holloway was like a re-run of Tunis. Again I was stripped and carefully measured. This time, though, I was given a bath, which was really enjoyable; a break in the continuing nightmare. I was shown into a white tiled bathroom with a great, generous, industrial-sized bath, compared to which the modern plastic stuff seems mean and chi-chi. I managed to relax a bit in that monstrous great bath, even meditate.

Afterwards I was made to dress in a prison uniform. I'm still not sure why this was, considering I was a remand prisoner; perhaps my clothes were not considered suitable, perhaps it was because I was supposed to be destitute. The uniform included a tan tee-shirt, a bottle-green cardigan, and a terrible short grey skirt made for a 44-inch hip. I was 36 inches at the very most, I can't think why they had bothered to measure me. There were lisle stockings with no suspenders, so that they constantly fell around the ankles. Elegant it was not. Then there were the shoes, 'sensible' brown ones in very hard ox hide. They had lace-holes but no laces – an odd arrangement, the sort of confusion you get in prisons and, I am told, in armies. I suppose you can do yourself damage with a shoe lace if in a depressed condition; but then why issue shoes that need them? I had a red star pinned to my shoulder signifying that I was a first offender. Then I was taken to the remand wing where I was locked in a cell, alone thank goodness.

The first thing I did was to write a letter. Not to my parents or to Rob Roy, who I was sure would still be in India; I simply wrote to anyone who might be at the Beaufort Street address, saying where I was and why. It seemed hardly more hopeful than putting a message in a bottle.

The prison was the Kingdom of Noise: pails clanking, keys rattling, shouted orders, every now and then a woman screaming in hysterics or wailing in despair. My wing contained people who were on remand and

51

also some who were serving sentences for all manner of things, from motoring offences to grand larceny and causing grievous bodily harm. There were tarts and child abusers; I think there were one or two murderers. Many of the prisoners were funny shapes; some had gigantic bottoms making them look like potatoes or Jerusalem artichokes, some were rotund and topheavy like turnips, others were cylindrical like leeks. Alcoholism or a heart condition produced one or two beetroots as well. Holloway was a kitchen garden on legs. Hair was worn lanky, usually slightly greasy, hanging down the face or scraped back. But among all this apparent variety there were only two main kinds of prisoner; the hard brazen ones, toughened, barging through their time in prison like armadilloes, and the delicate little butterflies, all limp and hurt and nervous with bitten-down nails. The yang and the yin; there seemed to be no middle path.

It was only at certain times that I saw the others; most of the time I was locked up and left to myself, because as a remand prisoner I had no work to do. In some ways this made things worse, for a job would have given some structure to my day; but on the whole I was pleased to be alone. My cell had an iron bed in one corner with two army blankets, a chamber-pot in the other, bars on the windows, broken glass. The floor was of stone, heavily stained. There was central heating, but the wind whistling through the broken pane made it cold, the time of year being mid-January.

Pigeons flew in and out a lot through the broken windows; they dropped their messes impartially on prisoners and screws, which did not worry us much but did annoy the wardresses, who had their dignity to maintain. Some said the pigeons were the souls of lifers come back to plague the place and take revenge on the screws with their droppings. I rather liked the pigeons, I think most of us did. They seemed to bring a message of freedom.

At 5.00 am we were turned out of our cells for ablutions; urine could already be smelt long before we got to the sluices where we emptied our chamber pots. For breakfast we queued along the corridors round the central stairwell, on each floor above and below us were identical queues, seemingly to infinity. Trays were doled out by prisoners on the kitchen staff from an aluminium trolley, one to each floor; the operation was overseen by a wardress. Each tray held a helping of thick unyielding porridge, a slice of Mother's Pride, a disc of margarine and a dash of marmalade, a mug of weak tea with the strange taste of bromide and no milk. They put bromide in to suppress the prisoners' sex drive; whether it does this I can't say, but it certainly makes the tea nasty. Every day breakfast was exactly the same; every day I would queue for it, collect it, then scurry back to my cell like a rat with its find.

Apart from this, I was allowed out of my cell three times a week for a bath; I looked forward to this. Then sometimes I could go and select a book from the censored shelves of the prison library. I suppose I read more on remand in Holloway than ever before or since, because there was little else to do. I found a copy of Robert Graves's poems which someone had recommended, and enjoyed them greatly, but my favourite author was Beckett. His sardonic bleakness, the way he brings out the queerness of life to mitigate its gloom, exactly fitted the way I felt at this time.

The evening meant a helping of bread and butter pudding stuck through the door and another mug of bromide tea. The bread and butter pudding was appalling, mostly made of heels of bread; I have not been able to eat bread and butter pudding ever since. At midday, the aluminium trolley would clatter along the cell block giving off a whiff of pease pudding and cauliflower; it was as if all the inmates had farted simultaneously. Fat meat and gritty marrowfat peas were other specialities of the house. Altogether I would rather have had the Tunisian soup, it was less unhealthy. I am certain it was the diet that made the prisoners develop such strange shapes; this did not happen to the Tunisian prisoners.

I reported that I had been raped, and asked to be examined; I had not been looked at since my visit to the Tangier clinic which I did not altogether trust. I was taken to the prison hospital wing, given a bed and told to undress. The nurse drew the curtain, but I could hear what she said to the wardress who had brought me:

'What's this one, then? Gynaecological?'

'Alleged rape,' said the wardress. 'Happened in Morocco, she *says*.'

'Yes, well, it's what they all say, isn't it, coming from those parts. Some are easier to rape than others, I daresay,' and she gave a spinsterish sniff.

It was vile, but what could I do? If I had called out in protest they would have sneered a bit more, if I had been at all vehement they might have put me in a mental ward. In due course a doctor came and gave me a very thorough scraping. He told me nothing, and I felt too low and miserable to ask any questions; but I have sometimes wondered, since, whether or not I conceived after the rape, whether the scraping was in fact an early abortion. If so, I am glad I never knew, but there was something dreadful about the impersonality of the whole procedure, as if I was a carcase. The cleaners, trusty prisoners on long sentences also openly sneered at me as I lay waiting for the doctor. I remember one in particular, a little dried-up cockney, whose ash-blonde perm sat strangely on the end of three inches of straight black root.

'What's up with you, then?'

'I was gang-raped in Morocco.'

'Rape, you call it? Course you do; but you was on the game, eh?'

'No, I was not.'

'Yer, well, rape sounds nicer, don't it? What yer got, clap?'

I was silent.

'Look, you don't want to be toffee-nosed, it's all right, the game is; for them what can get it. Still, the wages of sin, eh, dearie? Not all roses after all.'

Eventually she got tired of this and went away. I had more of the same sort of thing in the breakfast queue next morning, after some nosey-parker had asked why I had gone to medical. It taught me that no-one in Holloway would ever believe anything but the worst of anyone. I had never come across an atmosphere like it; had I not quickly learnt to keep myself to myself, I should have come close to despair. The gossip was rank, the backbiting poisonous. I have never liked female chit-chat, but my violent aversion to it started in Holloway. It irked me so much I sometimes used to stuff my ears with cottonwool.

One morning a deep voice behind me said, 'Good morning.' I turned round and there was a man, a soft-looking old chap in a cheap suit, nylon shirt and men's shoes with his hair done short back and sides. How nice to find a gentleman here in Holloway, I thought, a male; I returned his greeting politely. But then I saw another one, and realized they were not men at all, but women, either on remand or with special permission to wear their own clothes. There was nothing sharp or snazzy about them, no elegance, no hint of expensive after-shave; they looked utterly ordinary old codgers. A pipe and slippers would have completed the picture. They were butch lesbians who had gone all the way; but they were not the only lesbians in Holloway. Romances were going on all over the place, causing a good many of the screams and sobs that echoed round the wing. I had never come across lesbianism before, and after the first surprise it didn't worry me. As far as I was concerned they could get on with it.

Night began at 8.00 pm when we were locked in and the lights were turned out. It was then that the caterwauling really started: yells, whines, reproaches, pleas for help, goodnight messages, all laced with four-letter words. It was pandemonium, but I soon got so that I could go quickly to sleep in spite of it. The stone walls kept me in, but at least they kept all this out. I felt starved of all understanding, doubly humiliated by rape and prison, degraded in my hideous uniform; sleep was my one escape.

Then one night, after twenty-eight days, my light went on at 9.00 pm, waking me from a deep sleep. A wardress was standing there, carrying the usual clipboard, and she addressed me in the slightly raised voice they used to affect.

'Susan Mary Taylor five-six-eleven-nine.'

'Yes.'

She looked down at her clipboard with an officious air, leaning back a bit to focus her middle-aged eyes. 'Do you know a Mr Rob Roy of Cadogan Square?'

I sat bolt upright. My heart leapt; it really did, it felt like a jumping shrew in my chest. 'Yes, I do.'

'He has offered to stand bail for you. Do you accept?'

'Yes,' I said.

'Then will you kindly dress as quickly as possible.'

I did so, kicking on my shoes. We made our way to Reception. I was searched in the usual indecent way to make sure I had no messages on paper napkins up my bottom, then allowed to put on my own clothes and taken to a small room where Rob Roy was waiting for me, in all his splendour. We looked at each other; no word was spoken between us, but joy surged through me like a fountain of champagne. We said goodnight politely, and left the prison together.

We got into his sports car. 'Sorry I didn't get in touch sooner,' he said. 'I'm only just out of hospital.'

'What did you have?'

'Acute hepatitis. I caught it in India; apparently I nearly died of it. My mother found out and arranged to fly me home.'

'How did you find out where I was?'

'I went round to the Beaufort Street flat to see someone about arranging a light show. Your name came up, and someone showed me your letter. That was about an hour ago. I got straight into the car and drove to Holloway.'

That was just like Rob Roy. He really is a wonderful person, I thought. We drove to the Contented Sole restaurant in South Kensington where we had a fish dinner, enjoyed by me more than anything I had ever eaten in my life. I must have looked like a scraggy bit of herring myself, but now I came to look at him, Rob Roy was not looking good, either; he was puffy, rather overweight.

'So what have you been up to, then?' he asked.

I told him.

'My God, what a story,' he said. 'Can't keep out of trouble, can you?'

He took me back to Cadogan Square and on to the scene again for the fortnight until my case came up. Perhaps it was a bit more sophisticated this time; Allen Ginsberg had been around, poetry groups were meeting at the flat. We went to the Worlds End fair and wandered round the antique stalls. But there was a sense of finality. I slept a lot, so did he; we were both convalescents. We shared a bed again and made love a bit, as old friends make love. He wanted no more; as for me, my love for him had always taken the form of seeing exactly what he wanted and providing it. I could do this perfectly, because underneath I was moonstruck, obsessed, desperate with love; a fact which, if he had even suspected it, would have put him right off me. Like a chameleon, I took on a protective colouring, toning myself down to be a mere friend.

My reward was that, as a friend, he could not have been kinder; he bailed me out, he put me up, he got a solicitor to represent me. But I now at last saw things as they were. Being left at Istanbul had shown me the truth for an instant, but the months without him had let my illusions steal back. It was clear; his kindness and generosity, which were among the things I loved in him, were not just for me but for any friend in distress. Any casual acquaintance even; he would give milk to a stray cat. I was grateful, and let him know it; what I kept to myself was that I was also bitterly, miserably disappointed.

The solicitor was hardly cheering. I might well go down for a spell, he said, though if I did they would deduct the four weeks I had been in on remand.

'But surely I'm a first offender, in this country?'

'Yes and no. In law, yes; but unfortunately the Crown knows all about the Tunisian episode; the consul reported it back. You are still on suspended sentence as far as the Tunisian authorities are concerned, and I'm afraid it will affect our court's view when it comes to passing sentence.'

'What should I do, then?'

'Plead guilty, but bring in your recent experience in mitigation. You might get off with a fine.'

As we drove away, Rob Roy said: 'We must think what to do with you when the case is over.'

'I suppose so,' I said dully. Obviously he was not going to let me stay with him.

'You'd better go back to your parents for a bit.'

'Oh, no,' I said, automatically; but the fact that he made the suggestion showed that it was really the only thing I could do. 'Well, all right; but what do I do then?'

'You ought to go south to Formentera to get yourself together. Either that or north to Stockholm.'

We went to Heathrow magistrates' court for the case. My sister Wynson was there, for I had by now contacted the family; we waved to each other but she did not look very happy. My haggard appearance was what really shocked her, she told me later; even more than the trouble I was in. I did as advised; the court adjourned while a telex was sent to Interpol, checking up on my story about the gang rape. After half an hour it reconvened. A reply had been received confirming everything I had said. The magistrates were merciful; I was fined £50.

Perhaps I still had a glimmer of hope that Rob Roy would change his mind after the case, but he didn't. It would be far better, he said, if I caught the fast train to Manchester and recovered with my parents. He was on a different trip from me. I took it like a Trojan warrior, but as the train drew away from Euston I felt enveloped in emptiness. I still felt like this as the lights of Manchester appeared and I got on the local train for Shaw. The only thing I had left was his advice; south to Formentera, he had said, or north to Stockholm.

My parents were kind, as always, but asked no questions; they sensed that I needed to be left alone. I was with them long enough to see a top Manchester gynaecologist; it was Patrick Steptoe, who was later to pioneer test-tube babies. He found that I was undamaged and uninfected.

'You're not pregnant, either,' he said. 'Actually you look as if you wouldn't conceive very easily, anyway.' This opinion, years later, was to prove wrong.

I soon began making plans to travel. It would be Formentera, I decided; I was hungry for the sun, and I knew from others besides Rob Roy that Formentera was a centre for alternative people. Very likely it would be just the place for me. So as the April buds began to appear I was ferreting in my mother's attic. I found an old rucksack, packed it with a selection of clothes in the style of the Forties, withdrew almost my last £150 from the bank, and prepared to fly from Manchester to Majorca. I was not going to hitchhike; my nerve had gone. So one morning I took off in style from Manchester airport.

There was no direct flight to Palma de Mallorca at that time of year, so my first stop was Paris, where I had to stay the night before taking off next day from a different airport. I found a cheap hotel in the Rue de Seine, not far from the Invalides bus station. Soon after I checked in

there was a fearful racket in the street: shouts and bangs. I looked out of
my window. Masses of policemen were breaking up a student procession
with its banners and bundling people roughly into black marias. It was
part of the buildup to the 'Events of May', the attempted revolution of
1968; for this was the year when many young people began taking up
politics, the year when the innocence began to be lost. In London, too,
there was the great Grosvenor Square riot. I was glad to get out of Paris
next day; I wanted no part of this business.

The gorgeous, healing warmth struck me as soon as I walked off the
plane at Palma. I caught a ship from there to Ibiza, whose old harbour
looked appealing, but it never occurred to me to stay there. Rob Roy
had said Formentera, so Formentera it should be. I went straight on to
another, smaller boat for about forty passengers, which took me to my
destination.

# 7

# Isle of the Lotos-Eaters

Music that gentlier on the spirit lies
Than tired eyelids upon tired eyes;
Music that brings sweet sleep down from the blissful skies.
                    (*Tennyson, 'The Lotos-Eaters'.*)

Formentera seemed to be the domain of some great smiling mother-goddess: Isis the healer. Everything seemed yielding, pliable. The red fertile earth set off the dark of the pines, the vineyards glowed bright green under the smiling sky. It was early in April, the grass was still fresh and the wild flowers in bloom beside the paths, yet everything already shimmered in the heat. This heat, still gentle, would nurse me through the spring till I could accept the stronger medicine of the high summer sun. The island was, in a way, primitive, but not as the Third World is primitive, and above all not alien; it was Europe, I was still close to my roots. Rob Roy, bless him, had known what he was about when he advised me to go there.

It was very much a hippy island at the time; a large area of it in effect belonged to us. Somewhere there were one or two tourist hotels, but none of us ever went anywhere near them. Some of the *fincas* had been bought by like-minded Americans and others with money; the Pink Floyd had a house and a recording studio on the island. The local shopkeepers had learnt to sell us what we needed for our alternative lifestyle; brown rice was obtainable in the shops, bakers learned to bake wholemeal bread, pan integral. There was plenty of hash, of course; probably the highest concentration of it in the Western world. For the moment this worried no-one, though a few years later one used to hear of hippies being cleared out, kicked off the island *en masse*. All very unnecessary in a way, yet there were some wanted people on the island, one knew that; they were mostly draft-dodgers from America who didn't want to go to Vietnam and had no passports, together with a few who

59

didn't want to pay alimony or were avoiding their creditors. There must certainly have been hash dealers, but there was no gangsterism, no sign of any hard men or violent criminals. I can't think of anywhere I have been where I felt safer. But one knew, instinctively, not to ask personal questions. No-one ever had a surname; I was Susie, nothing else. Some others didn't even use their Christian names, but called themselves things like Hawkface or Aquarius or Lotus-flower.

I found my way to the only café in San Fernando, sat down, kicked off my shoes, grounded my heels, spread my toes in the sun, and basked in the peace of it. I looked around at the modest old whitewashed houses in the street; directly opposite was the post office, doing little business. There were some cyclists; very few cars, nothing bigger than a small SEAT or Volkswagen beetle. A tiny, ancient yellow van rattled by, full of empty bottles; then it went round the corner and there was peace, utter peace, in the sunny street. I decided there and then that I should stay for the whole summer. I had only about fifty pounds to live on, but this workaday worry seemed curiously remote, a tiresome problem of theory that had no relevance to the real world. In practice I knew I should manage; Formentera would help me to manage. As I nursed my coffee, my optimism unfolded in the spring sun.

Two American guys arrived, Al and Jim. We had come over together on the boat and chatted a bit, they seemed like kindred spirits.

'Do you know anywhere I could stay?' I asked. 'Not too pricey.'

'Come along with us,' said Al. 'We are staying at a little place with two girls. Perhaps there'll be room there.'

'No,' said Jim, 'it'll be pretty tight for us as it is; but if you come along the girls will probably know of somewhere, they live here all the time.'

So we set off in the shimmering heat; I was carrying my possessions in the big rucksack, but somehow it never seemed to get heavy even though we were walking, or rather ambling, for an hour or so. There was all the time in the world, no reason to rush; slowing down to a Formentera pace was luxury. We walked under the big pines past vineyard after vineyard. There were bay trees, lemon trees, grey-green aloe cactuses; there was thyme and wild lavender, rosemary and honeysuckle. Once or twice we passed a white dwelling with a flaming bougainvillea. The scented air hummed with bees. I kicked idly at the red dust and revelled in the generous island. The whole place seemed flat, there was no toiling uphill. Someone was dozing under an ancient olive tree with a flock of sheep close by, a black-robed figure with a bald head. As we passed I saw that it was an old woman; quite a lot of the Formentera women seem to go bald in old age.

The *finca* where the boys were staying was tiny, and there were several others besides Karen and Joanna, the two girls. I was made welcome; we all sat on cushions on the floor, joints were handed round. In due course a meal was served and I ate heartily of brown rice and ratatouille, washed down with water from the well. It had been decided where I should sleep; Joanna had the answer.

'I know where she can go; Kenny's loft.'

'Sure,' said Jim. 'I should have thought of Kenny. We'll take you round there when we've eaten.'

I didn't need to go through the ceremonial dance that straight people practise – are you sure it will be all right, shouldn't we let him know? and so on. For one thing there was no way we could have let him know; there was no telephone. Then again, people like us had a kind of freemasonry; if my companions thought it would be all right, it would be. I had moved into the Beaufort Street flat in just this sort of way. If Kenny and I happened not to get on, I could always wander off somewhere else; but this was unlikely as he was obviously one of us. This relaxed way of proceeding had a lot to do with getting me into bad trouble a year or two later; but that was in London, not Formentera. So Jim and Joanna escorted me across country to a tiny little house standing by itself in the middle of a field. Inside the open door, on one of three dusty oriental rugs, sat Kenny; he wore khaki shorts and cloister-creepers, nothing else. I don't believe I ever saw him dressed in any other way until the nights became nippy in October. His stocky body was deeply tanned and his brown walrus moustache was slightly bleached at the ends, by the sun. He parted his thinning hair in the middle, and this, in combination with his tan, gave him a slightly Red Indian look. He was whittling at a stick.

'Hi, Kenny,' said Jim. 'This is Susie.'

'Hi,' he said. 'Come on in.'

'Could she put up here a while?'

He looked at me a second or two. 'Yeah, sure, she can hang out here.'

We all sat down; he laid aside his stick, carefully rolled a joint, and passed it around. I looked about me at my new home. There was a canary in a little cage; the stick Kenny was whittling was evidently to be part of a new, larger cage for it, of which the beginnings stood on a little wooden table with a pair of African tom-toms. The only chair in the room was occupied by a tabby cat, fast asleep. There was a faded print of the Virgin and Child in a dusty frame, otherwise the flaking whitewashed walls were bare. To the right was a door to what I presumed was Kenny's bedroom, opposite the entrance was an open door to a small kitchen, to the left was a wooden staircase leading to a trap-door in the ceiling. Jim and Joanna left; I don't think I saw either of them again, or their friends, which was odd because I soon met a lot of people and became quite gregarious. It shows how fluid the scene was; people came and went all the time, it was just a question of whom one happened to bump into.

Kenny lifted his eyes and motioned with his head to this staircase. That's all he did, he was far too laid-back to go up with me and show me the place, as a host would in the straight world. I took my gear up, opened the trap-door, and there was the loft, gently lit by gaps in the tiles and full of sweet-smelling straw. From then on it was my territory, shared at times with Kenny's pussycats; the sleepy tabby on the chair was only one of several. He did later show me the well with its pump and the outside earth closet which were the washing and sanitary arrangements. It was all perfect; in that climate, in that atmosphere, who needs modern plumbing?

I just lived there, soon making friends with the people from the *fincas* round about. Most of the time I wore one of two white linen dresses in Forties style. I went around a lot with Ingrid, a tall Swedish girl with a mane of blonde hair who lived in the nearest one. She and I and one or two others used to walk most days to the sea to swim; it was some distance, but the walk was as delightful as the swim and involved climbing down one of several ravines, some of them pretty steep. There are no sandy beaches on that part of Formentera suitable for the bucket and spade or even sufficient space for picnic parties on the rocky shore. None of us bothered with bathing suits, men or women; and from the first I felt no self-consciousness. I do remember once or twice thinking of the Holloway potato-women and how dreadful the poor things would have looked without clothes; my companions, if not all prize specimens, were of normal human shape. There were no towels, either; we dried ourselves in the sun. We could always wash the salt off later with well-water, if we felt like it. The weather turned from warm to hot, from hot to very hot. I revelled in it.

Kenny was very good to me. I explained to him that I was just out of the nick and that previously I had been gang-raped, that I was feeling very raw. He was totally understanding, a real soul-brother. He left me completely on my own and never intruded; he too was very much one to keep himself to himself, so I in my turn respected this. Far from asking for any rent, he even fed me. Every morning he would give me a bowl of muesli which he made himself, a mixture which beat anything of Dr Bircher-Benner's; it was softened with goat's milk which he got from his neighbour and landlady, a balding Formentera widow like the one I had passed that first day. It was all I needed, and neither of us ate much else except when asked out. We smoked, of course; Kenny was very preoccupied with dope, and I liked it too. But it is amazing that he put me up for nearly seven months; I did practically nothing in return for his kindness except to cut his hair once or twice and help with what little housework there was, which was almost none. Perhaps at first he kept me out of pity and didn't have the heart to throw me out; I suppose in the end he got used to me. Every now and then he had a girl in, though never for more than a few days. Perhaps my presence discouraged them from wanting to move in more permanently, which could have suited him. But that is conjecture.

I often went out in the evenings. Sometimes Kenny came as well, sometimes not. Most of the island seemed to be within walking distance, and one came home at night without fear. Entertaining was simple; jasmine or camomile tea, perhaps some local wine, hardly ever any spirits. To eat there might be bread with tomatoes and olive oil, or a vegetarian risotto, or grilled fish; now and then someone would give a barbecue. Always there would be joints rolled and passed round; the smell of hashish blended with the island's herbs as we sat around outside a *finca* in the gathering night, and this is to me the fragrance of Formentera. Often someone would play the guitar and sing, inspiring me and others to dance. I also played drums, as in the Tunis prison. I brought Kenny's tom-toms along and accompanied the music with them, or simply played them alone for people to dance; it is a lovely feeling to originate the beat of a dance with fingers on a drum. Shaking a tambourine is fun, too; if there was one lying about, or some castanets, I would borrow them. The boundary between audience and performer dissolved in the great oneness we felt, but there were the movers and the sitters, the doers and the listeners, and I was usually a mover and a doer. Kenny and I never entertained; our place was too small and spartan. Nobody thought the less of us for this.

A lot of people were into cottage crafts, making sandals, weaving cloth, creating clothes. Very few did any agriculture, this was left to the islanders. I resumed my old profession; I had brought along my scissors and not forgotten my skills, so I became the hippy hairdresser, the barefoot barber. Alternative people are known for letting their hair grow, it is true, but a surprising number were glad to have a trim. I tidied a good few beards as well.

Formentera was for most of us a place for soul-searching, meditation trips, God trips. As in London the religion was often Eastern, but there was also a kind of nature-worshipping paganism, centred on the phases of the moon. Full moon was always a time for celebration. We came from all parts of all Western countries, from all classes, from all walks of life. We all did our own thing within a very wide range; about the only practice we all had in common was the smoking of hash. We didn't all speak each other's languages; English was the *lingua franca*, but a lot of people weren't very good at it. All the same, various as we were, we formed a tribe, with a tribe's consensus and a tribe's solidarity. The sound of drums often betokened a party, people would hear them from miles away and come along.

I remember my first full moon party; it was very powerful. Ingrid came by our door as the sun was going down towards the treetops. Kenny wasn't there.

'Are you coming to the party?'

'What party?'

'It's full moon tonight,' she explained. 'We always have a party at full moon.'

'Sure I'll come,' I said.

'Better bring a shawl or something, it'll get chilly at night.'

Strangely excited, I scampered up to the loft, brought down a shawl, scooped up the tom-toms, hung them round my shoulders, and we set off. Soon we joined other people going the same way, and by and by we heard the sound of drumming in the gathering dusk. We quickened pace; I felt expectant, almost as if I were going to take some sort of communion.

About twenty people were sitting cross-legged in a circle outside a big *finca*, more were arriving. I sat down at once and joined the drumming. Someone gave me a glass of mint tea, piping hot; I set it down beside me on the ground and drummed. Someone struck up a guitar. I drummed. Some girls got up and danced, static and sinuous. I drummed, making the rhythm more urgent. My neighbour handed me a joint; I paused for a long pull, passed it on and drummed some more. By now the great moon ruled the darkened sky, dominated it so that only the boldest stars were visible.

There was an interval while we were given risotto on thick earthenware plates. There was wine for those who wanted it, I drank my tea, we chatted normally, yet inside me there was this tide of rising excitement. In due course someone started playing a recorder, a pure pentatonic melody; a little later the guitar started again in harmony. I drummed again, others drummed, the dancing resumed. I put aside my drums, threw off my shawl, strode to join the dancers. The moon seemed to demand it. We danced and danced in the white light. The music changed; there was singing. We still danced. It stopped for a bit, the other dancers stopped, but the beat was in me and I went on, leaping and gyrating in a savage rhythm. Others started up again around me, centred on me. I danced on, tireless, inspired. The moon sank towards the horizon, and still we danced, I danced. . . .

Only a few of us were left, we drank water, passed joints around, and drummed. It had been, yes, a sort of communion. *Wovon man nicht sprechen kann, davon muss man schweigen.* If you can't talk about something you have to keep quiet about it. The moon had extended her mercy to me. A few days later my period came, for the first time since the rape. It was easy, natural – no curse but a renewal of grace.

The weeks passed, and the months. I felt myself expand like a flower, ripen like a fruit. I didn't look in a mirror for months on end; there wasn't one, anyway, though Kenny may have had a little one for shaving. All the same I knew I looked good, because I felt so good. I became browner and browner; I kept myself washed in the well-water. I never left the island, even to go to its bigger worldly sister Ibiza, which we thought of as the home of ego-trippers and boutiques and disco-dollies, of seeing and being seen, of tawdry tourism and boring urban vice. I went to San Fernando to buy some rope-soled sandals, and that was enough town life for me. I was totally content, prowling about like a wild lioness, fearless, fulfilled. My hair was like a lion's mane, its natural auburn-brown bleached in parts to a dark blonde. Formentera felt like a kingdom that was all mine. For days at a time I would speak to nobody; not sulking, nor because of some Trappist vow, but simply because I saw nobody. In any case we talked less than most people; we were free of that normal human need to disarm and pacify each other which causes so much empty, phatic talk. I had no love-affair, not even the beginnings of one. The lovely island and the easy companionship were all I needed, they were like a protective cast over my spirit as its wounds healed. I suppose one or two men did try to get closer to me, but I discouraged them and they did not persist.

There were a lot of wild mulberry trees on Formentera and in due course the mulberries ripened. I remember, on my way to swim one day, coming on a great old tree bowed down with ripe purple fruit. I picked some off the ground, I picked those I could reach off the bending branches; finally I climbed the tree and sat on one of its great limbs, then another, eating my fill. I pillaged that tree, plundered it, ravished it; yet I felt it approved. When I got down my white dress was patched in purple, several different shades of it, looking like batik work. It crossed my mind that the stains might be permanent, but they all came out with a good scrub that evening. None of the islanders seemed to bother about the mulberries; they left them entirely to us alternatives. Some of us used to gather the fruit and tread it in vats to make wine. At one of the full moon parties this wine was served, heady and fragrant; that evening, for once, I took an alcoholic drink, and got high on the essence of Formentera. As autumn approached there were no more mulberries, but the grapes in the vineyards ripened. The farmers never minded us taking a few bunches, and we would pick and eat them as we walked.

Then came the time to go. It was the beginning of November, the days were shorter, the warmth was going, many of the alternative people had departed. After seven months, the island had worked its magic on me. Kenny had begun wearing a shirt, now and then even a pullover. He had finished making his birdcage and the canary had taken possession; it was time for him to pack up his things and return, bird, cage and all, to Cincinnati. I left a day or two before him; we parted company as we had met, saying a friendly goodbye. It was one of those beautifully cool relationships, cool in the sense of *good*. He was a really open soul, and gave me back my confidence in men. I never saw him again, but wherever he may be he has my gratitude.

By boat and train I made my way to London, staying a night in Amsterdam. There was room in the Beaufort Street flat, so I moved in there. One of the girls, Chantal, was clearing out some of her old clothes and came on an old black coat she had worn at Roedean.

'That's a nice coat,' I said. Its clean, no-nonsense line appealed to me.

'You actually like it? I hate it, it reminds me of school. Well, you can have it.'

'Can I really? Well, thanks awfully.'

I put it on, looked in the mirror and liked what I saw. I liked my image in other ways too. My tan suited me, I no longer looked scraggy but fashionably lean. Then some of my Formentera mane came off and I styled my hair. The reason for this was severely practical; I needed a job to support myself, and thought I might get into the theatre. I had no acting background except my performances as a child; I also knew quite well that more people wanted to act than could find jobs. However, Formentera had made me look good and feel well; I was optimistic. I called myself Susie Potter as a stage name.

I went to the Arts Laboratory, also to the Round House at Chalk Farm which was the home of the Living Theatre. The happenings there were always fun and sometimes inspiring; *Paradise Now* was memorable, so was *Antigone*. I came to know Julian Beck slightly, and enjoyed most of what he did, though sometimes there was an unpleasant note of aggression against harmless people in the audience. This was part of a trend that disappointed me, the fading of flower power. In the time I had been away the London scene had taken on a bitter quality, moving on to radical objectives, social causes, militant feminism, anarchy. Julian Beck was into anarchy. None of this was my grab, and I felt I might just as well move on somewhere else.

I took in *Stage and Radio* for its advertisements, which always included one or two for people without experience. One in particular looked interesting, so I applied.

# 8

# Circus in Lebanon

'Beirut', said the advertisement. Dancers were wanted for a circus, no previous experience required. Well, it seems odd, but I did not spot anything fishy in this. Not being a newspaper reader, I had missed the stories in the Sunday tabloids about girls going to Beirut as dancers or hostesses and being forced into prostitution. Someone up there was looking after me, though, because it turned out that this proposition was straight, as such propositions go. The idea appealed to me for several reasons. It involved travel; it was a sort of entry into show-business; and the circus had always fascinated me. Then again, there seemed to be nothing for me in London. I wrote in and was invited round to a little office to be interviewed by a very respectable woman. My employer would be Mr George Prince, who ran the circus at the Casino du Liban; to be exact it was not at Beirut itself but at Mameltane nearby. The job was quite well paid, the air fare was provided.

'One thing, though,' said the woman, 'it's a twenty-four month contract.'

That was fine by me, I didn't even think of refusing. I felt that in the circus world I should at last find my niche. As a child I had done daredevil stunts on the high beams in the barn at Shaw; why should I not become an acrobat? I was agile and not easily scared. I thought, if I pass up this opportunity I shall always regret it.

'All right,' I said, 'I'll do it.'

The contract seemed straightforward; I signed it under my own name, but made it clear that I wanted to be known as Susie Potter. Two days later I was in Beirut, wearing my Roedean coat with a big red carnation in the buttonhole and carrying a plum-coloured hockey bag from my own schooldays. Mr Prince may have been a bit taken aback; my image was rather different from that of the usual run of trainee dancers.

He seemed a good boss. He allotted me a nice little apartment, really an independent bungalow set into the cliff above Mameltane. I would start rehearsals next day; in the meantime I had the evening to settle in. I went down into Mameltane village to get supplies for supper and breakfast. The winter sun warmed the cypresses so that they gave off a faint fragrance. I found a food shop and bought some black olives and lakni, which is something between cheese and yoghourt. Now for bread, I said to myself; and there behind a bead curtain was a lovely little shop, filled with the aroma of baking. The proprietor, in a jellaba and yellow Turkish slippers, stood smoking a hubble-bubble set on a table in front of him; behind him was the clay oven, and some shelves with warm loaves of leavened and unleavened bread.

'*Du pain, s'il vous plaît,*' I said.

He put down his mouthpiece and pottered over to the shelves, fetching loaves of various sizes between which I could choose. But it was then that I noticed another smell, more welcoming even than that of the bread. I pointed to his pipe; he smiled and nodded, and after a bit I left the shop with a little fresh cob of bread and a lump of best red Lebanese hash, almost the size of the loaf. This is my kind of place, I thought, and went straight back to the flat to roll a joint.

Next day I started rehearsals. I was in the dancing chorus and a raw trainee at that, right at the bottom of the heap. All the same, some of the dancers were needed to help with the circus acts and, as a new girl, I was tested to see if I could do this; for not all of them had the nerve. Luckily physical fear has never been one of my problems. I was given an elephant to ride, one of five or so that walked round the ring, each with a showgirl on its back. Later we were to get fancy costumes with plumes; there was already a harness brightly coloured in red and orange, not much to control an elephant but better than nothing. My elephant, Sally, needed controlling more than any of the others, though she was the smallest, nowhere near full-grown. I call her 'she' out of politeness and because she had a girl's name; in fact she was a hermaphrodite, with both sets of genitals and a double temperament to match. Sometimes she would be all female, graciously willing to do as she was asked; at other times a masculine, rebellious side would emerge and she would refuse to get down to allow me on, or step out of line, or stop still, turn round and quiz me with her beady eye. I'm glad to say she never tried to bolt, I'm not sure what I should have been able to do about that. Despite her quirks I became fond of Sally, and as the days went by she seemed to get used to me.

Another thing I did was to ride on the back of one of a team of strong men who did tricks on magnificent black Harley-Davidsons, each carrying a girl on his shoulders. The men were real experts, rock steady, absolutely reliable. It was exhilarating to see the hall whizz by, the bystanders' faces a blur, my ears battered by the insistent roar of the engine. I've never had anything to do with bikers, apart from this, but it showed me what fun they must have.

The dancing numbers, the ones I was originally hired for, were what I liked least about the job. They were coy and tasteless, just about suitable for plastic puppets. Our coach, Jack Cole, had taught Marilyn Monroe to dance, a fact he used often to mention. Poor man, he just didn't know what to do about me, for I was simply too bored to concentrate. Dancing, for me, had to be an exercise for body and mind. Disciplined, yes – I wasn't silly enough to expect freestyle, and I knew what choreography was for – but the discipline must be *of* something, a control of real energies to make a real effect, not this petty pedantic tittupping about. I remember one dreadful routine in which we were supposed to be teapots. We stood in line, facing the side, with one arm on the hip as the handle, the other bent and pointing outwards with the hand down to be the spout; we turned our faces to this side as in an Egyptian frieze.

'I'm a little teapot, short and stout,' we sang. 'Here's my handle, here's my spout.' (Three steps to the side.) 'Tip me over and pour me out.' (Three to the back.)

Jack Cole rapped on the floor with his stick, to stop the act.

'Susie! That's three steps *back*.'

'Sorry.'

'Start again,' he said to the pianist, and himself sang the idiotic rigmarole with us:

'I'm a little teapot . . . Susie Potter!' – and again he rapped with his stick on the floor.

'The hand points *down*, Susie, get it? So that the housewife can pour the tea, all right? Start again . . .'

Another rap. 'Susie! You are way out of line, way out, you ought to be here, get it? Here to the right of Marlene, to the left of Clarice. I even managed to teach Marilyn how to dance, yet I can't get Susie Potter to toe the line . . .'

But we spent most of our time sitting around in our communal dressing-room. There were hours during the day when we were on call, waiting for the practice rooms to be unoccupied or for Jack Cole or the pianist to turn up; or just hanging about. The other dancers spent a lot of this time making little adjustments to their face make-up. Nails, too, needed lacquering; the girls would devote to this a concentration worthy of a brain surgeon, then when the operation was completed they would fiddle with their hair, which most of them kept back-combed and bouffant. Mostly they were blondes, by nature or out of a bottle; one or two were henna-red. They had magazines to leaf through, back numbers of *Woman* or *Honey*. Otherwise they would look in the mirror at their own big creamy bosoms as they gossiped about their Lebanese boyfriends, dissected yesterday's party or speculated about tonight's. There was just one dancer who was different; lithe little Jenny, who had been with the Royal Ballet and was hired to do solo numbers. Her hair was short, and kept its natural mouse-colour; her bust was neat; she preferred doing ballet exercises to coffee-housing with the others. I brought hash in and smoked joint after joint, sharing it with those who wanted it, and spent a lot of time drawing, having bought for this a large supply of paper and crayons. Jenny and one or two of the others caught this interest, which must have made a change for them; after a bit there was quite a little group of us drawing and admiring each other's work. It passed the time.

The proper circus performers were a cut above us, but I got to know them and to like some of them. The motor-cycle team were all Lebanese. Mostly, I think, they were local tearaways recruited by Mr Prince for the act when they showed a bit of talent. The language barrier stopped me talking to them much, but there is something appealing about skill and strength and a trained body. Then there were the horsemen, eight or ten fine-looking Italians in spangles mounted on wonderful Arabs. They kept themselves to themselves. My main friends among the performers were a team of trick cyclists, husband and wife and son. They were a reminder of home to me because they came from Manchester, and quite apart from this they were genuine, sincere sort of people. I was less sure about Jan the lion tamer; a giant Afrikaner from South Africa, 6 foot 4 if he was an inch. His face was triangular, chiselled, handsome in a way but grim, like Boris Karloff. He never seemed to smile, his grey eyes were like stones. Sometimes his stare would light upon me, but I kept out of his way. This may have been fortunate, for he was later to strangle one of the showgirls in a fit of jealous rage.

On my days off I got about a bit, talked to one or two people outside the circus, sometimes went into Beirut. Lebanon was at that time a good place to be; some people called it the Switzerland of the Middle East because of its combination of banking and scenery. There were all the amusements money could buy, and the way the mountains went down to the sea meant, people said, that you could ski all morning and then find yourself by the Mediterranean for your afternoon swim. All the same, despite not being very interested in trends and current affairs, I couldn't ignore the sinister side of Beirut. Behind the smart shopping streets were vile slums; on some of the open spaces were clusters of pathetic shanties, swarming with destitute Palestinians. Nobody seemed to care a damn. To an English eye it was shocking, and worrying as well. What would happen to all those ragged children when they grew up? Would they be content just to go on vegetating? In a café in Mameltane I met a wise old man with a white beard and piercing dark eyes; we talked pidgin French.

'*Liban – foutu,*' he said, '*vous verrez bien.*' (Lebanon is finished, you'll see.)

Television pictures of the Beirut I knew, now raw ruins, make me think of that old man.

The showgirls used to hang around the gambling rooms at the casino, and their talk often concerned nights out with the high rollers. Sometimes one would be shown a bracelet or a pair of earrings. Now and then one of them would put in a specially arduous session on her face make-up, after which a character in dark glasses would turn up and take her off in a chauffeur-driven Mercedes. Often there were parties to which any of us who wished to go were invited; I remember the first one of these I went to. We all piled into black limousines and were taken to a large house decorated in an odd mixture of ultra-modern and Arabian Nights traditional: occasional tables in glass and metal cluttered with inlaid brass bowls full of flowers, brass ash-trays, snuffboxes and photographs in frames, three-piece suites covered with Eastern carpets, art deco painted wooden chairs, more carpets on the walls between sets of glass shelves crowded with chased silver beakers, Staffordshire figures, plates in porcelain and coloured glass. In a niche was a big jade Buddha, heaven knows what *he* made of it all. There was champagne followed by a heavy meal with red wine, then brandy. Soft drinks were available, thank goodness; some of these were delicious, especially the green melon juice and a red one that I couldn't identify. Afterwards we sat around, some of us getting amorous with the dull overweight men. The stifling smell of tobacco was everywhere – just tobacco, unfortunately. I thought, dare I ask for a joint? These are Middle Easteners, after all. Better not, I decided. A boy made overtures to me; he was quite winning, like a puppy, but flabby as a blancmange. Already at twenty or so he was getting a paunch, and there were rolls of fat under his tight shiny suit. He told me a terrible lot about his Aston-Martin. Then a man in his thirties came up, a hawk-nosed character, handsome in a sort of way. By noticing that my glass was empty and filling it, he got me away from the fat boy and talked about his yacht. I thought, never mind, fat boy, you may think you've lost out, but I'm not going with this one any more than I'd go with you.

I went to another similar party, all too similar, except that this time there was a sucking pig in the middle of the buffet with an apple in its mouth, ready sliced. I don't know what it is about sucking pig, but for me it always symbolizes luxury at its grossest. I accepted a slice, savoured its fat delicate taste, then thought of those wretched Palestinians in their hovels and felt guilty. After this I made my own amusements, as often as not just staying at home to dine on bread, olives and lakni.

This was not popular with Mr Prince; his circus was, after all, attached to the casino, and the casino liked us to amuse its customers not only by our performances, but out of hours as well. He had a little talk with me.

'You don't seem to be having much social life, Susie,' he said.

'Well, I'm not really a social person.'

'That's a mistake, you ought to get about more. I like my girls to have fun.'

'Well, it isn't much fun, sitting around drinking.'

'Nobody's asking you to sit around,' he said.

'Anyway they don't like my type, they go for fat women here.'

'Nonsense,' he said, 'you've got a nice figure. Only the other day Ibrahim was telling me – you remember Ibrahim, you went to his party – where's that nice girl, the slim one with the suntan, where's she hiding? – my son liked her so much.'

Idly I wondered, which was the son? The fat boy, or hawknose? It didn't matter. 'I didn't like *him* all that much.'

'All right, all right, there's other fish in the sea, though. Find someone you like better, don't waste yourself.'

This conversation did not appeal to me. I felt that I was being pressured, almost procured, and to me this was an intrusion. It was not only insulting but disgusting as well, when I thought of those soft, hairy bodies on top of me. Worst of all, it was just possible that in the end Mr Prince might win. How long, in that environment, would even I be able to go on saying no? The ease and spaciousness of the rich life did vaguely attract me. It would be nice to ride around for a bit in a chauffeured limousine, bedecked in jewels; not to mention the Paris clothes. If one of those millionaires had been a bit more attractive than the others, he might have seduced me with the handiwork of Dior and St Laurent. All the same I knew that such a life would become a hideous bore, sooner rather than later.

Of course there were good things: Sally the elephant, the thrill of the motor-bike act and the nice people from Manchester. Despite my fears for my own virtue, I might quite easily have stayed with the circus had it not been for what happened to Lynne and Marlene. These two fluffy blondes were a bit homesick, I suppose, and one day they simply weren't there. Mr Prince had, I think, gone through this before, so he knew what to do. He took a taxi straight to the airport, where he found them in the departure lounge waiting for a flight to Heathrow. He showed their contracts to the airport police, got an enforcement order, and brought the girls straight back in disgrace. I was relieved, though quite surprised, to note how little either Lynne or Marlene seemed to mind this; after a day or two of sulks and sniffs, they were soon their old selves. But the incident made me very worried for myself. It was clear that my contract, like theirs, meant exactly what it said, and was enforceable. I felt trapped, enslaved; I got into a completely negative frame of mind, and convinced myself that there was no way this life would fulfil me for twenty-four whole months. However, it was no good simply taking myself off, Lynne and Marlene had proved that. Mr Prince must be made to want to get rid of me.

So I set about my shoulder-length hair in front of the mirror. A few quick snips, and the tresses were on the floor. Then I gave myself a bob cut like they had in the Twenties; the *gamine* look of Mia Farrow, boyish. Tomboyish, one might say; pert, virginal, hard to get. For fun, I put a silver streak in. This did two things; it ensured that none of the Beiruti night-owls would look twice at me, and it annoyed Mr Prince.

'What the bloody hell have you done to yourself?' he demanded.

'How do you mean?' I asked, wide-eyed.

'Your *hair*, for God's sake.'

'Oh, don't you like it? I just thought I needed a new look. Also it's nice and cool.'

'Cool be damned,' he grumbled. 'I'll have to get you a wig for when you go on, I'm not having you look like that. And what are you doing in *pyjamas?*'

For I had also changed my style of dress, and was wearing a pair of striped pyjamas from India with tight bottoms to the trouser legs. Elegant, I felt, but certainly unsexy.

'Sorry you don't like them,' I said. 'I think they're rather nice, personally,' and I complacently stroked my flank, well knowing that my figure was totally concealed, which was of course the point.

My behaviour got rather tomboyish as well. I introduced the others to the game of hopscotch, learnt all those years ago in the Oldham streets. One or two remembered it from their childhood, the rest learned quickly. I am sure it was good for them, sharpening up their wits no end. Jenny soon became an expert and played with real grace, but it was quite funny to watch some of the others galumphing across the chalk squares like overgrown schoolgirls, their bosoms flopping about. Mr Prince did not see the joke.

'What the bleeding hell are you doing?'

'Playing hopscotch,' I said. 'It's fun; like to join in?'

'Like hell I would,' he growled. 'That's enough now, all of you! Back to your dressing-room at once.' As we filed in, he grumbled a bit more: 'Grown women going back to the bloody kindergarten.'

Then I began sabotaging poor Jack Cole's dancing lessons. Instead of being merely absentminded, I became deliberately obtuse, bringing him to the point of literally tearing his hair. He had a good wail to Mr Prince.

The costumiers came, a firm from Rome who were going to fit us out in our feathered and spangled costumes for the performances. I had a suggestion for them; wouldn't it be amusing if I rode Sally dressed in grey silk as a mouse? A mouse on an elephant, right? Naturally they thought this suggestion completely lunatic, and Mr Prince was informed.

'What's this nonsense about a mouse?' he said to me.

'Well, people say that elephants are scared of mice, I thought it would be a bit original.'

'Original,' he said, with an air of finality. 'Susie Potter thinks it would be original.' Then he raised his voice: 'but I'm not bloody having it, do you hear?'

'The smallest animal on the biggest one . . .' I started to explain, but he cut me off, shouting:

'I don't hire you to bury yourself in fabric, but to show yourself! Show yourself! Is that understood?'

He now began thinking of me as a serious nuisance, one he couldn't understand or handle. For one thing I was quite evidently not in the least scared of him. Again, as a mere untrained dancer my place was below everyone else, to the point where nobody ought to have paid me any attention; yet I seemed to be not only incurably eccentric, but also a bit of a leader. Others were taking to my strange ways, hopscotch and so on. It was fairly harmless so far, but I was the type who might take it into my head to lead a serious mutiny.

When I felt the softening up was completed, I went to Mr Prince and

said I was not really fitting in. I have never seen such an expression of
relief on anyone's face. He was only too glad to hand out my passport
and ticket to London; he even gave me an extra month's pay, a golden
handshake to make sure I went.

I had a thought. 'Just book me to Paris, could you?' I asked. 'Leave
the flight to London open.'

The reason for this was that it was January, and there wasn't likely to
be much doing in London. It seemed a good idea to go and look up old
friends at Katzenbrunn, maybe even to learn to ski at last, if my funds
ran to it. It would be nice to see Frau Loeffler again; also, of course, it
was quite possible that Rob Roy would be there. So from Paris I took a
train to Munich, and looked round there for a few hours; the place
appealed to me and I thought, some day I may stay here for a bit, it looks
as if there is quite a lot doing. Then I took a bus to Katzenbrunn.

Frau Loeffler greeted me warmly, of course she had a room for me,
how could I suppose she might not fit me in? Then came the bombshell.

'Our friend Rob Roy is here.'

'Oh, that's nice.' In a flash I realized that of course he was the real
reason why I had come.

'He's not staying here, he's in a flat in town with some others. You
know he's getting married?'

People talk about being *engulfed* in misery, and perhaps that is how it
takes them, but for me it is not like that. Misery is not a tide coming in to
overwhelm, but a tide going out, an abandonment, a loss.

'No, I've been in Beirut all this time. Who is he marrying?'

'Ruth, her name is; a nice girl, well-dressed. By the way, that's a
lovely overcoat you've got on.'

'Oh, do you like it?' It was a blessing for me, this change of subject.
Besides, Frau Loeffler was a great one for swapping clothes, and if she
took a fancy to this very ordinary brown coat from C&A, I might get
something really funky in exchange.

'Yes, it's very elegant. Let me show you something.'

She produced a fabulous coat of white sheepskins sewn together; far
too big, a man's coat really. But she was good with a needle and thread;
she said she would alter it for me in exchange for my brown one. Well,
that was something; I should love this coat, it would give me the wild,
free image that I needed after escaping from Mr Prince's vulgar yoke.

Naturally I went to call on Rob Roy and Ruth, his betrothed, in their
shared flat. He opened the door to me and welcomed me with such a cry
of delight that I was quite cheered up.

'Susie! It's great to see you, really great.'

'For me, too. You're looking good.'

He was, too; and his after-ski outfit of black trousers and patterned cashmere sweater looked tidy and conventional. Her influence, I thought.

'You must come in and meet Ruth, we're going to be married, you know.'

Thank God for masculine insensitivity. I couldn't have borne it if he had alluded in any way to my disappointment; I could even hope that he was unaware of it.

'Yes, Frau Loeffler told me. Congratulations.'

Ruth was in the flat's living-room, and Rob Roy introduced us. She was goodlooking, with a kind expression and a way of speaking that immediately made me like her. Her best feature was her waist-length black hair which she wore pinned up. She was not in any way alternative, but a straight person who shared Rob Roy's background; he could settle down with her, if he was capable of settling down at all. I at once thought of her as a friend; I still do.

# 9

# *Hair*

After a bit we all went along to have tea at the Scheune, the place in
Katzenbrunn where everyone goes for *après-ski*. From there I crossed the
road to a discotheque. I was feeling a flow of energy; the thudding beat
of the pop music gave an outlet for it. I was disappointed, but physically
happy; my mind felt bleak and my life uncertain, yet my animal spirits
surged and flowed, totally positive. I began to lose myself in the dance,
to enter a state of abstraction, of no-mind.

'Susie!'

It was the princess, my former employer, greeting me now as a friend.
She embraced me, kissed me on both cheeks in the continental fashion.

'Susie, my dear! I thought, who's that marvellous dancer? Then I saw
it was you. Sorry for the interruption but I had to say hello. *Wie geht's
dir?* You're looking fabulous! Where have you been?'

'Oh, lots of places; I've just come from Beirut.'

'Beirut! *Kaum zu glauben!* But you always said you would travel.'

'I've travelled all right.'

'Come and sit with us for a bit.'

The princess and her friends were sitting at a table near the dance
floor, and the music I had been dancing to was no longer an inspiration
but a noisy intrusion. All the same we managed to talk, and I told them
some of my experiences, those that I thought were fit for their ears.
'Hippies' were in the news quite often and I think they were interested to
meet one.

One of the party was a journalist from Munich, Annette Schelling.
She said to me, 'You know, you dance really well, also you've got that
hippy look. They are doing *Hair* in Munich, at the Theater der Kunst,
and I know they are often looking out for people to join the chorus. Why
don't you try to get into it? I believe you'd be ideal.'

'Really?' I said, flattered. *Hair* was the show we alternatives regarded as our own. It had captured Broadway and London, totally succeeded in the straight world without compromising our feelings and ideas. For me to get into it would be a kind of apotheosis.

'Yes, they have professionals in the name parts, of course, but they take amateurs for the chorus – flower children and so on – and sometimes they leave, there's quite a turnover. I've seen it; not many of them move as well as you.'

'Do you know, I just might try it.'

'I hope you do,' said Annette. She handed me her card. 'If it works out, get in touch with me.'

The more I thought about the idea the more sense it made. There was nothing doing for me now at Katzenbrunn, and to act in *Hair* would be totally fulfilling. All right, if one was to be realistic the chances could not be rated that high. All the same I might always find something else in Munich, and if I didn't it was on the way back home. So I boarded a coach next day.

I spent the night in the cheapest lodgings I could find, then in the morning I thought to myself, it was fairly mad to come here thinking I'd get a job in *Hair* on the suggestion of a casual acquaintance, but now that I *am* here I might as well go and have a look. So I put on my sheepskin coat and found my way to the Theater der Kunst. I went in by the stage door; nobody stopped me. I heard music and followed it to the stage, where the 'tribe' was rehearsing, and simply joined in; this was not as difficult as it sounds, for I knew the tunes, and the dancing was very free. At the end of the number the director came up to me.

'Who are you?' he asked.

'My name's Susie Potter. I thought I'd try for a job with you.'

'English, are you?'

'Yes.'

He considered for a bit. 'You sing in tune, you dance well, you look exactly right. You even speak some German; this is useful in case we want you to speak a few lines. The songs are in the original but the spoken words in German. Yes, we can use you. See me afterwards. Carry on here for now.'

I saw him in his office afterwards; he offered me a very acceptable wage.

'Have you got a work permit?' he asked.

Oh dear, I thought, that may be a problem. 'No, I only arrived yesterday.'

'*Ist gut*, just fill in this form for me, we'll get you one tomorrow.'

It was a classic wish-fulfilment dream come true, complete with

small, easily-surmounted obstacle; yet it was happening in real life. It
was, in the nicest possible way, really rather comical.

The first telephone box I came to, I rang Annette Schelling.

'This is Susie, remember me? We met at Katzenbrunn, and you
advised me to try for a job in *Hair*.'

'Of course I remember you, it was only two days ago.'

'Well, I thought you'd like to know, I'm in Munich, I did what you
suggested, and I've got the job.'

'It's not true!'

'Honestly! I've just come from the theatre, I'm starting tomorrow.'

'But that's marvellous! Where are you staying? You must come and
stay with me.'

'With you?'

'Of course, I've got plenty of room. I won't take no for an answer.'

So in a couple of hours my situation was transformed. I had woken
that morning unemployed in a sordid pension; I went to sleep that night
in the comfortable Schwabing flat of my new friend, having found not
just a job, but the best job that I could have imagined.

It was a lovely life; we rehearsed in the morning and played to packed
houses in the evening. We called ourselves the 'Tribe', and we felt like a
tribe; I was reminded of life on Formentera. There was no hierarchy, no
class distinction between the main actors and ourselves. I became friends
with Donna Summer, who had one of the main parts, and her husband
Ronnie. Donna became an international pop star, of course, and she will
have long forgotten me, but we were friends and I have always
remembered her kindly. One weekend I took a few of the tribe to
Katzenbrunn. It was a happy time.

But not everyone liked *Hair*. Its message against the Vietnam war
seemed to rightwingers to be designed to undermine the West in the
interest of communism. Some of them also felt that the show would turn
young people on to drugs, another way to weaken the West and promote
Soviet domination. There were also those who were shocked by the
scene when the whole Tribe appears nude on stage, even though all we
did was stand there in a dim light. Looking back, the attacks all seem
pompous and overdone, yet the show did flout convention, and flout it
deliberately. There were people who felt that a gauntlet was being flung
down, as in a way it was; and in Munich at any rate, there were some
who were willing to pick it up.

It happened during a scene in which some of us were sitting on potties,
wearing pompom hats on our heads and with dummies in our mouths.
Suddenly there was shouting: 'Eins, zwei, drei, vier, fünf!' It drowned

the music. About twenty young men marched on to the stage in single file, still shouting and unfurling banners with slogans – neo-Nazi ones, I was told later. The demonstration must have been fixed up some time before; the students had occupied a block of seats in the first two rows of the stalls. The orchestra stopped playing; Herr Schmidt called to us, from the wings, to leave the stage, and most of the cast immediately began to do so.

But I stood my ground, as did some others, all black; the rebels included Donna Summer and Ronnie. My action wasn't particularly political; I just didn't see why these youths should spoil everyone's enjoyment. Also, from close to, it was quite obvious that they were not powerful or dangerous; just spotty self-important adolescents, rather pathetic really. I walked up to one and placed a potty on his head; a few of us began dancing round him. There was a roar of applause from the audience. They were naturally on our side, having paid to see the show and taken the trouble to come, but this by itself hardly accounts for the cheers and claps. My idea had simply been that a jerry was suitable headgear for a Jerry. But Germans don't think of themselves as Jerries, or necessarily know that a jerry means a chamber-pot. Almost certainly the people in the audience were thinking of something quite different, namely the famous George Grosz cartoon from the 1920s of a retired general with duelling scars wearing a potty on his head; they would have been familiar with this, whereas I was not. In any case, the crowd were on their feet. The cast trickled back, so did the orchestra. The demonstrators had lost the initiative. What should they do? Each had to decide for himself; they had not expected any of this to happen, so no plan had been agreed between them to cover it. Also, there was no leader. Some crept sheepishly away; the others stayed for a bit, including the one wearing the potty, and took part in an unrehearsed ensemble. We danced round them, in friendly fashion, and they became quite friendly in return, even joined in a bit. Again the audience applauded wildly. The orchestra started up, the last demonstrators left, and the show went on.

The theatre management was livid; so was Herr Schmidt, who all the time had been ordering me to get off, first in a stage whisper, then in a shout that rose almost to hysteria.

'*Susie! Komm' hier! Sofort!*'

He concentrated on me, partly because I was only a member of the chorus, partly perhaps because he felt happier ordering a white person around than tackling the blacks. It has also to be said that, among the chorus, I was undoubtedly the ringleader. With hindsight one can see why he was frightened. He was a middle-aged man who had lived through the Nazi era, and the period just before it. In those days a demonstration like this could easily have ended in serious violence, bloodshed, even a burnt-out theatre. Then, the demonstrators would probably have been armed and the police might quite likely have supported them. Of course things were now very different, but people are marked by their past. However, Herr Schmidt ought to have been big enough to realize that in the changed atmosphere of 1969 we were right and he was wrong, that the police, if called in, would have been on our side and the demonstration was really nothing more than a feeble prank. We had called the boys' bluff and won a victory, of which Herr Schmidt himself was the main beneficiary, because but for us he would have had to return that audience its money. This he could not see; he felt he had lost face. He was determined to sack someone, and because I was the easiest to sack, it had to be me.

So I was again without a job. I got plenty of sympathy, of course, and some advice. Kind Annette let me stay on with her at Schwabing for as long as I wanted. I tried to become a model. A good many photographs were taken of me in my huge white coat; my hair had now grown again. Some compliments came my way; I had an interesting face, one photographer told me. All the same, he added, he didn't actually see where I should fit in. I was before my time, he thought. This may have been right; modelling in 1969 was still static, I didn't possess the stillness and passive grace that were required. The day had not yet come when models would be judged on their ability to move.

I learned that a production of *Hair* was about to start in Paris, and that they were recruiting for it, so I decided to go there to try my luck. Before I went, somebody advised me also to try Dorien Lee's model agency. So, armed with these two possibilities, I took the train, arriving on a Saturday morning; and had one of those wonderful strokes of luck.

The first thing I did was to ring Dorien Lee's agency, in case someone was there with whom I could fix an appointment for the Monday. A French secretary answered.

'Who are you?'

'My name's Susie Potter.'

'Yes, of course Miss Lee will see you. Come round this afternoon at two o'clock.'

I was staggered. Dorien Lee must be a real workaholic to interview a complete stranger, just a voice on the telephone, at two o'clock on a Saturday afternoon. But who was I to argue?

'I'll be there,' I said.

At two o'clock I went round to the address. The door was opened by a slim chic woman.

'Hello,' she said, 'who are you?' Funny, I was expecting to see my sister.'

'My name's Susie Potter,' I said. 'Your secretary told me to come round here for an interview at two, I'm looking for a job as a model.'

'Well, if that's not the darndest thing! She told me on the 'phone Suzy Parker was coming to see me and I was thinking what a thrill it would be to see my sister. She simply heard wrong.' She laughed. 'Come in anyway now you're here, and tell me about yourself.'

I said I'd been in *Hair* in Munich and had come up to Paris to try my luck in an audition, and to get a job modelling if it didn't work out.

'I've got two girls on my books auditioning for *Hair*,' she said. 'It seems to be the rage in Paris, there's a lot of competition. As to modelling, have you a portfolio?'

'No,' I had to admit.'Just a few pictures.'

'I don't know that I can do anything for you without a proper portfolio. Where are you staying?'

'Nowhere at present,' I said, 'I just got in this morning.'

'Well, I just might be able to help. There's a couple of girls, friends of mine, I think they've got room. Jackie Astor and her friend.'

She picked up the telephone. 'Jackie . . . ? I've got this girl here, Susie Potter, auditioning for *Hair*. Could you put her up . . . ? Fine, she'll be there in half an hour.'

I was amazed. 'Well, thank you very much,' was all I could think of saying.

She turned her bright smile on me. 'Come and see me Monday,' she said, 'and I'll see if I can use you, help with your portfolio.'

Again it was like a dream. I got in a taxi, went to the address in a smart quarter of Paris, was greeted by these charming people. Jackie Astor was very kind to me; I stayed several weeks during all of which time I felt sheltered, welcome, safe.

All the same, my stay in Paris didn't lead to anything. I failed to get into *Hair*, mainly because I had almost no French. Dorien Lee, despite her kindness, could not fit me in, nor could any of the other agencies I tried. I got to know some groovy people and hung about with them; I had quite a good time, but I was really at a loose end. Without at first noticing it, I began going downhill, losing my energy and willpower. If I thought about this at all, I blamed my lack of a job, my inability to get one. People like me who do not follow a fixed career or a path mapped out by society, can easily get the feeling that nobody needs them. Who, I felt rather than thought, would miss me if I was not there? This is a cold and dismal state of mind. Whatever fun I was having with my friends in the evening, there was nobody who wanted me enough to pay me, nothing for me to do that would be of real help to anyone else. All the same, this feeling takes time to sink in, and it might not have affected me at all deeply had not something much nastier been at work, something physical.

One afternoon I went to the lavatory. I happened to look down and saw this off-white, stringy thing. I knew very well what it was; a tapeworm. Feet of it. I had eaten steak tartare once or twice in Beirut, that is probably where it came from. In any case it was obvious that I had to go home and have it seen to. I said goodbye to my friends, went to London and then up to my parents in Shaw. One reason I have survived my vicissitudes is probably that in really dire emergencies I have always been able to go home to Mum.

# 10

# Vomiting

The tapeworm was no match for our Lancashire doctor; he gave me some medicine and after a few days I passed the whole foul creature, right to the head. It must have been a yard or more long, off-white, segmented, folded in loops. I looked at it, there in the lavatory, and vomited. Surprisingly, this didn't feel unpleasant, but somehow *right*. I felt cleansed, uplifted; and I remember thinking it odd to feel like this after being sick. Soon it was lunchtime; I accepted second helpings of everything till I felt heavy. Afterwards I again went to the lavatory and spewed it all up. Again I felt that gratification. I was vomiting in the faces of the rapists, the Holloway warders, the tapeworm. Also I thought to myself, after eating like that I'd have probably started putting on weight; I shan't do that now, I shall be svelte and elegant. I felt purified of all poison, mental as well as physical; a clean and airy energy buoyed me up. My strength was as the strength of ten because my heart was pure.

What a mockery this was. My vomiting became a habit, then turned into an addiction. At first I did it occasionally, then every day, then after every meal; soon I began to eat between meals and did it then as well. I cleared out fridges, raided larders, wolfed food in supermarkets before being checked out; in later years I was to be reduced, at times, to scavenging fruit in boxes discarded by market traders, even devouring what people had left on their plates in restaurants. I was to go on eating and vomiting like this for eleven years and more; even now I have only recovered from the addiction in the sense that alcoholics recover provided they don't drink. It is, of course, impossible not to eat, which made my cure harder than going on the wagon. Fasting was never beyond my powers, but the trouble with fasting is that if one persists in it one is not cured, but dead. Bulimia is what they call my trouble. It is a more complicated thing to cure than alcoholism and, as with severe alcoholism, the cure is never quite complete. I still have to watch my

85

diet. Eating too much, or the wrong things, or at the wrong time, still makes me sick.

Bulimia is now quite well known, but in those days only experts had heard of it. For years I didn't know it was an illness. What will seem odd is that I enjoyed vomiting, even the process itself; though the real buzz came immediately afterwards in the form of a rush of high energy, of euphoria. I could ride on the feeling as on a drug high, though the intensity varied. I would often do cartwheels or a crab or walk about on my hands after throwing up. I also took a pride in vomiting cleanly and, as I felt, gracefully. This seemed to make up for the over-eating which followed it and gave the vicious spiral another twist downwards. All the same I soon began to hate the habit, especially when I realized it was something I couldn't give up. It made me ashamed, and the shame grew while the pleasure diminished. This made me despise myself for weakness of will. There was another way in which the disease made me feel ashamed; the wastefulness of it. I felt this almost from the beginning, but most acutely in later years when I found myself in India and Sri Lanka among people who really were short of food. At all times, of course, I realized that if other people knew about my habit they would find it unpleasant, so I kept it as secret as possible.

I am talking about this illness now, and shall do so again when I get to the point where I began to cure myself. In between, I shall only mention it when necessary; but from this point it must be understood that every time I had a meal, virtually every time I had a snack, I went and sicked it up. I found, too, that the sooner I did this the better; if my food stayed down less than a minute or so it was bland and pleasant, because the gastric juice had not had time to give it that acid taste. It was lucky for me that the need for secrecy often made it impossible to spew quite so quickly; if I had managed this every time I should perhaps have starved, because my digestion could not have snatched any nourishment at all. Frequent snacks were a help here, too; my ill-used stomach must have managed to keep back some minimal amount each time. It was in prison, when I was confined to three meals a day, that I really came close to starving.

Bulimia is an addiction to food-plus-vomiting; a genuine addiction, as strong as alcoholism or drug dependence. It is odd that this should have been my addiction considering the drugs I have tried without ever getting hooked. I have taken cannabis, LSD, morphine (in the form of Romilar) and on one occasion a line of cocaine, just to try it; none of these made me dependent. Yet I became abjectly enslaved to food and vomiting. Addiction is still a great mystery.

Already when I was in Lancashire, at the very start of my bulimia, the regular vomiting began to harm the enamel of my teeth and damage the gums. I decided to have all my teeth capped. This was quite expensive, but I regarded it as an investment, not realizing that it would only be worth while if I gave up my habit. Then my parents took a spring holiday for three weeks, caravanning in the South of France, and I went too. This was fun in a way, though rather like going back to childhood; and all the time the bulimia was taking hold. I then moved back to London, where I stayed in various places; once or twice I even parked myself on Roger, the boyfriend whom Wynson had abandoned to go with me to Austria. 'Not you again?' he would groan when I telephoned him, but he never refused me a corner on his settee or his floor.

At this time I went most Saturday afternoons to the Dance Centre at Floral Street to take lessons from Lindsay Kemp in mime and drama. He only charged a pound an hour, which was really giving it away, for he was a maestro, a genius. We never knew quite what the lesson would be like. Sometimes it was gruellingly energetic, sometimes quiet and contemplative. One experience was particularly beautiful.

'You are walking along,' he said, and we walked round the stage.

'Now when I clap, each of you will meet with your death. You will die. How you die is up to you.'

In my case I died vomiting, spewing my guts out, contorting myself, struggling on the floor. Then with a twitch I was still, waiting for the next instruction.

'Now you are reborn, in paradise; you are all angels.'

I rose to my feet, and suddenly my consciousness shifted as when a switch is pressed; this thing was actually happening to me. I was in paradise, these people were real angels.

Then there was the Round House, the circular turning shed given up by British Railways to become for some years the most exciting theatre in London, fostering every sort of alternative and experimental performance. Audience participation was a feature; the boundary between audience and performers was fluid and easily crossed. One could almost live at the Round House, if one could find somewhere to squat nearby, and take part in environmental happenings, or the performing arts laboratory. It was there that I met John and Denis Myers, identical twins.

They were – they are – beautiful; beautiful is the only word that will do. Slim, with straight black hair and a gipsy-dark complexion, long fine faces, straight noses, deep-set green eyes with long lashes which they fluttered. It is not that they were at all effeminate; rather, they were other-worldly, eldritch. They loved women, especially Denis, and women most certainly loved them. Ken Russell had used them in his films, they had modelled, they were well known on the scene. They spoke in ways entirely their own. In conversation their style was dry, strangely military. The reason for this clipped and rapid speech was perhaps that, from childhood, each knew the other's meaning before he had finished speaking. However, when reading or reciting they spoke quite differently, very slowly and in a tremulous singsong. Those unused to this mannerism did not always find it easy to keep a straight face. The twins were – are – like nobody else, except each other. They are identical in the sense of having sprung from one egg; yet there are subtle distinctions between them, and fond as I am of Denis it was always John who most drew me to him. He reminded me of a great crow, his head moving independently of his body on a fluid neck. We never became in the technical sense lovers, John and I; our friendship is so deep and strong as to have bypassed the physical. Anyway I was never plump enough for him. In later years he would tease me about this. Frequently when we were in company he would feel my upper arm, not in the least amorously but like the witch in Hansel and Gretel, or my father appraising a bullock; and the result would always be a scolding.

'Womannn,' he said, giving a funny little hum to the final 'n' sound, 'you need more flesh on those bones.'

But I had no wish to look voluptuous, even to please John. What to him was voluptuous, to me would have seemed gross.

Summer had arrived, it was already June, so my thoughts began to turn towards Formentera. How would I get there, though? I certainly couldn't afford to fly. As so often, something turned up. At the Round House, the twins and I met a Frenchman with an eye-patch and a suitcase full of spiritual literature; he was a member of the Living Theatre. He in turn introduced us to a German count, who said:

'Why don't you all come down with me to Spain in my van? I've got a house in Cadaques.'

'Where's that?' I asked.

'On the northern end of the Costa Brava,' he said. 'It's where Salvador Dali lives; his father was notary there.'

Dali, the great Surrealist, the artist who unlocked monsters from the subconscious and twisted the forms of nature with his own special non-logic. He was a name to me, of course; someone who in his own way explored the interior of the mind, as we did. Had I known his work better and how intimately it is linked to the landscape of Cadaques, I should have paid more attention; but I only thought of my own plans. I said:

'I want to get to Formentera, somehow.'

'It's more or less on the way,' said the count. 'Do come, and stay with me a couple of weeks.'

It was a generous offer, and would show me a new place and new adventures; I accepted at once. Later that day the count fitted us all into the van; the twins, the Frenchman with his eye-patch, a man called Rick who dressed as a cowboy, and me. We drove quietly through France. Our host, knowledgeable and thoughtful, showed us the sights, taking us on a detour whenever there was an interesting monastery or church or castle. This fascinated me but bored the Frenchman, who dropped off at Lyons. After a few days we came through the Pyrenees and across the Spanish border, down briefly into the plain of the Ampurdan, then up again into the rugged foothills, where the road wound along, displaying one spectacular view after another of hills covered with green and brown scrub splashed with the other-worldly grey of olive trees. At last the count turned right.

'Just a few kilometres now,' he said.

We drove down bends by the side of a deep ravine. John played his recorder, I accompanied him on a drum. Angular strips of cloud were slashed across the sky; I was later to see this sky again in Dali's paintings and, more immediately, to associate it with the *tramontana*, harsh and bracing, that is the prevailing wind of Cadaques. By and by we saw the sea, then we came round the corner to where the ravine widened to take in an eminence with a church on top and houses grouped around its slopes. Then the road became a village street under noble plane trees, and at last we came out on the Rambla, the short avenue or tree-lined oblong that is the social centre of the village. Cadaques, in due course to become my residence and my refuge.

It did not seem a refuge on that first visit. Formentera had embraced me; Cadaques confronted me. It threw down a challenge with its harsh hills and the angular shadows in its steep streets like canyons. It was as tough as Formentera was soft; the yang as compared to the yin. The people I met, too, were much more worldly: stimulating, not restful. There was none of that hippy vagueness.

The Count's house was high and narrow and whitewashed near the bottom of a steep cobbled street that would not take cars. From there one walked down a hundred yards at most, under an arch, past the barrows of two or three fishwives, across the road to the stony beach and the twinkling sea. I stayed there for two weeks exactly, busily painting

and drawing. Conventional and well-to-do people came up from
Barcelona at weekends. Few, as yet, practised alternative lifestyles, but
there were many painters and writers. This had always been the case;
Dali was only one example. Lorca and Picasso both visited Cadaques
between the wars. The biggest of the cafés, the Casino, had on some of its
round marble-topped tables these marvellous pencil drawings, mostly of
people and faces; they had been doodled by the artist Maifren.
Nowadays the old table tops are hung up on the walls to preserve them,
which is sensible; but it was more fun when they were simply the tables
round which the customers sat drinking, when one spotted these
drawings underneath one's cup of coffee and imagined one had
discovered them, casually, for oneself.

Life centred on the Casino and the other cafés round the Rambla.
Each had its normal clientele; there were the ones where the locals went,
there was one frequented by the older foreigners and the Barcelona
business people. Then there was the Hostal, a rather chichi place
patronized by the young and artistic. It had been done up by a gay
Frenchman with reproduction antiques and oddly shaped bottles with
coloured liquid, and at night one could dance to a band or a hi-fi. What
made it amusing was that people didn't at all stick to their 'own' cafés;
everyone of all sorts went to all of them at one time or other.

Peter Hodgkinson was a young English architect who worked in
Barcelona and played the drums at the Hostal; it was his wife Geela, a
German artist, who introduced me and the twins to the mountains. We
walked south-west along the high coastal path to the little lighthouse, or
the other way, north-east, towards the big lighthouse on Cabo Creus
that warns shipping to avoid that dangerous headland. Since it was June,
the mountains were still green; all but the toughest shrubs would scorch
to a dun colour by August. All the same, and despite the remains of the
spring flowers, the scene was austere and rocky. Patient farmers, long
dead, had terraced these mountains, father and son and grandson for
generations; their long toil had shaped a whole landscape. The earth is
still held back by these dry-stone walls with little steps cut into them,
some no more than a couple of feet, others fifteen feet high and more,
covering endless square miles of what is now nothing but wild mountain
scenery. In later years I was to come to love this landscape, to explore it
in depth, make use of its mysterious stone houses. On this first visit I kept
to the paths, but I stored Cadaques in my memory as a place to come
back to, one day.

Formentera was an anticlimax; I stayed in a different part of the
island this time, and did not recapture the magic. A South American

lady employed me in an informal sort of way to look after her three children and their friends, in return for board and lodging. She was good at making paellas, and I ate large helpings only to bring them up, furtively, in the bushes. One day I felt in my mouth two hard objects like cherry stones. Alas! It was two of my newly capped teeth, detached from their roots by the hydrochloric acid.

Back in London, I visited the twins' studio behind Bombers, a boutique in Radnor Walk. I came to spend hours there. It was a tiny place, reached through a nondescript back yard. From the outside it looked squalid, yet inside it was marvellous. Nearly everything was antique, especially, I felt, the twins themselves; they seemed to be reincarnated from some unimaginably distant century. There were old box cameras, theatrical props, a fine chaise-longue in red velvet, shawls draped everywhere. A smoking jacket hung on a tailor's dummy, with a feathered woman's hat on the head. There was a huge blow-up of Sophia Loren and Marcello Mastroianni in *A Man and a Woman*. John had an easel where he painted. The twins did everything with style and grace, smoking the pipes from their collection and listening endlessly to classical music, especially Beethoven: the Eroica, the Emperor Concerto. Mahler's Ninth Symphony was another favourite. A guest would arrive and take a seat with hardly a word, slotting at once into the pattern, accepting a passed joint or rolling his own; then when he felt like it he would just leave. They let me paint in a corner of the studio, and though there was really no room for me to sleep they would sometimes let me curl up on the floor or on their chaise-longue. I also made friends with their neighbour Geoffrey Brett, a gaunt, grey-haired poet, older than us; a figure from the Fifties, dressed as often as not in a dressing gown and living on muesli and valium. His little place was austere, and much as I loved the twins' warm, old-world clutter there was something about Geoffrey's bleakness that appealed to me.

But my bulimia had settled in, and in addition I was smoking a lot of cannabis, which makes one fuzzy-minded, careless as to the morrow. The weather turned chillier, winter was starting, and I began to feel as I had in Paris, that I had no roots, no point. On the whole I kept this at bay, though, enjoying life on the scene with my friends in coffee bars, or in the Picasso restaurant in King's Road. Every day there was a new sight to see, a new sound to hear, another joint to roll, another picture to paint. To earn a bit of money, I did odd jobs for Universal Aunts and Solve Your Problem Limited. One met children on trains, took them across London; that sort of thing. On one occasion it was not a child but a parrot. Then in the evenings there was dancing, usually in the UFO club. As in Manchester in the old days, I would dance for hours at a stretch, tirelessly, wearing out one partner after another. I also went to the Round House; the Living Theatre was a joy, especially when I could join in through the audience participation.

One Chelsea figure of the time whom I always enjoyed meeting was Marc Chagall's son, also called Marc. He was a genial old fellow with a marvellous collection of walking-sticks and a fund of stories which he shouted at the top of his voice. Sometimes I think he confused himself with his father; he also, despite his age, very much fancied his chances with the girls. At first we used to find him in the Picasso restaurant; later he moved to a geriatric bed in a hospital, where John Myers and I went to see him several times. He had a number of his father's paintings for us to look at.

The people I knew in various parts of London would have been surprised to know that I was ill, and getting worse. They thought of me as energetic, which I was, but only I knew that this was partly due to the high from my vomiting; only I knew of my habit and the shame of it. As always, I walked erect, and nobody believes there can be much wrong with anyone who stands up straight. All the same, if I had carried on in the same way I could easily have ended as a tramp, a bag-lady. Part of my trouble was that I enjoyed being slim, and able to slide into the clothes of the twenties and forties which we were all wearing.

Up in Lancashire my parents worried about me, though without knowing quite why. One day, not long before Christmas, my mother sent me some money, enough to get to Spain with; she wrote me a letter saying that was what I ought to do. Of course I never went to Spain or anywhere else, but stayed in London, frittering the money on my food habit and puffing my guilt away *chez* the twins in a cloud of marijuana to the sound of the Pastoral Symphony.

# 11

# The Arm of the Law

One of the others who hung round the studio was Philippe, an eighteen-year-old French gipsy with lustrous black hair to his waist and two inch fingernails on elegant white hands. A friend of the twins had brought him along one day, dumping him on their doorstep like a stray cat, as it seemed to me, for the poor boy had no resources. Anyway he became one of the gang, and one day he said, 'Do you know Feliks Topolski?'

I was stumped, but Denis said: 'Of course, the artist.'

'He has invited me to come to his house on Christmas Day, and bring friends. Why don't you all come along?'

Denis preferred to stay with his girlfriend from Models One, but John and I decided to accept; it would cheer up our Christmas which otherwise seemed likely to be bleak, since we had no money. We walked in the direction of Feliks's house, not being able to afford a taxi; but it was rather a long way, so Philippe put out his thumb for a lift. People don't often stop in London, but since it was Christmas Day you never knew.

Philippe had the Midas touch. A Ford Escort stopped and the driver said, in a southern American drawl, 'Merry Christmas.'

'Merry Christmas,' we returned.

'I can give y'all a lift,' he said. 'Where you going?'

We told him. 'Sure you don't mind taking us all around the city?' I said, for perhaps he didn't realize how far it was.

'No problem,' he said. 'Ain't got nothing else to do.'

When we got in, I said, 'Are you doing anything today?'

'I guess not,' he said. 'I'm at my great-aunt's house, but she's not there. I'm alone apart from my father's secretary, and she's got a date.'

'Come with us, then,' said Philippe, for the invitation had been for any number. Feliks welcomed us warmly and gave us a lovely time. His house was fascinating, furnished in sumptuous East European style and decorated with wallpaper of his own beautiful design. By the time we left, it was as if we were all old friends. Our kindly driver, it transpired, was a postgraduate student on sabbatical, using his aunt's Eaton Place house as a base from which to pursue his hobby of motor-racing. When we left Feliks's he asked us back for a coffee. The house was grand but rather dingy; it had not been decorated for half a century and there was something reassuring about the solid furniture, the big round wooden tables. Our friend's aunt had been a sculptress; mounted on a pillar there was a big portrait head she had done of herself.

'Where are you living?' our host asked me.

'Well,' I said, 'John and Denis have got a place, but Philippe and I are dossing wherever we can. At the moment we are on somebody's floor.'

'Why don't you come and stay here?' he said. 'There's loads of room.' He was expansive, trusting, pleased at the good time we had given him.

That's how the trouble began. His aunt trusted him; he trusted us; we trusted others, and the end result was the death of trust. But at the time we didn't seem to be harming anyone. We lived at peace, brewing endless pots of tea and smoking joints. All the same, our numbers began to escalate, and I slipped into the role of organizer. John Myers brought Eveline, a French lady, fortyish, with South American connections who hung homeless round the King's Road. She was thin and nervous, practised Za-Zen and worshipped the twins. I felt for her as a fellow-dosser; naturally I gave her a room. Another afternoon, two more people came and stayed. A friend of Philippe's came when our host happened to be there, and charmed him into letting him have a room. Lance, he was called; a good-looking man with wavy hair and a moustache, dressed in period clothes. Unluckily he was a dope dealer. A small-scale one, right down the line, but a dealer all the same. He cut hash into squares and sold it, like the old man in Rabat; he also had fingers of red Lebanese, wrapped in silver paper. He was very discreet, but customers came, and the place became known.

This was the time when I finally wrote off my beautiful capped teeth. They had been falling out; but I saved the front ones, and stuck them in myself with gum. This was useless, so I tried again with sealing-wax. This hurts at first, but the wax soon cools and the teeth, for a week or two, are firmly in place. But I couldn't go on doing this all my life, so I got a set of temporary false teeth, big men's ones with one gold eyetooth so that the rest would seem more real. I meant to go back for a permanent set, but never had enough money. My present good set comes from a later date and a different dentist.

Feliks Topolski became a friend to all of us; we often went to his studio under one of the railway arches on the South Bank, just near the Festival Hall. He welcomed his friends on Fridays, starting about five o'clock. The place was like a warehouse, with its conrete floor, its high-placed window, its all-pervading dust. It was hung and piled high with paintings, drawings, gouaches on canvas, on cardboard, on paper. They were of all sizes; the walls were lined with the big ones, mostly unfinished, about twelve feet high, layered one on top of the other. The public know Feliks best for his impressionistic black and white drawings, but these don't show his magical sense of colour. In his giant paintings colour comes in swirls and waves as if on a wild ocean, then the waves will organize themselves to produce a sharply-observed face, the pink body of a glass-breasted nude, or George Bernard Shaw. You know how sometimes, just before going to sleep or when otherwise semi-conscious, one sees patterns of pulsating colour that are just that, yet seem at the time to have a deep meaning? Feliks's paintings often tell us that our everyday thoughts and images are not solid at all, but born of this many-coloured subconscious chaos.

The studio, at all events, was a chaos. He had a space cleared, after a fashion, under the window, so that he could paint where the light fell; but even that space was cluttered with tins of paint and easels and palettes. There was another space on the dark side of the studio where we sat on or around his red velvet chaise-longue and bed. Apart from that the entire room was covered in paintings, finished and unfinished, and piles of prints and periodicals, not to mention supplies of clean paper that were often creased and spoilt. The same was true of many of the works themselves; clearly someone had the habit of scrabbling under his piles for particular things, without caring much what happened to the rest, and that someone must have been Feliks himself, because nobody else would have dared. I use the past tense, but nineteen years later it all remains the same, except that the piles are deeper still and the treasures even more numerous. Disregarded treasures, for Feliks, though he won't throw anything away, doesn't seem to care whether it gets torn or creased. A creative artist doesn't need to preserve; if he tears something or loses it he feels he can always do it again, or something else as good.

Feliks himself held court on his chaise-longue away from the window, dispensing coffee or tea or wine, chatting, rapidly sketching someone when he felt like it. Philippe was a favourite model; he dressed in all sorts of clothes, sometimes even as a woman, and Feliks would grab his sketch-book and start drawing. One painting of Philippe shows him in a feathered hat. Feliks painted the twins too; all three of them feature in his monumental *Memoir of the 20th Century* now housed under an adjacent

arch, as typical figures of the late sixties. He did at least one painting of
me, giving me four hands; I didn't make the *Memoir* though, unless I am
one of the shadowy female faces near the others. Dear Feliks! His
friendship was a boon at a time when I was going downhill, but neither
he nor anyone could stop my descent.

It was 20 January, 1970. There were about ten of us, enjoying joints
and music; I was mildly stoned and on a vomiting high as well. The
beautiful sheepskin coat that I had acquired in a swap from Frau
Loeffler was draped round the pillar which bore the aunt's sculptured
head. The twins were not there, but three debutante followers of theirs
had turned up hoping to find them. Then there were Eveline, Philippe,
and Geoffrey Brett; others as well. Our friend Ian Goodman turned up
with someone new, who said he had something for us. This guy asked us
into the kitchen where there were drinks set out on the table: small
glasses of clear colourless fluid which could have been vodka. In fact,
each held an ounce of pure liquid acid – LSD. The normal dose of this
drug is a few drops, generally taken on a tab of blotting paper. We
downed the drug, in my case in one swig. Bottoms up; why none of us
was killed by this I shall never know. In any case from then on – BOY!

First oblivion; the room and the people dissolved. This stage could
have lasted seconds or hours . . . Then there were stars and stripes,
colours everywhere, swirling, billowing, changing. I felt rooted where I
stood, the world turned fluid around me. The banisters melted; people
shed garments, for LSD makes one feel hot. There was a power cut, I
think; at any rate all the lights went out and the music stopped. Someone
lit candles. In a corner was a group of sleek young horses; a chestnut, a
grey, a black one. Gentle fillies tossing their manes. I knew they were the
three debutantes who had come looking for the twins. Geoffrey and
anther guy took their shirts off and spoke to each other in Roman
numerals.

'X one one,' said Geoffrey.

'V one double one,' his friend replied.

'L X one V?' asked Geoffrey, with an insistent questioning note.

'C,' said the other firmly.

This conversation seemed deeply meaningful, but I could not follow
it, so I started to dance. I felt Hebraic, Greek, whirled back through the
centuries. Eveline was with me, her presence was intense; I cared deeply
for her and felt passionately at one with her. I saw athletes, Olympic
athletes running; and suddenly a feeling of disaster came. Precognition
of the shooting in Munich, perhaps.

'Can't you see?' I cried. 'The games! The Olympic games!'

The visions came and went; did I sleep? In that condition there is no knowing what is sleep, what is consciousness. Early in the morning I decided to paste my hair with henna, I thought it would be a constructive thing to do. As a trained hairdresser I knew just how to apply it, so I slapped it on with carefree expertise, gobs of thick dark greenish-brown henna which would make my hair bright auburn-red after it had done its work. Then after an hour or two the bell rang. I opened the door, dressed in my shift with carpet slippers several sizes too big and my hair covered with this gunk. It was the police; three of them, with a search warrant.

What had happened was that Philippe had taken my sheepskin coat off the pillar and gone up to the roof to look at the stars. After a bit he had thrown off the coat and stood there in the cold dressed only in his hipster bell-bottom trousers, his waist-length hair hanging down his back, his arms raised to greet the cosmos. An admiral in a flat opposite had spotted this odd-looking, motionless figure in the gathering light and fetched his binoculars. Yes, there was no doubt; it was a young man, long-haired, half-naked. He telephoned the police.

They searched the house. There was still a glass of LSD in the fridge. The guy who had brought the stuff had left. Then in Lance's room they found his stock in trade, a quantity of hash. This was more than enough.

We were shown into a black maria. I went first, still in my absurd outsize slippers and with my hair covered with henna, wearing my sheepskin coat over my shift. Later one of the policemen testified in court that I had excrement on my hair, and it did in fact look rather as if I had put a cowpat on it. As in my previous LSD trip, I felt I was in a film, a B movie this time. I seemed to be cast as the great madame.

At Chelsea police station I was in difficulty; for a time I even forgot my real name, though I remembered 'Shoe'. A policeman came up with this form for me to sign, but I couldn't hold the pen. Another offered me a cigarette; I stared at it. It seemed to be gigantic, a foot long, a strange, alien object. I waved it away. All thoughts of resistance, of self-defence, were in abeyance; the only reality was the present. Despite my surroundings, all seemed peace and bliss; the police in their uniforms with their notebooks, the cream tiles, the hum of officialdom, all seemed to have an extraordinary charm. I took in some of what was going on. The three debutantes, no longer horses, were taking turns on the telephone, mobilizing their mothers or their solicitors. Geoffrey Brett, the poet, was fiddling with his ballpoint and a piece of paper, but no inspiration seemed to come. He soon gave up and contemplated the silver sheen of his classy ballpoint. Lance adopted a military air, marching up and down the police station, caricaturing the fuzz and shouting from time to time. Philippe was impassive as a waxwork, Eveline was desperately nervous, fidgety, clearly heading for a bad trip. '*Mon Dieu!*' she kept repeating. '*Mon Dieu! C'est affreux!*'

Lance began abusing the coppers, so they put him by himself in a padded cell. I was glad to see him go, to tell the truth, for his shouts were annoying me. The rest of us were taken to ordinary cells in pairs; my companion was Eveline. Our cell was sparse, devoid of distractions; the tiles were a restful yellowy-beige, the bench was shiny as glass and rounded to the touch. It was monastic, the ideal place to complete a trip. I promptly lay down on the floor and put my legs into the full lotus posture for meditation. In this way I could drift and dream, allow the trip to unfold in this tiled womb with its little three-barred window in the door. I completed the remaining hours moving out of one twisted posture into another; I had at that stage had no yoga lessons, and most of my positions were simply those that felt right to me at that moment. Eveline, worried and tripping badly, was certainly soothed a bit by my calm demeanour; but I was only aware of her at intervals. Much of the time I was not in the present, but seemed to be back in other times and incarnations, away in other possibility-worlds. This body of mine, my present suit of clothes, proved obedient and adept, and I enjoyed the facility with which it twisted itself every way I told it. All the same I had this strong feeling that it was not me, but simply something I dwelt in. A mug of tea, a sandwich of fatty beef and a rock bun intruded; they were as a fly on the face, brushed away to be forgotten.

Night fell, we emptied our potties and were given blankets; then the light was dimmed to a silvery blue colour. This seemed a new delight, a new mystery; yellow had been predominant before, extrovert daytime yellow, and now it was replaced by the gentle blue of the night. I suppose I slept. Early next morning the henna had dried to a powder; it reminded me of the sand in my hair when I was a child by the seaside and came in from a game on the beach. Having no comb I rubbed my scalp hard, shook my hair till the henna was piled on the cell floor, a greenish powder like Japanese tea. My hair must have surprised the police; could this startling redhead have been the same person as the mud-headed vagrant they locked up the day before? At least I was now in a condition to tell them my name and sign their form, before facing the magistrate in the police court.

Friends turned up at the court; Ian Goodman had rounded up the necessary people to bail us out. The Chelsea scene was a strange mixture; on the one hand people would run like rats in fear of being busted themselves, but on the other there was a fierce fellow-feeling, a determination to help when possible. My surety was Nicky Ryman, whom I had only met casually, through the twins; we had visited him once or twice in his Pont Street flat. He was to renew his pledge throughout the ten months before we came to trial, bless him. Philippe was bailed by Feliks Topolski; I'm not sure who helped Geoffrey. The debutantes were whisked away by their families.

The magistrate told us all to turn up at the assizes in six weeks, and when it was over I dusted the last of the henna powder off my coat and stepped out into the street. A flash-bulb popped; news had reached Fleet Street, and a little knot of newshounds was waiting. The front page of the *Evening News* of 21 January, 1970, carries the story of the arrest, with a picture of one of the other girls. I had always remembered it as being me, but it isn't. Just as well perhaps.

# 12

# The Mahatma's Light

The twins were in their studio when I turned up later that day; John offered me a cup of maté tea from South America, Denis handed me a pipe. I told them everything that had happened and soon, under their soothing influence, my trouble faded. I couldn't quite forget it, of course; I knew very well that sooner or later there would be a trial and more trouble. For the next nine months my dread of this was an obscure but insistent ache. It did not affect my life except to make my bulimia worse; I now had a worry in the present to add to my hang-ups from the past.

A new person was at the twins' that evening, new to me at least. Venetia Stanley-Smith was a dark girl with brilliant black eyes and a quick sympathetic intelligence. I felt drawn to her at first sight. She was only eighteen and a debutante, but she had been lead singer in a pop group, and was a cordon bleu cook. She later showed iron determination and a pioneering spirit; qualities she perhaps inherited from her great-grandmother, Emily Pankhurst, or her great-uncle, Lord Curzon. Yet at this time the world was distressing and distracting her; she wanted to find the way to God. She was 'on a God trip', as we used to say in those days; not a good expression because it puts God on a par with a hobby, or even a drug. It says a bit about us Sixties people that we could talk like this. Because we were willing to try anything, we were apt to look on everything as being of equal value. We were all 'into' something, and it didn't much matter what; into hash, into carpentry, into rock, into health foods, into CND, into scientology. If Venetia's serious and humble quest for spiritual enlightenment seemed in a class apart, it was because her account of it was powered by her personal magnetism. She had come to the studio to tell us about the Divine Light Mission of the Guru Maharaj Ji.

'A friend of ours who used to be a colonel in the Indian army told me about this guru, Guru Nanak, and took me along. I was disappointed, and didn't know why. Now I know it was because his message was incomplete.'

'How do you mean?' said Denis.

'Nanak is a good man, no question about it, and he gives great meditations on light and sound, but that's all he does. It isn't really the whole answer, and for me Guru Nanak was a dead end, sort of. But I got talking to some of the people there, and found out about the Divine Light Mission. So I went round to this basement in Fairholme Road.' She paused for effect.

'And then?'

'Well, all I can say is that it's the real thing. Guru Maharaj Ji – ' she pronounced it M*arah*ji' – gives light and sound meditations as well, but he also gives meditation on the holy word, and on nectar. It's like nothing else in this world. He's a child, not more than ten, but he has followers all over the world. They call themselves premies.'

'A child!' I said. 'What is he like?' I thought of my vision of the Indian child in the Windsor café.

'I didn't meet him in person, he's in India, but I saw one of his people, Mahatma Charanand. He imparts the Guru's knowledge and he is – *radiant*. He radiates goodness and happiness, reflects the Guru's innocence as the moon reflects the sun. You must come and meet him, all of you. You too.' She turned her bright black eyes on me.

'I'll come,' I said.

The twins, too, would always try anything, so soon they and I went with Venetia to Fairholme Road. Various people were there; someone said:

'Mahatma's in the back.'

We went behind to the little kitchen and there he was, peeling potatoes. He was just a gentle old Indian in pink silk robes, but it was as if a 100 watt light bulb was turned on in my head. Every time I met him I was to feel the same.

Mahatmaji had served the Guru's father, also a guru, for many years. It was a family business, said the cynics in the newspapers when, a little later, they became aware that the Divine Light Mission was a mass movement worldwide; they fastened on the Guru's private aircraft and Rolls-Royce, insinuating that the family was in it for the cash. It is true that after the time I am describing the Guru's message began to be 'marketed' by hucksters who didn't seem to understand what it was about. These people repelled the intelligent but managed to convert many good and innocent people to a vulgarized version of the knowledge, a caricature. Mahatmaji was light years from all this, and too innocent and loyal to have understood it if anyone had ventured to point it out to him. The trouble is not peculiar to the Divine Light Mission; all religions suffer from something like it. Krishnamurti, in his day, walked out of his own organization when he realized that it could only corrupt his message, and the history of Christianity is the history of a Message that keeps getting buried in error and misunderstanding. There have been splits too in the Mission, again as in Christianity; at least nobody has been burnt at the stake. In any case, to me at this time the Mission was the Mahatma, and he was undoubtedly a holy man. I have since met others. Each had his own flavour, his own being; each dispensed the eternal wisdom in his own way. For me, though, Mahatmaji was the first, and I shall always revere him.

I went often to the satsang room in that basement, where for an hour or so I could let go of my restlessness and turmoil, suppress the worry about the coming court case, and prepare myself to 'take the Knowledge'. I made many friends there. Sister Sandy cooked for the mission; she it was who was in the kitchen with Mahatmaji when I first saw him. She was a renunciate, almost like a nun in her sober dresses with her hair scraped back. It was she who had been to Hardwar in North India and found the Divine Light Mission and the Guru's family who ran it. She had been on morphine at the time, hopelessly addicted; she came across the mission almost by chance, and they took her in. By and by she brought the Mahatma to Britain. There was another former addict, also cured by the mission; a young man with fair hair down to his bottom, carefully combed back. I, like these people, was coming to the Mission in a desperate state, addicted to my bulimia, weakened by rape and prison and with the prospect of more prison. So often those who seek the light are the weak and the weary.

Not that this was true of all the devotees. One who quickly became a close friend was Julian West, a beautiful, fine-boned girl who looked like a Sinhalese princess; which is exactly what she was, through her mother, her father being Aubrey West, the handwriting expert. Then there was Charles Cameron, a poet, who had the gift of putting the feelings of satsang into words; approximately only, no-one could ever do it exactly, but he enriched the experience of all of us.

Soon Venetia invited me to stay with her; I gratefully accepted. I came to know her really well. Though so much younger than me, she cared for me almost like a mother. But she had her own troubles.

'You know,' she said once, 'before I found the Guru I was on the point of cracking up.'

'What! You?' I asked in surprise, for she seemed so strong and stable.

'Oh yes, I was in a very bad way. It's strange, because the world seemed to be at my feet; I had money and friends, a good life, even a proposition to make a pop record with Frank Sinatra.'

'Honestly?'

'Well, I don't know if it would have come off. Anyway I didn't pursue it, that whole world seemed so empty. That's when I started searching.'

'And found Mahatmaji.'

'Exactly. And now I know that I am going to devote my life to the Divine Light Mission.'

She has done exactly what she said. A year or so after this, early in 1971, she went to Japan to establish the Divine Light Mission there, and succeeded. But that story belongs to a later chapter.

About this time I went along to Universal Aunts and landed a temporary job, a real plum; teagirl at Apple, the Beatles' company. This, to me, was like being taken on at Buckingham Palace, only more so. All the Beatles were in and out. Ringo was the only one I had any sort of conversation with. The first time I brought him his tea he looked at me curiously, cocking his head on one side.

'Are you Yugoslavian, then?' he asked me.

'No,' I said, 'I'm from Lancashire, like you. I was born in Oldham.'

'Well, how about that? I could have sworn you were from Yugoslavia. Or Poland.'

'Why did you think that?'

'I don't know, you've got that sort of a look somehow.'

Unfortunately the Beatles hated my tea. From the Divine Light people I had learnt to make proper Indian chai the way they do it in the East, boiling the tealeaves in milk with root ginger and cardamoms. I felt that my employers ought to like this, given their interest in the Maharishi Mahesh Yogi. But my beautiful chai took far too long to make, and didn't taste right when it appeared. The Beatles preferred the traditional quick-brew teabag slung into the accustomed mug of boiling water, and they expected to get it quickly. I only lasted about two days in the job.

Punctually six weeks after my arrest, in mid-March, the day of the Assizes arrived. I hadn't seen any of the others since the time we were all arrested, except Geoffrey Brett who was a neighbour of the twins. The organization Release, which helps people accused of drug offences, had provided me with a solicitor. He was a sympathetic character by the name of David Offenbach.

'Nothing will happen today,' he told me. 'They'll remand you all again for further evidence.'

'What further evidence do they need?' I asked. 'We were all bombed out of our skulls, and they know it.'

'Difficult to say, it's usually like this. I expect they want to know where the stuff came from.'

David turned out to be right. The proceedings only took an hour; bail was renewed, we were told to come back in three calendar months. Then we each went our separate way; an oddly assorted crowd, debs and down-and-outs, a poet, a neurotic French lady, a strange Gipsy boy, and myself, a hopeless case of bulimia. Seeing the others again I felt I was looking at them through the wrong end of a telescope; I no longer had much in common with them now that I had found Mahatmaji. He had shown me not in words, but in his being, that there is something beyond this material existence. I well knew that there was no escaping from what had happened, or from the trouble I was in, but I lived with it. I still danced at the UFO club, I still went to arts laboratories, alternative environmental happenings, and so on. I even exhibited about twenty-five of my paintings in a café belonging to a kindly Pole near Worlds End. They were not framed (I could not have afforded this) but I was pleased to see them round his walls, together with the works of a young sculptor. One or two were sold, mostly for about £2.50, £5 being the very top price. They were abstracts of strange swelling shapes, animals and birds, vaguely like sketches for possible living forms as they might have existed in the mind of the Creator, discarded drafts of organisms, melting into and emerging out of one another. Whether they were any good I have no idea. I wonder if anyone still has one.

# 13

# The Strongest Woman
# in the World

Lindsay Kemp was at this time giving his dance classes on the balcony of the Round House. One day he told us that a theatre group called Palais des Merveilles was expected from Paris, a burlesque circus act without animals. After the class, I wandered down to the cafeteria to see if there were some leftovers on the tables which I could wolf so as to give myself a free binge. This was something I often did; I was rock-bottom in money, there was no way I could have paid for my food habit, so I sustained it off other people's plates. I wasn't gross about it; I would prance up to the abandoned plate, look at it with a sidelong glance and then whip up the food in my fingers neatly and as if absentmindedly, perhaps talking to someone else at the same time. The Round House cafeteria was the finest place for this; no-one ever paid any attention, and also the food was all whole food, stoneground bread, organically-grown vegetables, free range eggs and so on. It is surprising what some people will leave. Anyway, this time I found the cast of the Palais des Merveilles there, and I got chatting to some of them, finding them a friendly lot of people. Naturally I watched their first performance next day.

There were two midgets, a man on stilts, a fire-eater who also jumped through a flaming hoop. There was an enormously fat girl with jet black hair and a prissy little mouth who dressed in a white ballet costume, complete with tutu, to perform a galumphing caricature dance to the music of *Swan Lake*. Another lady, of a certain age, wore bleach-blonde hair cut short to ear-length and marcelle waved; she wore men's boxer shorts and nothing else, and stood in a hip-bath playing the cello, her oversized breasts sagging over a floppy stomach. Her cello-playing was pure and beautiful, a poignant contrast to her dreadful body. Miss Lily was the opposite; a lanky six-footer, she wore sparkling leotards and had her black hair woven into two long plaits fortified with fusewire so that they stood out at the sides of her head like antennae. The master of

105

ceremonies, and the boss of the outfit, was Jules, a handsome man of
about forty with blue eyes and mousy hair; a cross between Burt
Lancaster and Kirk Douglas. His manner was hard, macho. He wore
white tie and tails, white gloves. He was as light on his feet as Fred
Astaire and as deft as a conjurer. He wore white face make-up with a bit
of lipstick and mascara. It was he who presented all the acts, held the
ring while the fire-eater jumped through it. Miss Lily worshipped him;
they made love a lot behind the scenes when not busy with anything else.
Nor did they keep their passion to themselves; a pretty girl would often
be seen leaving their dressing-room adjusting her clothes with the
dreamy expression of one who has been made very happy indeed.
Sometimes it was a nice-looking young man.

That first performance captivated me; thereafter I went every night,
and chatted with them behind the scenes. Part of Jules's act was to turn
a spotlight on someone in the audience and challenge them in some way,
ask them to flex their muscles, dare them to wrestle with one of his
midgets. One night I was suddenly dazzled; the spotlight was on me.

'Let's see if you've got a biceps,' said Jules.

Well, I remembered Ronnie giving me threepence for my biceps
when I was little. I stood up and flexed my bare arm; for a woman in
those days before the female bodybuilders of Pumping Iron II the
muscle stood out quite well.

Jules came up to me, under the spotlight, and said, 'So you think
you're strong, do you? I'm going to make you sit down.'

He pushed me. I resisted, determined not to give in. I must have
surprised him because he broke into French and said softly, not for the
audience, '*En effet, tu est bien forte.*'

He remembered this next day when he saw me in the restaurant,
picking up scraps from people's plates like a stray cat.

'How is the strong girl?' he said.

'All right.'

He looked me up and down.

'That's quite a pair of shoulders you've got. How would you like to do
a bit more in the act with us?'

'I'd like it, of course.'

'Come to rehearsal tomorrow, then.'

'I'll be there.'

We shook hands on it. His grip was firm; so was mine. Again I felt he
was testing me, trying me for size. I never lost this feeling with Jules; all
the time he was challenging me, on more levels than he ever knew. He
brought out the masculine side of me, and made me determined not to

let him see my femininity. He was not going to make me give in, not in any way. To be brutally precise, I was resolved never to drop my knickers for him in that dressing-room with Miss Lily watching. He was an attractive man; yes, there was a sexual attraction, but to give in to it would have been to knuckle under. I would be a colleague on equal terms, or nothing. Let him be a hard taskmaster; I should be equal to everything he wanted me to do, and more, but I was not going to be one of his concubines.

Punctually next day I turned up for the rehearsals in my leotard and long combinations. Jules greeted me politely, but for a few seconds it seemed evident that he had forgotten asking me to come. This might have been a ploy; ploy or no ploy, I wasn't having it. I looked him straight in the eye, used a bit of body-language with him, and he remembered.

It all hung on whether he could throw me over his back, or I him. We got in a clinch, and I held him to a stalemate. He looked at me thoughtfully, sketching out a possible routine in his mind. Then he said, 'Can you do a back flip?'

'I've never done one, but I will if you'll show me.'

He showed me. I followed him with ease because, whether or not I was all that strong, I was as fit as a flea from my constant dancing. When not at the Round House I'd be at the UFO club or somewhere similar, dancing to acid rock, sometimes for four hours at a stretch. My natural energy coupled with the effects of bulimia drove me to exercise more than ever till I was hard as nails. It wasn't many minutes before I did a decent back flip.

'You're on tonight,' he said. 'We'll bill you as the Strongest Woman in the World. Wait here till I've rehearsed the others, then we'll get you ready.'

So that night, there I was in the audience in a sleeveless dress and a raincoat, with a skullcap on my head.

'Who is the strongest woman in the world?' cried Jules.

I stood up, took off the raincoat and shouted, 'I am.'

The spotlight swivelled and rested on me; I flexed my muscles in the dazzling glare.

'Come and prove it!'

I whipped off the dress and stood there topless; they had painted rings of colour round my breasts so that they looked like two targets. My breasts were not large, but firm and prominent enough to prove I was not a man in disguise, in case anyone was wondering.

Then I walked into the arena. Jules and I got into a clinch, skull to skull, arms crossed over each other's shoulders, walking and pushing. One, two, three, then he heaved me over his shoulders and I did a roll back flip, ending on my back. He came towards me to gloat over his success but I jumped up, turned on him and tossed him over my shoulder: he lay on his back defeated. I put a foot on him and looked around the audience, flexing my biceps in triumph; then one of the midgets came up behind me, dressed in bright green with green make-up and a great eye on the top of his head, a green manikin from outer space. He tripped me up, pushed me down on my back, stepped up on to my stomach and stood there, claiming he was the strongest. The whole sketch was over quickly, in two minutes at the most, to rolls of the drum. Next thing you knew the spotlight was off us and on Jules, now holding the flaming hoop for the fire-eater. My sketch went down well, and I became a regular performer. At matinées I wore a leotard top, in deference to the children and their mums; it was only in the evenings that I appeared with my bullseye tits.

One day Jules said to me, 'I'd like you to appear in the finale.' He turned to Miss Lily. 'How shall we dress her?'

'I'll get some things to try,' she said, and ran behind stage, reappearing with a pile of dresses, skirts, tights, furs, spangled boleros. After trying several other things on me, she selected a blue feather boa and draped it over my shoulders.

'That's it,' he said. 'With her blue leotard.'

'How about this?' I said, for an idea had occurred to me that would really be in the spirit of the show. They liked the macabre; very well, they would see something they hadn't bargained for. I put my hand in my mouth, removed my set of false teeth and gave them a wide, slack grin to show my bare gums.

'*Ça, alors!*' said Jules, genuinely surprised. He and Miss Lily looked at each other. They appreciated my sacrifice of personal vanity for artistic effect.

The finale was in two parts. In the first, old records from the Thirties were played and we invited people from the audience to dance; waltzes, quicksteps, foxtrots. I had the blue boa draped over my painted breasts and blue leotard tights to match; my face was painted dead white with red patches on the cheeks and I fluffed out my henna-red hair so that it was like a lion's mane. At the very end we all stood still to take a bow; and that was when, grinning broadly, I removed my teeth, no longer the wholesome dolly-girl but another weirdo.

I moved into a squat opposite the Round House, a flat that had belonged to Suzy Creamcheese, an underground press figure whom I knew. For a week I housed the big fat ballerina there; she was rather a dear, only eighteen years old but I suppose she had glandular trouble. It was an odd place, all sorts of freaks had inhabited it. There were all these lengths of cloth; somebody had been cutting them up at one time, dressmaking presumably. We used them as bedclothes.

My squat was a godsend, because it meant I could easily get away from the troupe's dressing-rooms and in particular from Jules. The fact is that at this time I was frigid; what was more, I was frightened of sex. Nobody would have guessed it; there was nothing of the repressed little spinster about my image or, come to that, about my inner nature. I was not timid or defeated; I never for a moment thought of creeping back to Shaw and getting a sensible little job in hairdressing, though come to think of it this might have helped in my coming court case. In every respect except the sexual, I could look the world in the face without flinching. All the same, I was frigid. I couldn't possibly have gone in with Jules and Miss Lily on their orgies; it would have reminded me of the rape, I might have lost control, had hysterics. Yet Jules was not the sort of man to whom one could have said, 'Look, lay off, can't you? – I've been raped.' His reaction would very likely have been, 'So what?' Even if, against the odds, he had been understanding, to appeal like this to his mercy would have been to show weakness, to climb down from my pose of invulnerability. I felt I could not afford to lose this attitude because of the sort of people Jules and the others were: heavy smokers, meat-eaters, lovers of wine. They weren't into dope, but they drank a fair bit. They didn't wash much; powder and eau de cologne were more their grab. Mystical feelings were entirely foreign to them; what they'd have made of Mahatmaji I can't think, they'd probably have hardly noticed him. They were not flower people but street people.

I didn't mind this a bit, in fact I responded to it. Jules attracted me as a professional who challenged me to equal his professionalism. In one way he and the others were my kind of people; the trouble was that there were whole areas of my consciousness that were entirely closed to them, so I could only accept them on my terms. But on my terms, I really loved them. They were never off stage. When we went at lunchtime to the pub opposite the Round House, it was a stage performance; Jules would pay theatrical court to the barmaid, Miss Lily would seat herself on the lap of some solitary drinker, the others would engage the customers in backchat, and soon everyone in the pub was drawn in. It was marvellous to be part of the Palais des Merveilles, to feel that I was becoming more proficient with every day that passed.

Jules decided we should boost attendance by marching in the street

with banners, so we all dressed up in our costumes and paraded, playing
music on a cassette. The weather was unpleasantly chilly, though it was
late in May. The fire-eater ate his fire. I wore a leotard and had my red
and white face make-up, and my hair fluffed out. I did cartwheels down
the street, which warmed me up; then I recovered my blue boa from the
person who was carrying it, and joined the others in blowing kisses to the
passers-by. As we were parading in this way down Oxford Street, the
BBC interviewed us, an unexpected boost.

One day I took the group to see Feliks Topolski. We turned up on one
of his Fridays. He was thrilled to see the troupe, and at once started to
sketch some of them. For me it was a joy to see him again. Later he came
to one of our performances and he must have enjoyed it, because his son
Danny turned up later saying his father had recommended it.

Then Jules had another idea for me, for the matinée. The purpose, so
he said, was to make the whole thing more lighthearted and suitable for
the children; but he had a curious mind, and I'm not sure that the new
sketch really had this effect. At any rate, I was to be a flying fairy who
was dead, a whirling corpse. I was sandwiched between a couple of
boards tied together by two ropes with slip-knots attached to the end of
another; an outsize white satin dress was pulled over this contraption. I
looked fairly stout, but that couldn't be helped. My face was made up
doll-fashion and my hair done in two silly plaits. My long supporting
rope was attached to a central pulley high in the air. Jules pushed me off
the balcony, then I flew round the theatre in decreasing concentric
circles. My arms and legs hung limp, my head lolled. Finally I came to a
halt in the middle and dangled there inertly while the children shrieked
and clapped below. It was quite scary, the nearest I have come to
jumping from a parachute.

In due course it was time for the Palais des Merveilles to go back to
Paris. Jules tried hard to persuade me to go with them.

'You must come,' he said. 'You are one of us now.'

'I'd love to,' I said, 'but no, I can't.'

'Why not?' Jules was pressing. 'We are well-known in Paris, we
should get you on the films. As soon as we get back we have a date with
someone who wants to make a film of us.'

'I've got my court case coming up, I'll have to be back for that.'

'Well, when is it?'

'Quite soon, another preliminary hearing, but the real case comes on
in the autumn.'

'All right, you can work with us in the meantime. I'll see you get back
when you're needed.'

Our conversation went on for some time; I felt more and more miserable, too miserable even to be boosted by his good opinion. I knew I could not accept, for reasons quite unconnected with the court case. It was the bulimia that stopped me going; it removed my inner confidence, fed my paranoia about the rape. Of course I ought to have gone off with them and taken the chance, and it tortured me that I knew this perfectly well at the time. What stopped me was a fear of being sexually assaulted or, if not exactly assaulted, then pressurized, expected to join in. In the long run, I felt, this would be the price I should have to pay to get in with Jules and Miss Lily. I wondered where I should stay when I got to Paris; probably it would be somewhere provided by Jules, in which case I should be in a weak position. Perhaps these fears were quite misplaced, but they were there, and I couldn't override them. So one Saturday evening I waved my friends an emotional farewell. Back in the squat, I sank down on my strange bed of rags and cried as if my heart would break.

# 14

# Under Observation

After the Palais des Merveilles left, I began going more and more often to the Mahatma's basement in Fairholme Road. Soon I asked if I might 'take the knowledge' so as to be accepted as a fully fledged premie. This privilege was granted me on 18 July. It was a profound experience, but there is a sense in which I was not ready for it. It gave me a key to certain doors within my consciousness, but I had no idea how to use it until much later. What the Mission had already done for me was to introduce me to some friends who were more worth while than anyone I had come across, people who gave me comfort and hope, and were to provide a direction for my life when I left prison.

That evening there was a fair in one of the London squares, and I wandered along to it, wearing the red spot the Mahatma had put on my forehead. Lord Lichfield was taking photographs, lots of smart people were there, one or two of whom I knew by sight. I floated through it all, utterly at peace with myself, seeing everything for the first time like a new-born infant. One thing that did disappoint me was that I continued to vomit as before; for an instant I thought the knowledge might cure the habit, but it did not. It did give me a power of acceptance.

I was soon to need this. Towards the end of July we were summoned again to the Assizes, and again I sat with my companions of the previous February. Soon after the hearing began I needed to be sick. It was urgent, there was no way I could hold it up, so I was allowed to leave the court with a policewoman. Then at the end of the hearing the judge singled me out. He remanded all the cases on existing bail conditions until a date in early November – 'except Miss Susan Mary Taylor'. I was to be kept for a month in the psychiatric department of Holloway to have my condition checked out. Nobody has ever told me why this happened, but it must have been because I had been sick. Heroin addicts are sometimes given to vomiting, so presumably they wanted to

112

check whether I had this trouble. Down went the judge's hammer; I stood transfixed with shock.

I was taken out of court into the sunshine, then shown into a black maria and driven to Holloway. It was the same experience as before; I was stripped of my possessions, my head was measured, my body intimately searched, I was locked in a rabbit hutch. After a bit the door opened and a mug of bromide tea and some bread, margarine and jam were put on the floor. Then came the bath in the great white bathroom, as before the only moment of comfort. This time I was taken downstairs, underground, into the psychiatric department, and locked into a cell there. Under observation.

At least this time I was allowed to wear my own clothes; a black top, a red skirt and a monkey skin round my neck. That was an improvement over my previous time in Holloway, but the company was a thousand times worse. There were people going mad, people who had gone mad, disturbed people, dizzy people, people like zombies after electric shock treatment, sad people who had lost their memories. Now and then in the exercise yard, or in the waiting room into which we were herded before being given various tests, some monstrously misshapen greasy-haired creature would come up to me, grimacing, shoving her face into mine and breathing putrefaction at me across her rotten teeth.

To be not only in prison but also among the mentally ill is painful; being underground made it claustrophobic. However, there was some opportunity for taking exercise, besides walking round the small yard. Some of the less disturbed kept fit with a lady who came to teach physical jerks, and there was a game, remotely related to tennis, which we used to play in a wide corridor, There was no racket, naturally; a racket could be a weapon. A string was placed across the corridor to represent a net, and over this we would throw a beanbag for the opponents to catch.

The madness of my companions and the deadly routine of the institution with its sickly smell soon began wearing into my brain. The Divine Light meditation helped me, it was an inner resource, but it did not exclude all the pain. No wonder people who become institutionalized in madhouses end up as zombies; it is far worse than becoming institutionalized in a prison. Criminals have their faults, but one can relate to them. A normal remark will usually get a normal answer, there is communication. But with the insane there is not. There were women there who were press-ganged into having electric shock treatment; they had no choice if the doctors prescribed it. I remember one friendly girl who seemed entirely normal; she told me as if in passing that she was going to have shock treatment that afternoon. When I saw her next day and said hello, she looked through me with dull eyes having clearly forgotten me completely. Then there were the people who talked constantly, at first seeming normal but then showing by some sign that they were completely loony. One well-spoken girl had embezzled a lot of money, and told me her story to justify what she had done. She told it vividly; it was an interesting tale and one that made me feel quite a lot of sympathy for her. Then next day she told it to me again, and I thought to myself, oh dear, no story is as interesting the second time, when suddenly I realized that she was using exactly the same words as before, even the same tones of voice that had sounded so natural. It was exactly as if she had a long-playing record in her head; every time she found a listener she put it on the turntable. After she had caught me a few times it became unbearably creepy.

Then there was a religious maniac. Her parents were in the Salvation Army and had stuffed her full of religion; in defiance she had gone on the streets and been picked up by police. Now she was obsessed with the need to recover her place among the elect of God.

'I am defiled,' she kept saying.

'I'm sure the Lord will forgive you,' I said.

'Ah, if only I could still hope for the forgiveness of the Lord! But I am utterly cast out from His sight, cast into outer darkness, there shall be weeping and gnashing of teeth.' And she began to cry.

A phrase came back to me from the Prayer Book. 'His property is always to have mercy, we are told.'

'If I could believe that!' she said. 'But I sold myself, defiled myself. I knew what I was doing, my mum and my dad brought me up in the way of the Lord and I sinned against His light.'

I said, 'Mary Magdalen was forgiven.'

But nothing I could say helped her in the least. She performed odd little ceremonials, kneeling down, banging her head on the floor, crossing herself violently. These conversations upset me, because I felt she had a beautiful soul.

As to the people who were supposed to be keeping me under observation, they took samples of my blood and urine to test for this and that; they never told me the results, that isn't their way in prison, but I am pretty sure they found nothing organically wrong, and certainly there were no drugs in my veins. About my illness they did nothing at all.

A week before I left I was moved to a big dormitory; this was an improvement. Everyone there was due to be moved or let out soon, and they were very young; at twenty-six I was about the oldest there. Above all, they weren't noticeably mad. Most of them were in for petty theft to get drugs. Often they came from broken homes or orphanages and their stories were sometimes heartrenderingly sad. One, a sweet young girl, suffered from nothing worse than a hasty temper; her boyfriend had got drunk and violent one day, and she had hit him on the head with a heavy ornament, smashing his skull. She had not meant to kill him; if the ornament had been lighter or his skull stronger, they would most likely have kissed and made up next day. The doctors must have satisfied themselves she was not insane, for she was about to be sent to an open prison to serve her life sentence. I felt so sorry for her; it was like seeing a bunch of spring flowers, still fresh, on a rubbish heap, for that charm of hers would fade long before in her mid-thirties, thoroughly institutionalized, she would at last be released.

I took to singing for them, all the show-stoppers I knew, mostly from folk artists like Bob Dylan, Joan Baez, Joni Mitchell and Tom Paxton, and sometimes going back to Elvis Presley. It gave me a feeling of release, and it cheered the girls up. Eventually they sang with me, and the atmosphere seemed transformed. We were all moving off to various destinations, none of us was sure of the future, but singing made us happy in the present. I was also allowed crayons in that dormitory and did a lot of coloured pictures, especially of lions.

Finally the time came to leave. I weighed in at a stone less than when I had arrived, and I had already been underweight. Prison is quite dangerous for anyone with bulimia because, without snacks to replace the meals that have been lost, bulimia becomes equivalent to anorexia. Now that more is known about the illness, perhaps special arrangements are made for bulimia sufferers in prison; certainly this ought to be so. It is true that I later came through eight months of prison with no special arrangements at all, but I easily might not have done.

It was a relief finally to emerge into the heat of late August. After a day or two I went by bus to Cadaques. It is lovely there in September; the pressure of people who crowd the place in the high season is lightened, the sun shines without burning. Usually I sat outside the Hostal under their canvas canopy on a comfortable swing seat, whiling away the hours in warmth and freedom. A tall man in a caftan loped along the Rambla. Alexander Mosley. He ordered a Cuba Libre, Bacardi and coke.

'I'm ready for this,' he said. 'I've just run down the mountain.'

'Down the mountain?'

'Yes, down the Pani.' That was the mountain to the south of the village with the two balls of the radar station on top. 'You know the white house high up, not far from the balls?'

Of course I did; it was quite a landmark. Sometimes people called it San Sebastian, sometimes Casa Guinness, the Guinness house.

'It belongs to my brother, Jonathan Guinness; I'm staying there without him.'

This name was not to mean anything to me for some time to come.

The twins were in Cadaques too; they had come to know Dali. One day they took me along to his strange, rambling house with its big garden above the jetty at Port Lligat, half a mile from Cadaques proper. From outside one sees the yard-high white plaster egg that is one of his symbols, and a Michelin man. We went up a flight of stone steps by the side of the house and Denis rang the bell. The door was opened by a maid in traditional pink uniform with a white apron; quite a rare sight now anywhere, but in Cadaques a real curiosity. In the small hall was a stuffed polar bear festooned with costume jewellery – gold chains, strings of imitation pearls, turquoise beads, sticks of coral – standing by a very odd-looking settee upholstered in green.

'Mae West's lips,' explained John, and as he said this I saw that the settee was like a huge Cupid's bow mouth.

'But why green?' I asked, as we went up the narrow whitewashed staircase.

'Originally it was pink,' explained John, 'but he had it re-covered.'

Gala, Dali's wife, was a slim Russian fox, ancient but with a dry, hard sexuality. She openly fancied the twins, and spent the whole evening fawning on Denis. The other men guests got little attention and the women, including me, none at all.

But on the whole I just sat outside the Hostal, nursing a coffee and watching what went on. This might be French or Spanish bowls, or the *sardana*, the circular folk-dance all Catalans love. I came to love it too, though only as a spectator; it looks simple, but the steps need to be accurately counted, and when over-confident and ignorant foreigners join the circle they can mess it up. This must annoy the practised local dancers, but they are usually patient and take it in good part. The band, to anyone new to this music, sounds out of tune; sharp, like a salad dressing with too much lemon juice. However, when I had heard the music a few times I realized that it was in tune all right, but in a special way.

One day the English contingent organized in the Rambla an event which was even more mysterious to the Catalans than their *sardanas* are to outsiders; a cricket match. The players had to use a tennis ball and refrain from hitting too hard otherwise the windows of cafés and parked cars would have been in danger, not to mention those of the Guardia Civil headquarters.

I told the story of my arrest and coming trial to a new friend, a writer, who played the role of tempter.

'Why go back to England?' he kept saying. 'Why not just stay on here?'

I could have done this. There would have been problems, of course, especially when my passport ran out; but I had met plenty of people on Formentera who got by without papers, and lived perfectly fulfilled lives. I dreaded going back and appearing in court; it was clear to me that I should probably go to prison. Nor did I have any feeling that I deserved prison; the Eaton Square incident now seemed utterly remote and trivial, really just a matter of bad luck. However it might look to others, to myself my part in it seemed entirely passive; I had neither dealt in marijuana nor introduced the supply of LSD.

But if the idea of skipping bail attracted me at all, it was only for a moment. My writer friend only knew half the story; specifically, he didn't know about my bulimia. To me, though, it was clear that a life on the run would be impossible for me. I needed help. Although my disease was not yet familiar to the public, and I didn't even yet know what it was called or that it had a name, I was, by now, aware that I was ill. Surely I thought, the court will recognize this. Probably they will send me somewhere, a psychiatric hospital perhaps, where I can be looked after and perhaps cured. Better than that would be some kind of craft centre where I might be allowed to treat and cure myself as well as doing creative work, painting, potting . . .

None of this had anything to do with real life; and what was odd about it was that I had learnt what real life was like, in the penal system. My month in the Holloway madhouse should have taught me. They had fiddled about looking at drops of my blood and making me pee in a bottle, and not bothered in the least either about my vomiting or about my weight-loss or indeed about my state of mind. The fact that this lesson did not sink in shows that I remained, deep down, just a good old-fashioned girl, and naïve with it. I might follow fashion in calling the police pigs, but that was all on the surface. Underneath I still felt that the authorities were on my side, that if they knew my problems they would want to help. There was something in this, as a matter of fact; not much, but something. In pockets here and there, there is goodwill in the system. All the same, my fantasies were crediting it with a degree of sensitivity and imagination that it simply did not have, and probably never can.

Another reason not to skip bail was my bail surety, Nicky Ryman; the money he had pledged for me was possibly not much by his standards, but he had helped me, and I should not have liked to let him down.

The chill of autumn hit me when I got back to London. I suppose I seemed the same as ever, but inside I felt weak and ill. Bulimia makes one feel the cold; there is a shortage of fat in the body. The condition became more unmanageable; to escape from my dread at what was to come, I pursued the high-energy buzz more desperately than ever. After the buzz, the black shame returned, so that I sometimes caught myself actually wanting to be locked up so as to be prevented from bingeing.

My lawyer, David Offenbach, was quite hopeful.

'They may send you down, but I don't see it being for long,' he said, 'even though you've got a record.'

'I hope you're right,' I said, 'because I really am ill.'

'Yes, and of course they know it, that's why they sent you to Holloway for observation. I really think they will take your condition into account.'

'That's a relief,' I said.

'It would help if you could find a character witness, someone solid and respectable. Do you think your father would agree to come to court?'

'Would that help?'

'Very much so.'

'Oh,' I said, 'I'm sure he will do anything he can.'

'Good, and a letter from him would help as well, if he'd just say that he has a secure job waiting for you and a place in the family home.'

But I was in for a shock. Ten days later I went to David again.

'Your father has written,' he said. 'He refuses to help.'

I went cold inside. I had asked my father for bread and been given a stone. And this was not just any old father; this was Ronnie, my loving Ronnie, the anchor-man of my whole existence. He had failed me; abandoned me. He didn't want to know me any more. It was an enormous new fact in my life, one that I should need some time to take in.

'Oh, no,' I said.

David Offenbach tried to cheer me up. 'Well, it's a pity, but some of the older generation are like that. Never mind, we'll do the best we can. I still don't see them sending you down for too long.'

'How long?'

'Two months, three months maybe, less one third for remission. We might even get you off because of your sickness.'

That evening I telephoned my father, though not to plead with him, because that is not my way and anyway I knew him well enough to be

Jive practice

Father's shop

My parents, Anne and Ronnie, in 1942

My family with the pony and trap (I am in the hard hat)

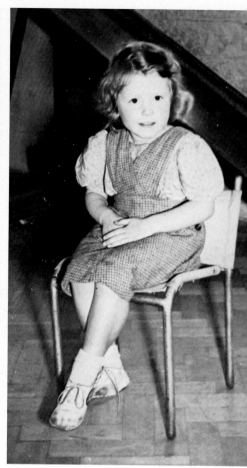

In Ronnie's arms

Aged 4

By the Schloss with the cook and
gardener

As Prince Charming with my
sister Wynson

Jean François, as a Buddhist monk, in Japan

Members of the Japanese ashram

With Anne Fleming on an elephant in the Guru's procession

Outside the twins' studio in Radnor Walk

The Guru Maharaj Ji

In Feliks Topolski's studio; Shoe, Denis, and Philippe studying
his portrait

With Dr Brian's children in Sri Lanka

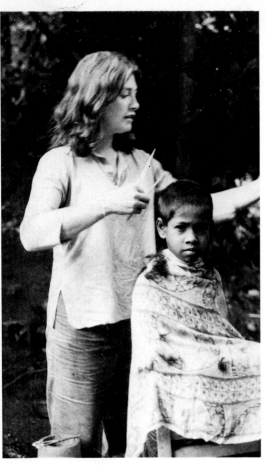

Cutting hair in Sri Lanka

Meditative in Japan

By the stone hut, Cadaques

My massage tent at the Bahamas ashr

Jonathan, Shoe and John, 1978

With Bracken and Lady Betjeman          On the beach with Diana

Aster, Diana and Thomas (courtesy of Tony Weaver, the *Sunday Express*)

aware that it would do no good. It was important to me to know what was in his mind. Could it really be that he was so angry with the disgrace I was bringing on the family that he was casting me off? It seemed like that, but I couldn't believe it, deep down. In my misery there was an element of quite cool curiosity; what was he playing at?

He said, 'A spot of porridge is your last hope. It'll get you off that old rope you smoke, get you away from that London crowd you're with, give you time to sort yourself out. It'll be your last chance.'

Was it my imagination? Probably it was, but I thought I heard a catch in his voice.

'I'll visit you,' he said. 'I'll send you everything that's allowed, your mother and I will look after you when you get out. You know that.'

'That's good to hear,' I said; without irony, for the tone of his voice had wiped away my bitterness.

'We'll do all we can, and a bit more,' he said, 'but in the end it's up to you. Chin up, lass.'

So he wasn't really rejecting me; he simply thought that a spell of prison was needed to sort me out. Damn him for an arrogant swine, I said to myself; he's not the one who is going down. Then I thought no, in his way he still loves me. Something even whispered to me that he might be right in what he was doing. He was right, for when I got out I kicked the drug habit at once and for good. All the same, it was years before I completely forgave him. He later told me that the decision was the hardest of his life. It was a gamble; he was staking my life on one throw. He calculated that I could still bounce back, but he might have been wrong; he knew it, and suffered.

At last the trial came up at Bow Street court; it was 29 October. There were all the others, my friends from what now seemed a past life. I was clad in a black cape to my ankles and wore my monkey-skin collar. They called me to give evidence; I declined, because I thought it might do more harm than good. I felt that once I was in that witness box the affair would be out of control. They might tie me in knots, make me incriminate others. The idea of grassing on other alternative people revolted me. Injustice would probably be done and to me in particular, but so be it. I should at least not need to blame myself. The way I put it makes it sound braver than it was; mainly I was just fatalistic.

Unfortunately the others were not, nor were their legal advisers. As the days went by it became clearer all the time; it was everyone for himself. Each new witness incriminated me deeper, because of my role in organizing the household in Eaton Place. They may not have meant to do this, but it is how their evidence worked out.

'Who opened the door to you?'

'Shoe Taylor.'

'Who served the tea?'

'I think it must have been Shoe.'

'Who switched on the television?'

'Shoe.'

They also said that I was the one who kept getting things out of the fridge; this was right, of course, because I was going constantly to the fridge for a nibble. Nobody knew the name of the guy who had brought the LSD. In the end my refusal to give evidence began to look more and more like proof that I had something to hide.

On the third day of the hearing I changed my image, discarding the black cloak and monkey skin for my faithful cream riding mackintosh from my teens. I thought it might look straighter, more mainstream. It was clear that the case was going badly for me. I was saddened by the way my friends kept coming out with my name as a quick answer, an escape route to help them in the cross-examination. Yet I didn't blame them entirely, for I saw how easy it was to become intimidated and entangled by the prosecution lawyers, tempted into the easy escape by the defence ones.

My worry and depression did not stop me observing the lawyers and the judge. They seemed strange to me in their wigs and gowns, subtly deformed because they clearly lived entirely in a head space. For years they had stuffed their minds with pages of small print as a goose is stuffed with food to swell its liver, and they had become like heads without bodies. Their cold parchment faces hinted at skulls and dry decay. All body consciousness seemed absent; their get-up highlighted the bodyless head effect, for the body was obliterated by the robe, while the periwigs drew attention to the head. When the judge came into court it was as if he glided on castors.

On the fifth day, judgement was pronounced. It seemed interminable. Throughout the case I had needed to go and be sick from time to time; that last day it was worse, quite out of control, and I remember kneeling over the lavatory retching helplessly with nothing to bring up. I came back into court more dead than alive. The sentences began; one person had a suspended sentence, another was fined, and so on; nothing very severe, it seemed. By and by the judge reached me.

'Susan Mary Taylor!' said the judge, and I stood to receive the verdict.

'It has become apparent that you were instrumental in a major way in bringing together this party of nine people, that you aided and abetted in intoxicating them with LSD. In the light of the evident severity of your stomach disorder which has caused you to leave the court on many occasions throughout this trial, I am exercising leniency.'

This sounded hopeful; for a second I felt a little cheer.

'But for this, I should have been minded to sentence you to two years' imprisonment.'

I hardly had time to be flabbergasted at this, for now came the crunch.

'As it is, you will serve a period of twelve months.'

Bang went the hammer.

# 15

# LSD Mary

They handcuffed me to a policeman before escorting me to the black maria. The handcuffs clicked home; this time the pigs had really got me. For as far ahead as I could see, I should have to live on their terms and at their orders. My prison experience up to then had never been for long enough to get on top of me; I had only sampled prison, not experienced it in depth. This was going to be different. I would learn the meaning of the word 'subordination', what it is like to live for a long time in the power of bossy and unimaginative people. Faceless people, they seemed; the other prisoners were very individual, but the screws were like machines. They varied a bit in height and looks, and they must have had names. But they never smiled, never passed the time of day, never bothered with the small-talk with which normal people make themselves agreeable. The screws ruled; they had no need to make themselves agreeable, and their manner was designed to remind us of this. At least they were very rarely cruel to anyone, and never to me. This is a compliment to the British prison system, when one thinks what happens in some other countries.

Arriving at Holloway I felt like an old hand. Again I handed in my things, again I was body-searched. This time the wardress's fingers seemed to linger just a trifle longer than strictly necessary in my private places, back and front; one of the 'trusty' inmates who was assisting gave me a hard stare and an insolent half smile. I stared back; my private parts had in their time suffered worse things than a few seconds of furtive lechery from a wardress, and her malicious little sidekick wasn't going to put me out of countenance. The prisoner had a typical 'lifer's' face, the hard mouth, the dull complexion, the dead hair, the rat-bright eyes with awareness but no feeling. The screw didn't push it, her bit of surreptitious fun was soon over; it would have to have been much worse before provoking me to complain. Again I relaxed for a bit in that generous comforting bathroom with its plain white tiles. Again I was made to put on prison uniform, which fitted no better than last time. Again I was taken to a cell and locked in.

My cell smelt the same as my other two and at first glance it looked the same; but suddenly I noticed that this time there were graffiti, etched into the plaster so that repainting could not quite efface them. Anna loves Charlie, Lynn loves Doris, Margie Woz Ere, Watson is a Cow, Suck Me Sarah. None of the graffiti would have been chosen for those little collections publishers produce for the Christmas stocking trade, yet they provided company, of a sort.

Next morning it was back to the breakfast queue with the vegetable women, the pigeons flapping and diving overhead. Someone got a dollop of guano in her porridge as she was returning to her cell; she marched back to the trolley to get it changed.

'Sodding pigeons!' said one of my neighbours, amused. A little brightness had come into her day.

Again I noticed the butch lesbians dressed as men. One of them gave me a bit of a shock; this one really is a man, I said to myself, noting a tightness at the crotch of the trousers, and he's got something that looks uncommonly like an erection. Then I noticed another bulge at the side and worked out that there was a hairbrush in the trouser pocket so arranged that the handle poked upwards in the centre, making the person look, as Mae West might have put it, pleased to see us. There was something rather winning about these *ersatz* men with their tattooed arms, shaved heads and breastbinders, grotesque though they looked. They were so *happy*, the only happy people in Holloway. Every day was Christmas to them, surrounded with sex objects without any competition. They had a cheery word for everyone.

'Hi Jean . . . Morning Jenny . . . See you later, Judy.'

One of them came up to me. 'What's your name, then?'

'Mary,' I said, for I had decided to use my second name during my prison sentence. This was to preserve Susan/Sue, my family's name for me, and Shoe, the name I was called by my friends, from a sort of defilement. I gave the name of Mary in the same spirit as I put on overalls to work in my father's slaughterhouse.

The Holloway population had become more varied in the two years since 1968. There were more people with black faces and brown ones. Often they were doing time for breaking immigration laws. There was a group of Arab women in flowing robes and shawls; Lebanese, it appeared. They were on remand, as I had been in Tunis; I wondered whether their experience of Holloway was better than mine in prison in the Arab world, or worse. The food was nastier, but at least they had each other to talk to and they were free of the fleas and the stifling heat.

I got a visitor the first day – David Offenbach. He was carrying a parcel.

'I'm really sorry,' he said. 'It was terrible we didn't do better for you. He really came down on you.'

'It wasn't your fault,' I assured him. 'You did all you could. I suppose I ought to have gone in the box.'

'Perhaps, perhaps not,' he said. 'One never knows quite how it will go. It might have helped, or he might have taken you apart. Anyway that's over and done with; we've got to think of your situation now. One consolation for your long sentence is that you'll probably get the opportunity to go to open prison.'

That sounded good. 'I suppose I should go, if I can?'

'Certainly; nearly everyone prefers open prison to Holloway. It's in the country, there's a softer regime, and there are more facilities.'

'Anything would be better than this place,' I said.

'Quite. Now, in open prison you'll be able to wear your own clothes. I've brought you these, courtesy of Release.'

In the parcel was a sturdy pair of green corduroy trousers and a dark brown polo neck sweater. I was allowed to try them on, before handing them to the invigilating wardress to put with my other things. They fitted all right, though the trousers were a bit tight round the waist.

'Thank you very much,' I said, 'I shall wear them, they are much more practical than my own things.'

'That's what we thought,' said David. 'And they'll help to preserve your things for when you get out.'

We talked a bit more about Geoffrey and Philippe; David was their solicitor as well as mine. Both had got off more lightly than me, which was a good thing as far as it went. It was a comfort to be able to talk to someone from outside, even for a few minutes.

Finally he said: 'I must be off now. Don't get too depressed; with remission you'll only need to do eight months, it'll go faster than you think.'

'Thanks for everything.'

'Goodbye, and good luck.'

I've never seen David since, but I've always remembered him kindly. He did his best.

After a few days a wardress told me that I was to be interviewed for open prison, and next day I was taken before the Governor. I must have succeeded in presenting myself as stable and reliable, because in a day or

two my name came on a list outside the Deputy Governor's office; I was
to go to the open prison of Moor Court. I was happy about this, for old
Holloway was the pits. I still have nightmares about it; not so often now,
perhaps about twice a year, but I always wake from them in a cold
sweat. This makes me quite neurotic about keeping within the law; my
parking tickets get paid by return of post, and the sight of a police car on
a dual carriageway makes me slow to about twenty miles an hour.

'So you're going to open prison, then?' said my neighbour in the
breakfast queue next day. She had seen my name on the list, but I was
surprised she knew who I was. You get people like that in institutions,
people who like to have their finger on the pulse and find everything out.

'Yes,' I said.

'That's a pity, you'll miss the Christmas party.'

'There's a Christmas party, is there?'

'Yes, it's quite a good do, considering. Des O'Connor is starring.'

'Tom Jones,' said another know-all.

In the next few days there was quite a lot of talk about this party, but
nothing would have made me want to stay for it, not if they had billed
the Rolling Stones, the Beatles and the immortal Elvis himself.

One Thursday, a fortnight after my arrival, I handed in my horrible
uniform, changed into the clothes David had brought me, and with
some companions climbed into a black maria to be driven straight to
Moor Court, which is in the Potteries district near Stoke on Trent. The
journey took about three hours, and I enjoyed looking out the front
through the bars, at the fields and the hedges, the sheep and cattle, the
wintry trees.

Moor Court was a Victorian country house set in good grounds of
about twenty-two acres including a little farm with cows and hens where
some of the prisoners worked, as well as a netball pitch. It didn't have
Holloway's appalling hugeness; there were only about eighty inmates,
all first or second offenders doing two years at most. The body search was
done in a much more considerate way. The screws, too, were a
pleasanter model; they came from the rural areas round about, looked
less pasty, and their Midland accents were closer to my own Lancashire
one. Of course the similarities were more important than the differences;
the same big bunches of keys jangled at their waists, they had the same
big feet in the same brogues and shared the same humourless and
pedantic approach.

After the search came the interview with 'Admin', a woman behind a
desk who asked an interminable list of questions. I said I was a
vegetarian, thinking cheese might be more appetizing than prison meat.

I was asked my religion and said 'Buddhist'. I had a hunch that this might qualify me for a cell by myself, where I could spend some of my free time meditating on the Divine Light. Whatever the reason, I was given a single cell, which was a relief. I was also given my dorothy bag or 'dolly bag', an object which was a sort of fetish with the authorities, and therefore a minor instrument of torture.

'You must keep this with you at all times,' said the screw. 'Be careful not to lose it. There will be periodical inspections to see that your bag and its contents are in order.'

There were not only inspections, but random spot checks; a screw could stop one in the corridor at any time and look in the bag. If there was any contraband, or if one was caught without it, one could lose remission. It was a soft cotton bag with a sugar-bag neck fastened with a string pulled tight, and a long handle. I disliked it on sight, especially because it smelt unwholesome. Some attempt must have been made to clean it for the newcomer, but there was a musty, rather fishy odour to it. Some prisoners let their bags get so grubby that no amount of cleaning would have sufficed. It was for washing things – a half-cake of buttermilk soap, some prison-issue toothpowder, a toothbrush – and other permitted personal possessions including cigarette papers, matches, and a tobacco tin for the meagre allowance of a quarter of an ounce a week. People used to fight with their dolly-bags; when the tobacco tin was cunningly placed, its corner would give the opponent a satisfactory gash. Nearly everyone smoked; I did at that time. Smoking in prison was a minor science; to eke out the pathetic tobacco ration it was necessary to make a roll-up as thin as a reed. We were also kept desperately short of matches. Scouts and Guides are taught to light fires using one match only; a prisoner would laugh at the idea that using a whole match was any sort of economy. The first thing we learned was to use a pin to separate each match into four exact quarters, and to use only one of these per roll-up without breaking it. Woe to those who were not neat-fingered.

After getting our dolly-bags we new girls were ushered into the big dining-room for tea. Everyone turned to see what we looked like, to see if there was anyone to make friends with or laugh at, and in the case of the lesbians to see what the new talent was like. Some attempt had been made to pretty the place up; there were small square tables for four with cheerful plastic florally patterned tops. The mugs, I noted, were not enamel on metal but thick white pottery; that's something, I thought, though I was to discover that the tea in them had the same aftertaste of bromide as the Holloway brew. I collected my mug of tea and bread and

cheese, then stood hesitating between the small tables to see where I
might sit.

A gruff voice shouted in an educated accent, 'There's a place over
here with us.'

It came from a small, squat figure, a woman in her sixties with grey
hair cropped in a Twenties bob. She had kind eyes, many chins, an
ample bosom, and wrists as plump as a baby's. She wore a man's jersey
over a tee-shirt, tracksuit trousers and men's shoes. Intrigued by her look
and especially her voice, I went to her table.

'Hello,' she said. 'I'm Rachel. I'm doing time for kidnapping.
Josephine here is a pro, and this is Annie who got done for passing dud
cheques. Come and join us. What are you in for?'

Her directness was like mountain air blowing through a long-closed
attic; her use of prison talk in that perfect Queen's English was also
deeply comic.

'My name's Mary,' I said. 'I'm in for drugs, LSD.'

From then on my name in that place was LSD Mary.

The prostitute had an olive skin and lovely eyes, dark and twinkling.
She was all curves; no prison allocation clothes could hide the
sensuousness of her figure. There was something refreshing about her;
she had no false shame, she was what she was and would never be
anything else. The cheque passer was very different: nervous and thin,
with bleached blonde hair growing out at the roots to reveal two or three
inches of dull brown. Her nails were bitten to the quick.

But the interesting one was Rachel: Dr Rachel Pinney, general's
daughter, qualified physician, child psychologist, Quaker, eccentric and
saint. Sometimes I call her the Eighth Dwarf. She has since become well-
known as the inventor of the technique of 'creative listening' and the
author of *Bobby*, an account of how she helped an autistic boy to join the
world outside. What a find she was for me, in that unpromising place!
She became a friend for life, and a good friend is always a gift; but that
the gift should be delivered exactly there, when most needed, can only
be seen as a special favour from God. She was my confidante and my
guardian angel. I could tell her everything, including everything about
my bulimia; she later stopped me doing something very foolish that
might have been the end of me.

Sometimes she needed to be defended. There were those who resented
the way she could talk to the screws and the Governor on their own
terms, even suspected her of being an informer. This was untrue and
unfair, for she was always on the side of the prisoners against the system.
Even so one can see how the suspicion arose; she was quite thick with the

authorities, though in entirely harmless ways like playing chess with the Governor. The tough Glasgow gangster-molls took it out on her; they would push her around, sneer at her accent, turn her the cold shoulder. One brute stole her dolly-bag and hid it, getting her into trouble; another snapped her glasses in two. I made a point of talking to her when she was ignored, and sometimes gave one of her tormentors the rough edge of my tongue. It was strange that someone with such a strong personality should need this support, but so it was. Though she was a lion when dealing with anyone in authority, equals or inferiors could walk all over her. Her own accent inhibited and embarrassed her, it associated her with all she most disapproved of. Being on the side of all rebels, she had no will to resist prison bullies. She turned the other cheek to them, and the hard cases took advantage of this, to my fury. There was another side to this, though; occasionally I could understand why Rachel was resented. As a psychologist she liked finding things out about people; she asked intimate questions that were not her business, and there were those who saw her as simply a nosey-parker. She was in prison for kidnapping one of her young patients from his mother; an action she had performed with love and a conviction of being right, though the mother did not see it her way and nor did the law. She was, in her own eyes, a prisoner of conscience. It was wonderful to have someone to talk to who was not only clever and kind, but one of the great characters of our time.

On Wednesdays I had to do without Rachel's conversation, for she never talked. A keen nuclear disarmer, she had decided that until the government dismantled its nuclear armaments she would refrain from talking for one day a week. She still keeps this up.

I had by this time learnt one or two yoga postures, and I taught them to Rachel. Despite her unpromising shape she was surprisingly limber. She was best at the 'Plough', in which one lies on the back and places the feet on the ground behind the head. One day she did this in the corridor completely naked; it was a pretty strange sight, and she was naturally reported to the governor. However, no regulation could be found specifically forbidding what she had done, and she got away with it.

Turning Moor Court into a prison had not harmed its exterior, but inside there was little trace of the pleasant mansion it had been. Everything was painted in buff and cream, and printed regulations were hung in the corridors. The reception rooms still had their high ceilings and big plate-glass windows, but they were littered with nondescript little tables and cheap chairs. One of these rooms was the dining hall, two more were the main recreation rooms, each containing a big television set, one permanently tuned to the BBC and the other to ITV. In the television rooms, besides hard chairs, there were one or two easy chairs upholstered in vinyl. Two newspapers were provided daily, one copy each of the *Daily Express* and the *Sun*. These circulated round all eighty of us; if one happened to be seventy-ninth, all the pages were in the wrong order and greasy as well, as if they had been used to wrap fish and chips.

Most people passed their evenings watching television in one or other of these rooms, but there were two other possibilities. In the loft there was a chapel where we were allowed to pray; there were those, more than you might expect, who spent some time there. My choice was the music room, an old tiled bakery furnished with a bench and a ping-pong table. This was used by the minority which didn't want TV but preferred to listen to pop music, or play table-tennis, or talk. It had vast cold ovens and a dumb-waiter; it was unheated, or almost. There was an antique record-player with a stack of outdated singles and a few LPs, including numbers from as far back as Johnny Ray. Trini Lopez featured, and the Tijuana Brass; there was a lot of Elvis Presley. I remember a reggae single called Fat Girl:

'I wanna fat girl tonight.'

This was played over and over again. I can hear it now, and see the black girls of Moor Park shaking to it.

The music room was also the resort of the lesbians. They crowded on the bench to smooch, Jean cuddling Joan, Betty groping Maureen. Recreation time lasted from 6.00 pm when tea ended till 8.30 when we went to bed, and I soon got into the habit of using every minute of that time to dance. When the black girls were dancing I would join them, otherwise I danced by myself to whatever music was on. I would do folk dance, gipsy dance, Latin American; I would leap like Mick Jagger, twitch like Jimi Hendrix. It was a workout and more than a workout, a dynamic meditation. Now and then I would gesture to those on the bench to join in, but they never did so; there was not a performer among them. Yet I often saw some of them watching me, out of the corner of their eyes; it soon came home to me that they were an audience, an audience that in a sort of way I held. This gave me a secret feeling of mastery; these streetwise women thought themselves tough, but when it came down to it they were scared to get off that bench in case someone laughed at them. I dared to do something they would not venture, they and I both knew this. As a result I never feared any of them, and they never harassed me.

We denizens of the music room were the oddballs of Moor Court; all sorts of strange things went on, totally against regulations. There was one woman who tattooed some of the others with ink and a needle; there were a couple of Irish girls who made packs of cards with Izal toilet rolls. They were very poor packs, being both floppy and transparent, but for card freaks they were much better than nothing. Proper packs were banned as was any form of card game.

During the day we worked. There were jobs in the kitchen and on the farm, but most of us, including me, made dolls in the 'dolly-room'. The work was harmless but boring.

Not long after I arrived it was Christmas. A nativity play was organized; Rachel was chosen as one of the Three Kings, but it turned out that the play was to be performed on a Wednesday, her day of silence, so she had to be demoted to the status of shepherd. The Governor and the screws tried to make Christmas Day as pleasant as possible, but the result was faintly macabre. For lunch there was turkey, Christmas pudding, and paper hats to wear. The screws were in civilian dress, and waited on us; they had all been at the sherry-type so were slightly, but noticeably, tipsy. Afterwards they handed round water-pistols so that those of us who wished could squirt them, and each other. I avoided accepting one of these; the false jollity of the celebration set my teeth on edge. The Roman Saturnalia, when masters waited on their slaves, must have been just like it; the slaves would have known, as we did, that one step out of line would end the whole silly farce. The business was the gloomier in that quite a lot of the prisoners, those with children, were in floods of tears at being away from their families. About the only person really enjoying herself was my neighbour, a quiet little pensioner.

'It's lovely to have a real Christmas dinner,' she said.

'Not so good being in here, though.'

'Oh, I don't know, it's a good place, this is. Soft. Nobody bothers you. It's warm, as well; I can't keep myself this warm at home. Matter of fact,' she said, and put her face closer to mine, giving a little knowing nod, 'I do a bit of shoplifting in the autumn so I can pass the winter in the nick. This is my third offence so he sent me down for eighteen months, the sod, but at least they've put me here.'

A few weeks after this I got out of the dolly-room, taking the opportunity offered to get on an educational course. I had a choice of two, upholstery or secretarial. I should really have preferred upholstery, but it would have meant being moved to a tougher prison at Style, Manchester, and so I opted for the secretarial course. For this, six prisoners from Style joined us at Moor Court. One of them I knew; she was the girl from the Holloway madhouse who had smashed her lover's skull. Of our people, fifteen were accepted, myself among them. I entered the course with mixed feelings; on the one hand it was an escape from the dolly room, on the other it was back to schooldays again with no blond maths teacher to admire.

An interesting change came about in most of the class; we spruced up as each of us began to see herself as the perfect secretary. Some credit for this must go to our teacher, a sensitive soul who was so frightened of us that we could smell the fear; she sweated in self-defence, poor thing, like a skunk. She was afraid to check disorderly behaviour, pretended not to notice the paper aeroplanes thrown by the unruly element. She had, perhaps, some reason to worry. I remember a Scots lass who got her ribbon in a twist, and next thing we knew a large black Remington typewriter was hurled across the room in the teacher's direction, followed by sheets of foolscap and accompanied by bloodcurdling Caledonian oaths. This particular story ended happily; after two days in the hospital wing the girl returned to the class and came top in the final test. What I enjoyed most was essay time, when I could let my imagination roam. Filing and accounts I am afraid defeated me, but I did come away knowing how to touch-type, and the course saved me from the dolly room for four months of my sentence.

I was still vomiting every meal, usually within five minutes though sometimes I played games with myself and kept it down for ten. Unable to eat between meals, I soon began to lose weight. True, after a bit I gained the confidence to wander round the tables after meals, eating leftovers, as I had done in the Round House canteen; and sometimes I secreted a slice or two of bread in my bra, though I gave most of this to the little birds that came to my cell window. All the same, the sweater and corduroys given me by David Offenbach, at first quite a tight fit, began to hang loose. In prison, my vomiting habit gave rise to a humiliation I had not known outside in that everybody knew about it; with the communal lavatories, there was no way I could keep it secret. People disliked and despised me for my habit, but they couldn't hate me more than I hated myself.

After lunch was the time for the daily organized walk, a quarter of an hour round the grounds. There would be a rush to the cloakroom to pick up one of the navy gaberdine raincoats; there was no time to think of fit or shape, the things were communal property, and I usually seemed to get a tight one hardly covering my backside. These raincoats smelt of body odour and rancid grease; they were never cleaned. We must have looked a depressing tribe, eighty women in badly fitting raincoats. We

formed up in threes and set out, accompanied by three screws. It was not
much of a walk, yet fifteen minutes out of doors was better than a kick in
the pants. Rachel usually walked with me, chatting incessantly unless it
was a Wednesday. Rachel was a special case, she talked sense, but there
was something annoying about the way the other women nattered.
There in the healing vastness of the fresh air was the green countryside.
Especially when spring came one could feel the force of it, the force (as
Dylan Thomas put it)

    . . . . . that through the green fuse
   Drives the flower.

  I needed to meditate on this force. Nobody else seemed to pay it a
blind bit of attention. They couldn't detach themselves from their
situation to marvel at the splendour of the outside world, but blathered
on about their prison preoccupations; they might just as well have been
sitting in the television rooms. Apart from everything else, gossiping
only uses a fraction of the lungs; it is no way to inhale the glorious *prana* of
the open air. The right thing, I felt, was to pace in silence and take deep
regular breaths; at the time this simply seemed what I ought to do, it was
only later that I learned that deep regular breathing is an important
technique in yoga.

  A month or two after I came to Moor Court I became quite disturbed,
and knew it; I felt I was heading for a breakdown. I was badly
undernourished through my vomiting, and at the same time on an
exercise high with my frantic dancing every night. Even sleep, that
priceless source of comfort in prison, was fragmented and disturbed;
sometimes I had insomnia, now and then I would virtually pass out in
my bed, in a sort of coma. My odd state of mind again made me think I
could turn to the authorities; if they knew of my plight, I thought, they
would help me. The feeling that I was cracking up grew more urgent; I
must *do* something, I must do it *now*. There were no words to express my
panic, so I stood in the corridor and screamed: Arthur Janow's primal
scream, high-pitched, louder than the firebell. A screw came, spoke to
me; I took no notice and screamed a bit louder. If I do enough of this, I
thought, they will take me away and put me somewhere where I can
dance and paint, somewhere green and gentle . . .

  Through my scream I heard a voice. Rachel Pinney.

  'Leave her to me.'

  There was authority in the voice, and the screw was trained like a
gundog to obey an educated accent; relieved, too, that someone else,
even another prisoner, was willing to tackle this screaming lunatic. I
thought, stop it, Rachel, you're interfering, you don't know what my

game is, I'm not doing this because I'm mad, I'm only pretending to be mad, I'm doing it so they will take me away. But I didn't say any of this because I was too busy screaming.

Rachel bellowed:

'Shoe!'

My own name, my private name. Of course Rachel had got it out of me, she got everything out of everyone. It was Rachel calling me, my friend Rachel; and it was me, the real me, that she was calling. My scream was my defence, the ring of fire I put round me against the outside world. Now that Rachel was there I could take it down. I stopped.

'Never do that again,' said Rachel to me, more roughly than I had ever heard her speak; and to the screws – there were three of them now, all looking grim – she said:

'She won't do it again, it's all come out.'

'She'll have to go to the Governor,' said a screw.

Rachel said to me: 'Look, I know it's hurting, but you've had your scream, if you do it any more you will only make it worse for yourself and everyone else. When we can do it, I'll give you a Listen.'

She was talking of her technique of creative listening, where the listener simply hears what the other has to say for five minutes, without answering except to get the exact meaning clear, then repeats it back. She did this to many of the prisoners, often in the lavatories. It didn't matter to me just what she was offering or whether it would do any good; it was the intention, and only the intention, that touched me and perhaps even stopped me screaming again. If there was somebody out there who cared about me, cared personally, I could do without my ring of fire. Certainly it would have been disastrous if I had gone through with my intention of making them think I was mentally ill; after my Holloway experience I ought to have known this.

The Governor sentenced me to be locked up for twenty-four hours. It could have been worse, she could have taken some of my remission away.

'You'd better take a tranquillizer,' she said.

I did that, and my twenty-four hours of lock-up passed as if in a dream. This is the answer, I thought to myself, and took to going every night to the dispensary. My name for this was the 'toffee shop'; tranquillizers, anti-depressants, mind-bending pills of all sorts were handed out more or less on demand. It suited everyone; us because it dulled the pain and blurred the boredom, the screws because it made us easier to handle. For a week or two I joined the toffee-shop queue every evening. I slept better, I was calmer, protected somehow.

It was the other pill-takers who made me worried about this solution. God knows Moor Court wasn't a centre of sparkling conversation, but these women in the queue were dumb and numb; their bodies were soft as puddings, their minds were vague and confused. They seemed only half alive. I thought, much more of this and I shall become like them, and I'd better kick the habit at once or I shall no longer even care. Rachel worried me, too; as a doctor she told me that the preparation I was taking could eventually cause kidney failure.

I missed the pills at first. Rachel helped me through this, purely by talking with me. But one day I felt an irresistible desire to turn on; if I couldn't get a joint, or something similar, I felt I should go crazy. If the toffee shop had been open I might have gone back there, but it was the wrong time. It's said that there is hash around in prisons, and possibly if I had known the ropes I could have got some at Moor Court. The trouble was that I had resolved, when I went down, never to touch an illegal drug again, so I had made no inquiries. I thought, 'tea' was Forties slang for hash, wasn't it? Perhaps smoking ordinary tea might turn me on. I cadged a supply of tealeaves from a friend in the kitchen, and as soon as I was in my cell I put some in a cigarette paper, rolled it, lit up, inhaled deeply. Then spluttered. There was a strong taste of tea and of burning; it was curiously nasty and had no effect at all.

I might have gone back on the pills that evening, but somehow I kept away. I danced instead in the old bakery, frantically, leaping and whirling and back-flipping till the lesbians stared openly and the ping-pong players forgot their game. Nothing was available from outside myself to give me a high, so I was thrown back on the ecstasy that came from inside, conjured by the beat from my exploding sinews. The discovery that I could get a high like this helped my self-confidence and was an important reason why I never took drugs again after being released from prison.

# 16

# Prison Hairdresser

One day I asked if I could cut the other prisoners' hair; I felt it might make them happier, and would also be a good distraction for me. Rather to my surprise, this idea was approved. The Governor had to ask permission from the Home Office, and it was granted. I was grateful for this, and still think that it was enlightened and quite brave of her to trust me with scissors after my screaming episode; possibly Rachel Pinney encouraged her to take this chance. Anyway, one Saturday, punctually at midday, I set up shop; I was open to customers every Saturday until my release. It wasn't exactly Vidal Sassoon's; scissors were my only equipment, there were no dyes or curling-tongs or hairsprays. Like the Israelites in Egypt, I had to make bricks without straw. But it is amazing what can be done just with scissors, especially with the aid of a little sugar and water to use as setting lotion.

I gathered a flourishing clientele. Bouffant tops were in demand; I was proud of the way I managed to make these look right, using my home-made syrup in a plant watering spray. The lesbians often wanted a DA, duck's arse to you; sticking out at the back like a duck's tail and with the sides short and chamfered. Some styles were easier than others; waves and curls were liable to straighten out after a bit, for lack of the proper equipment.

People usually came to me when they were expecting visits. We were allowed a visit once a fortnight, and the prison arranged it rather well. The visiting room was the most civilized in the place, with china cups and saucers on pretty tablecloths. Prisoners and visitors were allowed as many cups of tea as they could drink, and there was no taste of bromide to it. Biscuits and Mars bars were available for the visitors to buy and give to the prisoners.

Ronnie turned up for my first visit; he enjoyed it as much as I did. He hardly asked after my welfare at all, which took me aback a bit, yet it suited me. He leaned back in an armchair, looked round as if he owned the place, asked about the other people in the room.

'What's that one in for, then? She looks hot stuff.'

'Shoplifting. She goes in for suede, used to take away three suede jackets under her jumper every Saturday morning till she was caught.'

'And that one over there?'

'She's a call-girl.'

'Get her number for me, I could do with her.'

'Now, Ron, you're to behave yourself.'

'What about that feller, then?'

'Don't be daft, that's not a feller, that's a man-woman.'

'Lay you ten to one in fivers it's a feller.'

'I wouldn't take your money; this is a women's prison, remember?'

'Well, you could have fooled me.'

'You want to do a bit of time yourself, Ron, learn what life's all about.'

'Not me, lass; I'm the one that got away.'

I laughed at him, laughed with him, loved him. It was as if I wasn't a prisoner but another visitor, amusing myself with him, observing all the odd people. By his magic he gave me for that hour the sensation of being a free woman.

'Look at that one over there, that fat one! Did you ever see anyone scoff Mars bars like that? How many do you think she's put away?'

It was a petty swindler, a shy, lonely person. Her sad grey husband had bought a supply of Mars, and she was gorging herself. In another mood I'd have been sorry for them, but under Ronnie's pagan influence they became figures of fun.

'Those in the corner look a hard lot, I'd not want to run into them on a dark night.'

'You're right there, Ron.'

He was looking at a little rat-faced Scot inside for receiving. Her visitors were a peroxide blonde with the same hard look, perhaps a sister, and a couple of sinister men. Italians or Maltese by the look of them, wearing rows of gold rings like knuckledusters, who could have walked straight on to the set of a gangster film and no questions asked.

Time was almost up when Ronnie got round to asking me if there was anything I wanted.

'I'd like a little radio,' I said, 'a little pocket radio, as small as you can get it. And some green knitting-wool.'

'Rely on me,' he said.

After that he came almost every fortnight; he really enjoyed the visits, he was mad keen to get there and see the women and their families. Apart from this he kept his promise of looking after me in every way he could. For some time during my sentence there was a postal strike; he often had business at Uttoxeter cattle market, and when this happened he delivered letters for me. I was often the only prisoner to get any post.

Once I had a visit from John and Denis, the twins. They were the only London friends who ever came, and I was really touched that they made the journey. They gave me as much of a lift as Ronnie did, though of quite a different sort.

We were allowed to knit, and to be sent wool from outside. Like everything else it meant queueing for a form to be submitted to the Governor, but permission was never refused. There was also wool from the stores, but this was either pale pink or powder-blue, because most knitting was done for babies. Soon I had a green polo-neck sweater, as well as my brown one from Release. Meanwhile, Ronnie had not forgotten about my radio. One Uttoxeter market day he delivered it – a tiny one just like I had asked for, smaller than my hand, with a little microphone on a string that could be stuck in one ear. He had acted quite against regulations; we ought to have got the Governor's permission beforehand. Some prisoners were allowed radios in their cells, but they had to go through the hoop to get permission. Ronnie simply drove up to the gate in his overalls and charmed Reception into accepting the radio. I was summoned to the Governor and given a bit of a lecture, but she let me keep it. Soon afterwards, for some reason, the authorities stopped allowing any further radios, though I was allowed to keep mine, thank goodness. Why they made this change I don't know, but I am sure it was a mistake. My radio kept me sane, I'd have been harder to handle without it.

After a day or two I never changed the tuning, but kept it permanently on Radio 3, the classical music programme. I don't really like pop music except to dance to, and traditional songs are for singing along, or belting out by oneself; for passive listening, classical music is the thing. It comforts, stimulates, inspires; it opens strange splendours to the imagination, provides an escape hatch from reality. The explanatory commentary did me good, too, though I was impatient when it went on too long; I learned a bit about the music and the composers who had written it, without particularly meaning to. All the money I earned in the dolly room went on batteries for my radio. At first I mainly used it to soothe myself to sleep at night, then I began to smuggle it into the dolly-room. It sat in my bra; there was room for it, because my breasts had shrunk to almost nothing. The mike fitted snugly in my ear, its lead was well hidden under my shoulder-length hair and the polo neck. So from then on I had my own 'Music While You Work' in the dolly-room, provided by the world's great composers. Mozart's music is said to make cows give more milk, and it certainly helped me churn out the dolls; but if I had been discovered they would have taken away the radio and probably some remission as well.

I sent for some more wool. Someone taught me how to crochet, and I made this monstrous circle of Lovat green and purple in concentric bands, with a hole in the middle for my waist. I stopped when it had got to knee-length and made a pair of braces to fix on it; it became a skirt. I made a purple cloche hat with a green band. Mary Quant, I thought to myself. The skirt dropped when I started wearing it; in the end it came more than halfway down the calf. Then I acquired another funky garment, this time from the prison stores; a sage-green jacket in Forties style with a velvet collar, a halfbelt and a deep pleat at the back. With its padded shoulders it would have looked perfect in the late 1980s, but in 1970 it was unusual.

These clothes helped me to feel individual, but often the prison monotony got to me. Walking back to my cell at night sometimes felt like walking along death row. It was so predictable, the same long corridor, the same rail to hold. Every night at the same time, the same walk. This sameness becomes a sort of brainwashing, a voice whispering: fit in, give up, admit that you are nothing. I was there for eight months, which seemed a long time, but when you think that some people are in prison for five, ten, fifteen years . . .

Once we were taken on an outing to the theatre; we saw *Major Barbara* done by the Stoke Repertory Company. This was an immense treat, but it made me worried about myself, about the effect that prison was having on me. It was as if I was one of a group of monkeys let out of the zoo. In the intervals we could go to the loo, herded by a wardress of course, and we couldn't control our hands as we passed the ashtrays with the dog-ends. I got four. Whoever had discarded them hadn't realized how generous they were being; the lovely fat things were bulging with tobacco, enough to make at least six of my wispy roll-ups. I pulled myself up short; could it really be me, scrabbling for dog-ends? Would I always be like this? My whole attitude to the outside world seemed to have changed, and I dreaded that it might never change back.

The only pretty thing in my cell was an azalea plant sent me by my family; it had fuchsia-pink flowers, and ever since then a pink azalea has always been very special to me. I was depressed no end when the flowers eventually fell off. But there were also birds; starlings, chaffinches and sparrows used to visit me. Had I had a longer sentence, I might have imitated the Birdman of Alcatraz. It was cupboard love on the birds' part, of course; they liked the bread I gave them. There is no prettier sight than a little bird on your window sill, especially if you are behind bars. Like the Holloway pigeons, they were a reminder of freedom.

I joined a painting class in the evenings. It was only once a week for an hour, not nearly enough for me, especially as the time taken to set up at the beginning and tidy away at the end seemed not to leave much more than half an hour for the painting itself. People liked painting food, cakes especially: French fancies, lemon meringue pies, New Forest gateaux. There was something very satisfying about having access to tubes of paint; it uncovered a curious savage greed. Just to feel a new tube of madder red, fat and virginal, gave me a buzz. I think many of us felt like this; people piled the paint on, producing works in the style of Berthe Hess or J.B. Yeats. The art master remarked to me that most of the pictures that lay about the room were still waiting to dry long after their creators had been released. I painted in this style too, especially at first, pulling out strange images from my subconscious and splashing on the oil paints as if they were going out of fashion. Craving more time to paint than this weekly class allowed, I nicked a little black tin box of watercolours with its brush, keeping it behind my cell locker, under the mattress, or sometimes in one cup of my unfilled bra, balancing the radio that lived in the other. I was constantly changing its hiding-place for fear it would be found, making me lose remission; but the danger was worth it for the sensation of sitting on my floor, cloche hat on my head, painting on an Izal toilet roll far into the night by the light of the ripe moon.

A cat I painted was awarded a Koestler Prize, one of the prizes instituted by the writer to encourage prison painters. Arthur Koestler had been in prison himself, before the war in Spain; he must have known what a joy it would be for a prisoner to win something like this. I bless his memory, and sometimes wonder what happened to that pussy-cat.

Over half the people in that place were mentally ill in some way; I include myself in this, because bulimia is a mental illness. We should really have had treatment, it was wrong just to lump us together and hope for the best. In the prison system, such treatment as there is seems to be concentrated on serious offenders. These, though, are usually not going to be released for a long time, so society benefits less than if more was done to cure the petty criminals who are going to be let loose at any moment. There were women in Moor Court who were complete alcoholics just sent in for cold turkey without any special care. Some of them were going bananas, pulling their hair out for desperation, sadder than any bag lady at Charing Cross; lost souls waiting dully for their sentence to finish so that they could get their next bottle of meths or rum after which, naturally, they would get into trouble again. In the meantime they sought comfort at the toffee shop. The shoplifters were going to offend again, too. Most of them did it regularly, often because they enjoyed the thrill of danger, and were simply waiting to be released and have another go. As to the prostitutes, their talk was of getting laid.

'Five more days,' one of them said to me, 'and I'm on that train from Stoke. And do you know what I'm going to do, Mary?'

'No, what?'

'First bloke I see it's down with my knickers and in with his cock, and the second and third one and all. And I'm not charging, the first day.'

In some cases the authorities did behave with compassion, as with the woman across the corridor from me. She had a mania for cleanliness, and spent most of her time vacuum-cleaning the prison, which was what she wanted; what was more unusual was that she was allowed to take the vacuum cleaner to bed with her. I think this shows that the Governor was a genuinely kind woman. However, there was no effort made actually to treat this prisoner, or anyone else. It was not provided for in the system.

One or two of us prisoners tried to help others. Rachel Pinney was the best at this by far, being professionally qualified; but I, too, used to find myself in the position of psychological dustbin. Often it was one of the prostitutes who needed to tell me of her screwed-up life between her punters and her pimp. Prostitutes ranged from the single mother who charged £5 a time to get toys for the children to the high-class whore who was the star of some establishment run by a madame. We had a couple of madames as well; the tarts treated them with great respect, just as rank still counts among prisoners of war. The girls from the brothels were lazy; every day they grew fatter on the peas and potatoes of prison. Their flesh was soft from their cosseted indoor lives, their minds were empty and complacent. The streetwalkers, in contrast, were lean as alley-cats and tattooed to show that they were tough. This toughness, though, was only on the surface; underneath they were sad and wounded. Most worked for pimps; often they had simply fallen for the wrong man. They pined for these pimps and could talk of little else. They were addicted, utterly subjugated to an extent I found amazing and rather disgusting. I had myself been in love, of course, but this willing sex-slavery was something I had never met.

The person I was sorriest for was a vulnerable girl I shall call

Gwen. Though superbly educated, she had turned to crime, and failed at it. Her boyfriend had deserted her, her parents wanted nothing more to do with her. She never had a visitor. In prison she was disliked for her intellect and her polished accent, like Rachel Pinney; but she lacked any of Rachel's zest for life or willingness to muck in. She felt more left out than anyone, especially as she had no intellectual equal in the entire place; no-one, that is, who could talk literature or history or philosophy with her. Even Rachel had no interest in those subjects; like Sherlock Holmes, she didn't bother about anything that was not to do with her profession. I couldn't help in this way either, of course, but I was drawn to Gwen as one is drawn to a wounded bird. Soon we struck up a friendship.

'You know, Mary,' she used to say, 'one day you're going to be such a happy girl, I know, I can see it in you.'

'And you have an old soul, you have seen many incarnations.'

I felt this; it showed in her face which was not beautiful, but wise and gentle. She was thirty, but it was clear that she would not look much different at sixty. What's to become of you? I thought, anguished. She had nowhere to go when she got out, no hope any longer of a decent job, and perhaps worst, none of the bounce that she would need to come back.

One thing she did like was driving; and to cheer her up I suggested that when we got out we should start a mobile fish and chip shop together. This, absurd as it sounds, gave her a sort of vision where she had none before.

'We'll get a van,' I said, 'and some red and white striped overalls with hats to match.'

'Fish and chips,' she said. 'Well, they're very popular.'

'Yes, and think of all those people in the countryside, they'd love to have a chip van come by. We'll call ourselves the Chip Chicks.'

'It might work, like mobile libraries.'

'Of course it'll work,' I said, warming to the idea. 'We'll start just with chips, then when we've made a bit of money we'll embark on the fish ...'

'Great licks from the Chip Chicks,' she said, and we started thinking up silly slogans. She built on the vision, certain now what she would do. I think it helped her at the time, though I knew that if we actually put the scheme into practice it would fail at once; with my bulimia I should have eaten us out of profits in a week.

There were other sad cases, particularly those who clung to their respectability. One pensioner had pinched a few rashers of bacon and a couple of eggs out of straight hunger; she had no money till her pension came next day. Instead of longing for release like the rest of us, she dreaded it; she would have to meet her neighbours.

On the whole people chose friends who were in for the same things; the tarts stuck together, so did the shoplifters, so did the dippers and the fences and the kiters who passed dud cheques. There was only one other in for drugs besides myself; a cheery plump black girl with a shock of woolly hair. There was no harm to her, but we never got intimate because she was still into hash, whereas I had decided to give it up.

Friday evenings were for religion. The Church of England vicar and the Methodist minister from the village of Oakamoor, a rabbi from Stoke and Sister Patricia, a Roman Catholic nun, went round the television rooms tending their flocks; touting for customers, said the cynics. The Methodist scored with me; about half-way through my sentence I renounced Buddhism and joined his church. Ronnie had been brought up a Methodist, switching to the Church of England when he married my mother, so I could tell him I was returning to my father's old faith. This was not quite honest, for my conversion had nothing to do with Ronnie. The fact was that the Methodists were taken on Sundays to the chapel in the village, and I would do anything for an outing. We went in the prison minibus and sat with a wardress at the back, away from the village parishioners who were at the front. The hymn-singing was lusty and sincere; I enjoyed it.

Later I made friends with Sister Patricia, who was Mother Superior at a small convent half a mile from the prison. She had been a prisoner too, she told me; interned in France, though when or why she did not say. She spotted the unhappiness behind my aloof façade, and it was not long before she included me in her invitation to tea at the convent. I went every other Saturday after that, till I was released. Sister Patricia's nuns were charming to us; they treated us so humanly, so normally. I became attracted to Roman Catholicism; a religion whose devotees could be like Sister Patricia must be worth following. But conversion to Roman Catholicism takes time, and before instruction was even half completed, I was relased. All the same I kept up with Sister Patricia. I visited her convent from home after my release, lunching with the nuns and cutting their hair. We wrote to each other every Christmas thereafter until her death in 1985.

Hot pants were the fashion craze for 1971, and as the weather warmed up the fever swept Moor Court. People sent out for knitting wool, queued for the supplies in the stores, and the place was alive with the clicking of needles. The results began appearing on the prisoners' bottoms, in garter stitch, feather stitch and stocking stitch. The pink and blue wool from the stores was not really suitable; prison-fattened rumps and thighs heavy with cellulite do not look good in woolly pink shorts, worse than a seaside postcard. But I can't talk. I made myself a pair in mustard and black stripes; kind friends told me I looked like a bumble bee. The hot pants got on the Governor's nerves; after a bit she banned them.

As release approached I got *gate fever*, that frenzy that creeps over all prisoners before they are let out. The night before you leave you are locked up at teatime for your own protection, to prevent rough celebrations. People get excited, their hidden envy turns into aggression and they can tear your clothes, ruin your possessions, even injure you.

I had quite a few things to take away with me; my paintings, the garments I had knitted and crocheted. They gave me a bag to put them in, also let me take the clothes I had drawn from the prison store. I was allowed to select another garment as well; I chose a green greatcoat in Forties style that I had worn to *Major Barbara*. Getting my personal things back was a queer experience. My bracelet, my ring – I remember looking at them with new eyes. I had forgotten all about them, didn't feel they were really mine, fingered them greedily as if they were Cartier's choicest.

They asked me where I wanted to go. After a moment's hesitation, I asked for a ticket to Manchester, to my parents. My mother had written kindly, making it clear that I had a home with her for as long as I wanted it. I knew I shouldn't stay long, but it would give me time to adjust.

So I ate (and lost) my last prison breakfast, and at eight-thirty I was taken in the minibus to Stoke on Trent station. The duty officer took me on to the platform, gave me my ticket and £2.50; before I went in it would have been £2.10/-, but the currency had now been decimalized, I should have to get used to that. We shook hands, and she was gone.

Feeling like a child playing truant, I bought a packet of ten Players from a kiosk. Then I stood at the front of the platform rigid, like a soldier at attention; I still felt part of that institution. In a sense it was as if it had abandoned me.

The train arrived; I staggered on with my big bag, put it down opposite a businessman also going to Manchester. He looked at me; I was sure he knew exactly where I had come from. I opened my packet of cigarettes, got one out, stared at it. I was struck by its fullness, its fatness, the way the tobacco was packed in with reckless generosity. That cigarette was to me like a Havana cigar. I lit up; this luxury felt wicked, decadent. In Manchester I changed to a double-decker bus for Shaw, then I walked the couple of miles to Clough Mount, alone with my bag. I went slowly, step by step. I felt exposed, skinned. At the door I put down my bag – it had become heavy – and rang the bell.

My mother opened the door in her familiar flowered apron, neat and stocky as a little Rhode Island hen.

'So you're here,' she said in her quiet voice. 'You've just caught me at cleaning time, can you vacuum for me, downstairs and up?'

That was all she said. When I had finished we had a cup of tea, but she still showed no curiosity at all. To her, prison was an incident that was closed and must stay closed. Perhaps it was as well.

# 17

# The Divine Light
# Ashram

Rob Roy invited me to stay at his house on a Hebridean island, and it was not very long before I was on the train to the north. The house crouched by the shore under a bracken-covered hill; not far away was the sea, seething against granite boulders and withdrawing daily to expose a waste of brown bladder-wrack. There was scarcely a living creature to be seen except the timid quick-footed sheep and the planing gulls. Only the wind and the waves disturbed the immemorial peace. Rob Roy and Ruth had a baby now, a little girl, and it would have suited me to stay a few weeks with them all in that quiet place. But my period of recuperation in the Hebrides was cut short, entirely by my own choice.

'There's a Krishnamurti congress in Saanen,' said Rob Roy as soon as I arrived. 'Switzerland. He's speaking in person. I'm going to hitch out there the day after tomorrow. You can stay here of course, as long as you like; but I must go and hear him. He's old now, it might be the last opportunity.'

Krishnamurti! We all revered him. The theosophist Annie Besant had found him as a small child and brought him up to become a great master. His followers had made an organization, but he had abandoned them because he distrusted all organizations. His view was that people must find their own way to wisdom. If they were helped by listening to him, well and good, but he disowned his own message when it was packaged and presented, even by sincere followers. There must be no followers. We seekers felt this attitude made him one of us.

Of course my master was still the Guru Maharaj Ji. I put his photograph on the mantelpiece of my room; his smiling face radiated blessing.

'Who's that?' asked Rob Roy.

'Guru Maharaj Ji,' I said, 'the Boy Guru. I took his knowledge last year in London.'

I said no more at that stage, I didn't want to push it. In any case what interested me at that moment was Rob Roy's plan to see Krishnamurti; I decided to go with him. It was as old friends and fellow seekers that we went together, nothing but that. My fondness for Rob Roy was by now transformed like a flower when it has been pressed in an album. So I was no more than two days on that tranquil island before we set off early in the morning with our rucksacks. We got a lift to Inverness, then suddenly Rob Roy announced a change of plan.

'We'd better fly,' he said. 'It will get us there at once, save us two or three days. We don't want to miss any of it.'

Life with Rob Roy was always full of surprises, good and bad; this was a good one. So we went to a travel agent, planned our trip then and there. Rob got out his cheque book and by that night we were in Saanen. We slept rough among the seekers; to be with them was to me like coming home. We sang to guitars or sat in silent friendship, people of all sorts, all ages, all nationalities. Krishnamurti was a guru despite himself. He gave his discourses in an enormous marquee, sitting on a hardback chair and dressed informally as an Englishman of his age would dress, in a white open-necked shirt and flannel trousers. A Krishna without a crown. He spoke simply, clearly and with great depth, then walked away alone, without any ceremony. It impressed me profoundly.

Rob Roy was also impressed, but did not feel that Krishnamurti was his guru; he needed to find someone who would accept his commitment. He asked me about the Guru Maharaj Ji, and I talked to him of the Divine Light Mission and my beloved mahatma. We had intended anyway to spend a night in Paris on our way home, so when we were there I took Rob Roy to the Paris ashram where I knew we should find my friend Charles Cameron. We got plenty of satsang (instruction, holy discourse) from Charles, and Rob Roy decided to take the knowledge. From Paris we went to London where by this time the Divine Light Mission had left its old basement and set up an ashram in Golders Green. There were two powerful new Indian mahatmas there. The ashram was full, but we camped outside it (*honi soit qui mal y pense*) in a bread van belonging to one of the premies, while Rob prepared himself for initiation. Finally he was ready, and took the knowledge.

After that he went back to the Hebrides. I was not quite sure what to do. I didn't fancy going home, still less to Chelsea. Rachel, before leaving prison, had given me a telephone number. She had said that if at any time I was in need or at a loose end I should get in touch with her friend Honor Butlin, a Quaker who lived near Kettering and always had an extra pint of milk left for the stranger at the door. I rang the number.

'Honor Butlin speaking.'

'My name's Shoe Taylor, and I'm a friend of Rachel Pinney.'

'Oh yes, she said you might call. So you're the famous Shoe.'

'I need somewhere to stay for a bit, and she said you might be able to help.'

'Come along then,' said Honor. 'And you can tell me how she is. I expect she ran the prison by the end.'

'You could say that.'

'You must have some good stories to tell.'

I was soon on a train to Kettering. Honor met me, took me to her house a few miles away, and put me up in a caravan in the garden. She set me to work helping her collect, wash and iron second-hand clothes; these were either sold in the Quaker meeting house for various good causes, or made into parcels and sent to refugees or the underprivileged. I went to Quaker meetings as well, and to poetry readings which Honor held in her house. I also baked bread, and made some figurines in the pottery at the end of the garden which belonged to Honor's daughter.

My friends the twins came; they spent a week helping in the garden and mowing the lawns. They must have found life rather austere, for there was no alcohol, let alone hash. But John had some news.

'There's a jumbo jet full of premies going to India to see Maharaj Ji.'

He said this lightly, in passing. But I decided then and there that I should be on that jet.

'When are they going?'

'Late November, early December; they are staying over Christmas, a couple of months.'

In due course I felt the need to travel again; it was only August, I didn't want to stay in England all the months before my date with the jumbo jet. Kind Honor gave me a little old Morris van; I painted the inside a bright terracotta orange, filled it with cushions, and headed for Brighton where the twins were. Going through London I bought a *Stage and Radio*; I had got the Beirut job from an advertisement there, perhaps there might be something for the summer. There was; again it was a circus job. Presenters were wanted for a travelling company in northern Italy.

'You'll do,' said the lady who interviewed me, 'but you'll have to make your own way there, we can't pay the fare.'

In the end she gave me £40 towards my travelling expenses. When I got to Brighton, the twins decided to come too, on their way to

Cadaques. So did John's girlfriend and another man, a poet called Peter. The day before we left Brighton there was a blow; the cord of the handbrake snapped. Getting this fixed would have meant missing the ferry, so we set off anyway. It was a dangerous journey. I was the only driver, and there was one bad moment when I went to sleep on a major road and swung into the oncoming traffic, to be awakened by frantic hooting. It was worse when we got into the mountains; driving in the Alps without a handbrake is a bad idea. Even so the journey was magical. It took eight days, about double what one would have expected even with a van that only did thirty-five miles an hour. We spent the nights out in the woods and lived mostly on bread, cheese, tomatoes and olives. I don't ever remember it raining, not seriously. All of us were in perfect harmony.

The circus was downmarket compared to the Lebanese one, but it was fun all the same. The twins and the others tagged along with me. The ringmaster could not offer them all jobs, but John was put on to washing the elephants. He got an amazing amount of wax out of their ears. We all travelled from village to village, staying a couple of days in each doing a matinée and an evening performance every day; it was always over by 9.30 pm. Everyone was in some sort of vehicle, some more decrepit even than mine. There were big bosomy Italian girls with bleached hair, hooked noses, flashing black eyes; they juggled or danced on the wire or tied themselves in knots. There were some black men who dressed in Zulu leopard skins and played drums; I think they really were Zulus but their primitiveness was an act, off stage they were like anyone else.

After a couple of weeks the twins felt the call of Cadaques. Without too much difficulty they talked me round, so we all set off again at a snail's pace. When we reached Cadaques we did not bother to find accommodation but went straight through the village to a place where there are shallow caves. The twins took one, I took another, putting a cloak over the opening. We spent our time making little things to sell on Mondays in the weekly market; clay images and pipeheads for *seepsies*, stone beads. The clayware we fired ourselves in the embers of our fires on the mountain. Our things sold, usually within a quarter of an hour. Otherwise we swam in the sea or travelled here and there in the van.

Eventually we drove back to London, and I contacted my parents to ask for the cost of the trip to India; flight there and back on the Air India jumbo jet, and two months' stay in the Divine Light ashram. With their usual generosity they gave me the money, so I boarded the aircraft at Heathrow with 200 other premies.

So there I was, a package tourist at last after doing so much travelling by myself. It was rather restful, and these were all fellow-premies with the same beliefs and aims. We landed in Delhi in the blazing sun and were shepherded into coaches. Dusty spellbinding Delhi! The poverty hits you in the eye; even if all you have is a rucksack you still feel over-dressed, over-cosseted, aware of your own affluence, especially if you are seeing it all from a seat in a coach.

After a couple of hours we arrived in Hardwar. The town was crowded with brown people; angular men in loincloths, old army uniforms, turbans, Nehru suits and hats. Then after less than a mile there was a great gate with a sign in bold black and white saying 'Divine Light Mission Ashram', and a couple of guards with sticks outside it. The gate was unlocked for the coaches, then locked again behind us, and there we were.

It was neither the Ritz nor the Taj Mahal, but it was fine. We were each shown to a bed in a dormitory, also the big satsang hall. There was no dining-room; we ate outside, cross-legged on the verandah. We got up at 5.30 am, and our first duty was to pick half-opened rose-heads, neither buds nor blooms, or sometimes marigolds. The bittersweet scent of marigolds will always bring back North India to me. The flowers were weighed in, bought by a man from Hardwar and taken away in a pannier on his bicycle. Devout Hindus were the ultimate customers; after morning prayers and chanting, they set them in leaf-boats to float down the holy Ganges a few miles away.

Later in the day we were set to work in the printing sheds, pressing and printing sheets of paper. All the time we were supposed to be meditating on the mantra called the 'holy name', which I managed to do at times, but I have to admit that the work was mostly as boring as the dolly-room in open prison. In another way, too, the ashram could have been a bit like prison if I had let it, for we were supposed to stay in it more or less all the time. This was not compulsory, but there was a fair amount of moral pressure. A lot of us disregarded this; I'm afraid I took no notice of it at all. My favourite place in Hardwar was the railway station. A meal in the station café cost about 25p, and to me it seemed as good as a five star restaurant.

I love Indian railway stations; there is teeming life there, yet also a sense of order. The stations and the trains that pass through them are painted in beautiful colours. People live and die there, sleeping on the floor, cooking, making things and selling them. An empty baked bean tin will have a handle soldered to it and become a milk ladle. Everything is recycled before your eyes.

Usually all I did was to take a rickshaw into Hardwar for a snack in a
*chai* shop, but there were two afternoons when I played truant for much
longer. On the first I took a trip to Rishikesh, where there are a number
of ashrams, including that of the Maharishi Mahesh Yogi. But the one
which impressed me was the Sivananda ashram. The motto was 'Love,
Give, Serve, Realize, Meditate'. I arrived at lunch time and watched the
*swamis* feeding masses of people. It was in a big hall, everyone squatted
on the immaculately clean tiled floor and was given food on a large
green leaf; chapattis, rice and subji (Indian mixed vegetables), dal
(lentils). Liquid yoghourt was doled out from a bucket. All this was free
to any wayfarer. In a music room people were practising on sitars and
tablas (drums), and there was a pharmacy where ayurvedic medicine
was being prepared; the late Swami Sivananda was a qualified
physician as well as a holy man. The Sivananda organization founded in
his memory and ordered according to his principles now runs yoga
centres in many parts of the world; I was to come across it again.
Sivananda yoga teaching is, in my experience, the best all-round system
for beginners and intermediates. As regards advanced studies I am not
qualified to judge.

On my way back, after experiencing the Sivananda ashram, my
attention ought to have been devoted to religion. I have to admit that
instead of this, I went shopping for clothes in Hardwar. I found a
wonderful tailor from whom I bought several yards of rough raw cream
silk. He fitted me for a Nehru jacket and some shirts. Then I looked out a
length of striped material in cashmere and ordered another Nehru
jacket. By the time I got back to the ashram it was quite late. I was called
to a supervisor.

'Are you realizing how long you were out this afternoon?'

'No, not exactly; quite a long time, I suppose.'

'This place is not a hotel,' he said, 'and you are not here as a tourist,
but as a devotee of our Guru.'

'Of course I am devoted to him,' I said.

'In future see to it that you do not do it again.'

I was glad he didn't try to get a promise from me, for I should have
had to avoid giving it. I was not going to be cooped up again, so soon
after being released from prison. Also, I had not come all this way to see
no more of India than the inside of one ashram. I got another scolding a
week or so later when I went to collect my new clothes. They were well
worth the wigging. The supervisors took care not to enforce discipline
too rigorously. As it was quite a few people got fed up and simply left, to
tour India or go home early, particularly the Australians.

I did have a feeling of guilt, but it was nothing to do with leaving the ashram for the odd afternoon. It was because of my bulimia, which in this country seemed so much worse. There was no abundance, and none of the fast food which I did not feel so bad about wasting. Here food was grown and prepared in the old way, trouble was taken about it, love was put into it, and I was abusing all that. I tried hard to stop, but the addiction was too strong for me. I took to working in the kitchens; I particularly remember one of the cooks who made chapattis, a vigorous Sikh with abundant long hair. That man really worked, he could turn out 400 chapattis without batting an eyelid, standing there on his big feet as if attached to the earth. He had sparkling black eyes that reminded me of a devil, yet he worked without caring for self. I watched him, emulated him; soon I could do the job almost as well as he could. Often in the third world I was impressed with the way people worked; their energy reminded me of my Lancashire childhood. This job also gave me the opportunity for many a secret snack. Eventually it occurred to me that a better self-inflicted penance would be to clean the lavatories. These were revolting, partly because no-one did much about them, partly because the water supply was so poor. You flushed, but most of the time only a trickle came. I got hold of some Ajax and set to work, but there was a lot to get rid of before the Ajax could be applied. I hauled bucket after bucket along, flushed them down, scrubbed till each lavatory was spotless.

One day I went to the lavatories after lunch with my bucket and Ajax. Just as I started work Marnie came past, a big, rather overweight American girl; she entered the next door cubicle. I heard her being sick. Marnie was a gentle soul, cultured and well-educated; she had been married for a time, then her husband had run off and she had taken the knowledge of the Divine Light. All this I had gathered through casual conversation with her, for we were quite friendly. Now, though, one or two things pieced themselves together in my mind. This wasn't the first time I had noticed her vomiting; and again, she had a passion for her food, never left a single grain of rice. She *wolfed* it, this was the only word. Not so much if she knew she was being watched, there was a certain shame about it . . . That's it, I thought. It takes one to know one.

I didn't accost her then and there, for if I was right in what I was thinking this might have upset her. I approached her later.

'Marnie,' I said, 'don't take this the wrong way, but are you on a vomiting high?'

She looked down; it cost her an effort to reply. 'I have this compulsive eating trouble,' she said, 'and, yes, I do like to vomit, I guess you could call it a vomiting high. Bulimia's the word they use.'

'I'm the same, have been for years.'

She looked at me. 'You too?'

'Every time I eat I am sick,' I said. 'I can't resist it, can't do without that high. And you're the first person I've met with the same trouble. What did you call it?'

'Bulimia,' she said. 'I've been under analysis for it, didn't do any good. Say, it's great to have a, like, companion in misery.'

We hugged each other, cried a little, and from then on we were firm friends. She felt the same guilt as I did, and decided to help me with the lavatories; with two of us on them working hard, those lavatories were more shiningly clean than ever before or since. Marnie was a true buddy, yet in a secret part of myself I looked down on her. Her heavy figure indicated that she was not able to vomit with such *profundity* as I was, that she failed to reach my degree of purity. For yes, simultaneously with my shame I still felt a sort of pride in what I did, in doing it thoroughly and properly. So much in our lower existence is a parody of what is higher, and my bulimia was a perversion of my desire to overcome the physical. Like a Pharisee in the Gospels, when I compared myself to poor Marnie I felt 'holier than thou'. I hope she found some reason to feel like this about me. To live with self-disgust it is helpful to think someone else is worse.

Venetia Stanley-Smith was at the ashram; she had come from Japan, where she had been setting up a Divine Light Mission in Kyoto.

'How do the Japanese take to the knowledge?' I asked.

'Better in a way than people do in the West. You see they are Buddhist, the way of thinking is closer. You ought to come out.'

'I'd love to,' I said, at that stage only half meaning it.

The Guru used to appear on the balcony some time in the late morning with his mother; one could go and have an interview with him there, put some flowers at his feet. It was all very innocent; he was about eleven at the time, a plump little chap like a Michelin man, being politely mobbed by us Guru-groupies. He has since matured into a profound master, but at that time what I felt for him was not respect so much as an intense affection. Also, I can't claim that his ashram affected me on any deep spiritual level. There was a sense of unity with all the young premies from other parts of the world; and certainly the Mission helped me to realize that I could never live in Chelsea again, not that kind of life at any rate. I had done with hash and LSD, I was on my way to broader horizons. But I did not at that time see the Divine Light Mission as more than a temporary stage for me. There seemed something juvenile about it all, particularly the attempts at discipline, the fuss made if I left the ashram. The silly thing was that I was not in practice prevented from leaving, only nagged for doing so.

About 50 of us were taken to Rajasthan for a huge guru festival. We paraded on elephants, two to an elephant; my partner was my friend Anne Fleming. Soon after this, late in January 1972, our two months came to an end. We all gathered together for a final pep-talk.

'OK, kids,' said the supervisor, 'pack your bags, kiss the Guru's feet, spread the word, meditate on the knowledge. Jai Sad Sitanand.' That was it. We were shepherded on to our coaches and driven to Delhi airport.

Anne Fleming put me up in her flat in West Kensington, and after ten days or so I got an airmail letter from Venetia in Japan. She invited me to come and join her. The letter arrived on a Monday; that Friday the money for the fare to Kyoto arrived from my parents, next Tuesday I was on the aircraft.

This really was a leap into the dark. I had never touched a pair of chopsticks or sampled a bowl of tempura; I had never felt the pull of the Far East and knew nothing about Japan or the Japanese. Anne gave me a lift to the aeroplane, which took off in the early morning, and I'm afraid I gave her a difficult time. I freaked out; an odd experience, perhaps the closest approach to it being my refusal to go to Paris with the Palais des Merveilles. It was a surfacing of the insecurity caused by my bulimia; this was always there, but did not usually show. I clung to Anne.

'Don't let me go,' I sobbed.

Anne said: 'Of course you mustn't go if you are feeling like that, you can't possibly travel. We'll go to the desk, cancel your ticket, get your money back.'

But suddenly I pulled myself together. 'No, I'm being silly. Of course I'll go.'

'Are you sure?' said Anne, for I was trembling.

'Yes,' I said, 'quite sure,' but I changed my mind again several times before allowing Anne almost to push me through that barrier.

Once settled on the aircraft and unable to turn back, I felt better. The journey was to take more than 24 hours. We landed at Bahrain to change planes; suddenly the experience became scintillating, strange. The air was warm. Quite different people got on in different clothes, Arab or Indian, some even in kimonos. The meals became weird.

I must not get off at Tokyo, Venetia had said, but stay on for the short hop to Kyoto. All I had was an address on a piece of paper, in English and Japanese. It was a mystery land; foreign people, foreign language, utterly foreign writing. I found a taxi, gave the driver my piece of paper; he did not seem to understand it, but he opened the door for me and, rather doubtfully, I stepped in. Eventually he drew up at a big building; and there running down the steps, fresh as an English rose in her funky clothes, was Venetia. From that moment I knew it was going to be all right.

# 18

## *Shui-San*

The class of bright little Japanese salesmen was most attentive. God help them, I thought, I hope I'm some use at this. *Shui-san*, they called me; Miss Shoe. I was trying to teach them English pronunciation.

'Good afternoon,' I said.

'Gudu,' they repeated, humming a little before launching themselves like skijumpers into: 'afutanunu.'

'We had better do that again, one by one . . .'

Then I tried: 'The sky is blue.'

'Da – sukai – iss – buru.' Each word came out like a karate chop.

'That's *blue*, Mr Ishi.'

'Bru' – this with a happy grin.

Venetia had installed her Divine Light Mission in what had been the British Embassy in a select area of Kyoto, built for a past ambassador by his Japanese wife. As soon as I entered the place I felt I belonged. This was just as well, for the westerner arriving in Japan for the first time feels about as alien as it is possible to be; it was a boon to have a home base with friends who spoke English. There were young people from many countries; Americans, South Americans, English, an Italian, an Arab girl. Our diet was partly Japanese, partly Western whole food. Japanese visitors were welcomed; we gave hospitality to young people who needed it, as monasteries did during the Middle Ages in Europe. We meditated in the great assembly room, on the floor covered with clean and elegant tatami. There was a lot of music played on traditional Japanese instruments; I already knew the banjo-like *shami-sen* and the long deep-toned bamboo pipe or *shakahachi*, people had played them in Formentera. Venetia was trying to master the six-foot stringed *koto*. To see her playing this beautiful antique instrument in her kimono was to realize how acclimatized she had already become.

From this secure base I could revel in the strangeness of Japan. I loved

155

the kimonos; many people still wore them and shuffled about the streets in their *geita* clogs. The men often had sweat-bands on their heads, giving them the swashbuckling look of the old pirates in their bandannas. Japan seemed a mixture of past and future, missing out the ordinary present. One would pass a monk in his dark robes and *geitas* who might have stepped straight out of a Hokusai print; next minute one could be on the *shin-kan-sen* or bullet train which travels at 130 miles an hour and has heated lavatory seats. The trees lining some streets turned out to be artificial, made of plastic, with artificial birds twittering; big robot traffic cops with awkward gestures took the place of lights on some of the street junctions.

Shopping was difficult at first for one who spoke not a word of Japanese and understood not a stroke of the Kanji lettering. I found this lettering so beautiful that sometimes I just stood and enjoyed it; but until I brushed up on the art of finger-counting and pointing, I needed Venetia or some other interpreter. I've often shopped in countries where I didn't speak the language, but normally the numbers on the price tickets give a clue; there was no such help for me in the covered market in Kyoto where the farmers and fishermen sold their produce. Sometimes both the stallholder and I were left totally bewildered. As I became more adept, I started to enjoy it; my theatrical instinct was satisfied as I turned myself for the occasion into an imitation Marcel Marceau. There was little response to this, for the Japanese do not do much with facial expression and hardly gesticulate at all; but they did, now and then, understand, and when this happened it was a triumph.

Purely as a spectacle, the market was wonderful. Row upon row of stalls displayed food such as I had never seen. Miso paste, in the West, is a foreign delicacy; here it came in vats, and in several shades and flavours. There were kegs of seaweed of many kinds, green and brown, smelling of the beach. The vegetables, many of them quite new to me, were neatly ranged; there was a marvellous variety of fish and shellfish and crustaceans of all kinds in a profusion that was yet disciplined by an innate feeling for how things should look. There was poultry too and red meat, and plenty of rice. For the instant snacks I craved there was the tempura woman; I loved to watch her. She dipped a sprat or a slice of vegetable in batter, then whipped it on to the hot square pan where in a few seconds it would be done. She had this indescribable neatness and sureness in all her movements. No wonder the Japanese are so good at fitting minute electronic chips.

We at the mission sold some food of our own. We made brown wholemeal bread in loaves and cobs, and English marmalade. Together with lavender bags, we sold our produce at the fairs held monthly in the temples around Kyoto. These too were fun, dealing in all manner of things as well as food: live birds, antiques, parasols, fans, kimonos, slippers. All the same, there was one thing I couldn't find anywhere in the markets or shops of Kyoto, and that was a pair of shoes to fit me. Japanese women just do not have feet as big as size 8. Perhaps I could have found some in Tokyo, but I got my long-suffering mother to airmail me a pair from England, at considerable expense.

The mission needed to make money to keep going, so those of us who could do so went out to earn it. That was how I came to be teaching English pronunciation. The trouble was that language teaching is a skill like any other, and I did not have that skill. My method mainly consisted of hand gestures, broad smiles and laughter. This wasn't a complete failure; my class smiled and giggled right back at me and seemed to find it amusing to be coached in these outlandish sounds by the red-haired barbarian girl. All the same, it was evident after four lessons that they were not going to make much progress. With profuse apologies, the director told me my services were no longer needed.

Venetia was disappointed, but not for long.

'Never mind,' she said, 'we'll try you as a *geisha*.'

I wasn't sure about this, but she reassured me.

'It's quite respectable, honestly. All you need to do is sit there. You're not much more than an ornament. The money's good, too, it will be quite a help.'

It was exactly as she had said. I had to sit in a row with a few Japanese girls, all dressed up to the nines, then some little Japanese businessman would select me and I was expected to smile at him as he ate sushi, drank little cups of sake, and perhaps tried out his elementary English. My tipple was fruit juice. An American guitarist played background music. It would have been deadly dull except that it was so strange; I was fascinated with the immaculate traditional costumes of the girls with their whitened faces, elaborately coiffed hair and tiny little feet. Did they spend their time packed in silk-lined boxes, emerging only in the evening? There seemed to be no sex-play at all. Admittedly I did not understand what was said, but I certainly never saw a man touch a woman, or vice versa. One of the things I liked about Japan in general was how sexless it all seemed; this suited my mood at that time. Presumably the sexlessness was more apparent than real. Japanese people are discreet and subtle in love-play, so no doubt I missed a number of signals, especially through not knowing the language. In any case I found the atmosphere restful. It seemed like a civilization for children. I liked the co-operative spirit too, the way everyone seemed to fit in. There was no rudeness, no yobbishness.

I soon began to be bored in the *geisha* house, just sitting around; the girls who had at first looked picturesque began to seem birdbrained, the men all resembled each other. But then I made friends with the guitarist; he had with him a pair of tomtoms.

'Can I drum in with you?' I said.

'Sure, why not?'

So I progressed from dummy to drummer, which suited me much better. All the same the place remained a mystery to me. The customers paid lavishly for what seemed so little. They talked with the Japanese girls in a decorous and stilted way; was there some special charm in this conversation? If this was the point, what was I there for, sitting like a waxwork? Did anyone get it together? Perhaps some did, but my impression was that most of the customers just went there to relax and be pampered, to unwind after the office. Then again, some people like to be seen by their friends at an expensive place. It closed punctually at midnight.

Then Venetia started finding me modelling jobs. I can never blame those in Munich and Paris who turned me down as an ordinary clothes model. This could never have been my profession; I am far too fidgety and my hands are too big. But what I did in Japan was more interesting. They used me as the Great White Wonder, the Girl of the Golden West.

The American occupation had brought beefsteak to the Japanese diet, and Kobe beef was supposed to be the best. I was employed to promote it and the Mission collected £200 per session. This was strange work for a fish vegetarian. I sat in an American-style steakhouse and was filmed putting away a three-quarter pound Kobe steak with chips and tomatoes. What was more, I had to wash it down with a glass of foul white wine, and I was even less used to that. I vomited it all up as soon as possible, which was painful; I had forgotten how to chew steak properly, and my guts ached all the next day.

The next job was really odd. One day Venetia asked me, 'Would you agree to being modelled in plaster?'

'Anything for the cause.'

'Good, there's two hundred pounds in it for us, plus another hundred if you agree to let them do your face.'

'What do I have to do?'

'You go to this laboratory where they've invented a new modelling plaster: some sort of liquid which does the job of plaster of Paris. They want to make a mould of a European woman. It's a hundred per cent safe, they say, and I'm sure they are straight, they are very respectable people.'

'Fine,' I said, 'of course I'll do it.'

'Including the face?'

'Certainly.'

At the laboratory I was received with the utmost courtesy by three men in white coats. I undressed completely and was at once wrapped in white towels and taken to a room where there was a long tub, the right size for a human body, with a raised portion for the head. They attached a thin harness under my shoulders. Suddenly it began to seem as if I had walked into a Hammer horror movie, but it was too late to back out; so I took a deep in-breath and lay down, wondering if this tub would be my coffin. I felt creamy cold liquid rising around my body. There was a modern electric clock on the wall, I kept my eyes riveted on the red second hand. The gunk tightened quickly, I could feel it. After about half a minute they pulled me out horizontally by the harness, breaking the mould at the shoulders. Two of them quickly stuck the bits back while the third whipped the towels on me to cover my nakedness. Then I had to take an even deeper breath and press my face in a bowl of the stuff, and that was it.

Afterwards I looked about me and saw what an odd place I was in, full of plaster arms and legs and heads and torsoes and glass eyes, uncannily real though bloodless. Everything in the room was white, including the technicians' overalls and my towels; it was a pure white experience. My mould was to be used to make dummy Western women for shop windows; I wonder if after all these years one or two dummies with my wide shoulders and prominent deltoids still linger in the Tokyo suburbs. As I was driven back to the mission, I felt calm and statuesque, as if influenced by the stillness of the dummies that were to be made in my shape. It was a good feeling; all the rest of that day I was grounded.

Next I was hired to help open the first McDonald's hamburger palace in Kyoto. They dressed me as a cowgirl in a big stetson hat and Texan boots, miniskirt and cape. The place was much grander than any hamburger joint I have seen in the West; it had rosewood panelling, ceramic tiles and gleaming brass fittings. A wide red carpet led to the door which had an enormous satin bow on its brass handle to be cut by whoever was doing the opening; this could have been royalty, the officials behaved with such ceremony. One had to remind oneself that this was only a McDonald's fast food joint being opened, not a major state occasion. I was one of six models who stood outside during the opening; each of us was given hundreds of tickets for a free hamburger, to distribute to the public afterwards. Word had got around and by the time the people came through the cordons they were a huge crowd, dense and eager. Everybody likes a freebie, and they all pushed and shoved in a most un-Japanese way. All I saw was a mass of yellow hands, clutching for tickets. I handed them out rapidly, deft as a conjurer, trying to be like the goddess Kali with her multitude of arms. But after a bit it was too much for me, I was worn down by the sheer numbers of people pressing against me and their demanding hands like hungry yellow tulips. I'd had enough, I wanted out. I threw my remaining tickets high in the air; they fluttered down, the crowd caught them as they fell and scrabbled for them on the ground. It was a relief to walk away, board a tram and return to the peace of the mission. I had earned them £150 that day.

My illness still ruled me completely. Rice cakes, sushi, tempura, cream cakes imitated from the West, strange viscous sweet-meats based on rice flour – I ate them all and threw them up. I liked Japanese green tea, but felt utterly unworthy of the stately Japanese tea ceremony. I had travelled ten thousand miles but the monkey on my back gripped me as firmly as ever, I might as well have stayed in Shaw boning out the beef. The nights are my relief; the sweet clean scent of the tatami floor matting by the futon that served as mattress filled me with serenity. The fragrance of those Japanese nights brought hope; then with each day came disappointment as my addiction resumed control.

Where might I find a cure? People talked again of George Ohsawa's macrobiotic system that Rob Roy had adopted in Chelsea all those years ago; perhaps that might be the key. Someone told me of a *dojo* (learning centre) which specialized in the macrobiotic diet; it was run by Oki Sensei, a famous Zen master who knew many healing arts. He took in people with all sorts of things wrong with them, mental and physical: sufferers from radiation sickness contracted at Hiroshima or Nagasaki, jilted wives who needed to be kept from suicide. About thirty patients were there at any one time.

I decided to go and see it. This meant leaving the shelter of the mission, and I still spoke hardly any Japanese. All the same, I have never been one to turn down an adventure, and apart from the hope of a cure I was keen to see more of Japanese life. So I took a deep breath and set out with a mission brother who also wanted to meet Oki Sensei and see his *dojo*. I only took a small bag packed mainly with gym wear, for I had been warned that it was very spartan, a gymnasium and little else.

The place was down a cul-de-sac in a small village called Mishimashi not far from Tokyo. A small stream ran by it, a temple roof was visible and there was a monastery next door. The building itself was of three storeys, covered with scaffolding; it looked unfinished. Spartan it certainly was; there was no ornamentation at all, not even a statue of the Buddha. The partitions between the rooms were made of *shoji*, rectangles of heavy duty translucent rice-paper stretched on frames of black-painted wood. Sliding panels also of *shoji* served as cupboards. There were two dormitories, one for men and one for women; for beds each person had a futon, rolled up and put away behind the sliding panels during the day, when our dormitories became day-rooms. The floors were covered with tatami matting and that was it. It was enough.

Oki Sensei was one of the hardest men I have ever met, totally *yang*. To get some idea of what he was like, study a martial art. He was a real healer, though. He greeted us with a gruff friendliness; luckily he spoke a certain amount of English. From his face I judged him to be well into middle age, but his hair was completely black. This, I learned later, was because he had it dyed – his one concession to personal vanity. Though ascetic, he was certainly not celibate; he had a wife his own age and a twenty-five year old mistress who visited him once a week from Tokyo, with his wife's consent.

My friend from the mission stayed a few days, then went home. I stayed four months, the only Westerner in the place. It was generous of Oki Sensei to keep me, for I had no money to pay him and at first there was no way in which I could be of any use. He had travelled a bit in the West, and perhaps he was interested to see how a Westerner would take to his regime. My illness, too, was a challenge to his techniques.

The life was extremely tough, but it suited me. We got up in time for *sotos*, or prayers, at 5.30 am.

'*Oko noko go ko so ko*,' we chanted, over and over again.

Then we had to run a mile down the road and back; some people splashed themselves in the stream on their return. Breakfast followed, always the same; a bowl of *misoshiru* soup with *osoba*, buckwheat noodles like spaghetti. I still usually have this for breakfast.

Most mornings we did gymnastics in the big *dojo*. We crawled along a slippery pole about ten feet up; Oki Sensei roared with laughter if anyone fell off it. Or we hopped across the room with a leg tied to a partner's, as in a three-legged race. Sometimes we were made to roll across the floor, up to the point of exhaustion and beyond. Anyone who was lazy, man or woman, Oki would seize by the clothes and swing round until dizzy. We had lunch kneeling all together round a big low table. By way of grace before eating we knelt up, clapped hands loudly before the face and shouted '*Gasho!*'

Our food was all macrobiotic; brown rice, soya beans, seaweeds, vegetable tempura, bananas, melon. Every other day we were given soya milk. We were not supposed to snack, but I soon nosed my way to a food shop about a mile away. When I could get there, which luckily was not all that often, I stuffed myself with fast foods. However, this was not enjoyable; some of what I bought turned out to be too Japanese for me, an acquired taste which I had not acquired, and some was a wretched imitation of Western confectionary. All of it began to seem nasty as I got attuned to the purity of the macrobiotic fare at the *dojo*, but this aversion never quite overcame my food fixation. After one of my outside binges I would jog back to base and cleanse myself by swigging cup after cup of rice tea.

Some fine afternoons we would go off to a field a mile down the road and play games out of doors. One was a race between pairs of people sitting on each other's shoulders. The 'horse' tried to reach the winning-post first while still carrying his rider, the rider tried to push the other riders off. As prizes Oki brought a bunch of bananas; he would fling one to each of the winners, exactly as if they were chimpanzees, and growl with displeasure if anyone failed to catch his banana in mid-flight. It all toned up the cardiovascular system no end. On other afternoons he would give us all adjustments, my name for his version of chiropraxis or osteopathy. He thought all our bodies were unbalanced, and he would remedy this with snaps, clicks and wrenches performed with a fierceness which, though superbly controlled, hinted at a streak of sadism. The first time I felt a bit worried, but everybody bore it impassively without so much as a murmur, and when my turn came it didn't hurt at all. After this came a session of 'Oki yoga', his version of hathayoga. The poses were the same as in normal yoga but they were done quickly, dynamically, and usually in pairs so that each person worked against the body weight and power of the other. The system is still taught by his pupils.

Late afternoon was acupuncture time. We all stripped to the waist, and he came up behind each in turn to diagnose the weak meridians, marking us with crosses where the needles were required. He did this with a matter-of-fact air as if he were a teacher writing an equation on the blackboard. Then we all lay flat and waited for the needles. In England acupuncture is one in each ear once a month, probably as a cure for smoking, £25 a time. Oki stuck six or seven needles into each of us every day. After a while he made me his assistant. My task was to apply the burning mugwort. Each needle had at the blunt end a little receptacle like the holder for a child's birthday cake candle. I put mugwort in this and lit it so that it smouldered and gently warmed the inserted needle, giving out a powerful and seductive fragrance.

Another treatment was suction. Glass hemispheres with stems, each like a wineglass without a base, were heated and applied to the patient's back. The idea is to introduce blood to the areas where it is needed. The suction pulls out the flesh and brings the blood to the surface so that the patient seems to have gigantic boils.

In the evenings we sometimes listened to lectures, which of course meant nothing to me, or we sang to traditional Japanese musical instruments. Then there was the hot room where we took oatmeal baths. We sat together in sunken tubs set in an area of concrete cobbled with stones from the beach. Into the water, which was so hot as to be only just bearable, we poured sackfuls of oatmeal that turned the water creamy. This was supposed to be good for the skin. After this we had a cup of tea; *o-cha* (big tea) or *ko-cha* (little tea). There was no evening meal.

Oki always closed the day with a session of laughter. We knelt and sat back on our haunches, Japanese style, and Oki started to laugh. One by one we all joined in, finally the whole *dojo* was laughing. At first I had to force it, but in seconds it became genuine, a torrent of side-splitting laughter. It is a good way to end the day; I often do it with my children, before putting them to bed.

It was at Oki Sensei's *dojo* that I first discovered massage. This was not part of his regular work, but a couple of people at the *dojo* were experts and one of them gave me a treatment. It was a revelation. I felt relaxed yet vigorous, utterly positive. I decided to learn how to do it myself. I watched, then practised, tentatively at first but soon with growing confidence. It became clear that I had an aptitude for it.

Oki Sensei had another *dojo* by Mount Fuji; the mountain made a splendid backdrop. When we were there we did more outdoor work, including walks or six mile runs through the spectacular scenery at the mountain's base. Some days we went to the sea and spent the time swimming. One visit to Fuji was very short; Oki gave us a yoga session, then made us pack up, get into the bus and come straight back to Mishimashi. One never quite knew what he would do next.

For me, it was four months virtually without talking. Nobody spoke any English apart from Oki Sensei himself, and I only spoke to him personally about once every two weeks when he gave me a private session in one of the little box rooms. This silence helped me notice my surroundings more and taught me to communicate non-verbally. It also helped his remarks in these private sessions to sink in. His English was not good, but was enough to get his ideas across.

'I want to make you capable of change,' he said. 'This is Zen, never to become fixed in your habits.'

I thought of my life and its variety. 'Am I fixed?'

'You are very fixed, Shui-san; all of you are fixed, you more than anyone. Every day you vomit. To stop vomiting, you must first stop being fixed; you must become pliable.'

'How can I do that?'

'Why do you think we went to Fuji and came straight back?'

'To shake us out of routine, I suppose.'

'You make your own cage in your mind and run round it like a rat; I bend it, but I cannot break it. You must break it yourself; it is from your own mind that the change must come.'

Another time he said: 'You want to cure your habit, Shui-San?'

'It's what I want more than anything in the world.'

'Bind your mind.'

'Bind my mind, Oki Sensei?'

'Binding your hands would stop the habit, but you cannot live with hands bound. A clamp on your teeth would stop the habit, but you cannot live with clamped teeth. Binding your mind will stop the habit, and that you can do. Bind your mind.'

He disapproved of suicide.

'Many people in Japan kill themselves,' he said. 'They used to do it with swords; *seppuku*, what you call *hara-kiri*. Now they do it in other ways. I try to stop them. They say they do it for honour, but it is stupidity.'

A few years after this Oki Sensei became well known in the West, travelling to the United States, to Holland, to London, teaching his techniques and especially his Oki Yoga. He died in the same way as Hermann Hesse's master of the Glass Bead Game; of a heart attack while swimming, I believe it was off the coast of Sicily. He was a great master.

After my stay with him I went back to the mission in Kyoto. I had not achieved the cure for which I had hoped, but I had learnt a lot.

Not long after my return there was tremendous excitement.

'Great news!' said Venetia. 'The Guru is coming.'

This really was great news. She had for some time been scheming to get Maharaj Ji to Japan to bless and sanction her ashram. The food chainstore Fuji Dinari, the Japanese equivalent of Sainburys, had agreed to sponsor the visit. They covered the flat roof of their store with red carpet, erected a platform decorated with *ikebano* flower arrangements in front of a white satin backdrop.

And there in the crowd was Jean-François! The friend who had shared my horrible adventure in Morocco was now a Zen Buddhist monk; I had written to him at his monastery suggesting he might come to hear the Guru, and here he was. He left before the end of the satsang, but we managed to exchange a few words, and it was clear he was happy with his life in the benign shelter of the Buddha. He still sends me a card every Christmas.

The Guru was twelve now, and gave us an address; I think it was his first public speech. He charmed us all with his round Himalayan moon-face, inherited from his Nepalese mother. He was like a little fat laughing Buddha, as ancient as Mount Everest yet as young as apple blossom; his message was of peace and light. He and his party stayed three days, fitting in a meeting on another supermarket roof and another at a temple in the heart of Kyoto where he gave a beautiful discourse and we devotees slept in the temple precincts. To my joy, he had brought with him my revered Mahatma Charanand, who had given me the knowledge in London. I had the privilege of taking the mahatma to visit Oki Sensei. To be at that meeting was one of the great experiences of my life; it was fortunate for me that their common language was English so that I could follow what they said. The mahatma's wisdom was yielding and gentle. Oki urged us to be pliable, but he could never attain the degree of pliability that was natural to the mahatma. His genius was strong, hard, bold. Yet each of these two men beautifully understood and respected the other.

Soon afterwards it was winter again, and time to leave Japan. It had been a scintillating experience, yet I felt I still understood nothing of the country. I remember it with awe and wonder.

We homed in on the Hardwar ashram in India, meeting other premies who had flown from London as I had done the year before. Julian West was there, and she had a great plan afoot. Inspired by Venetia's achievement in Japan, she was going to use her connections in Sri Lanka to start a Divine Light Mission there. She had some family money there as well, which could not be exported. Would I come and help her?

Of course I would. So I accompanied her back to London, stayed with her for a few days and arranged for another subvention from my mother. Julian and I then boarded a flight for Madras, from where we took the train and boat to Sri Lanka.

On the train, Julian looked at me thoughtfully. 'You're very thin,' she said.

'It's because I'm sick all the time.'

'I know, and I'm sorry, but it may come in handy. Could you stick these film spools up your jumper?'

'Why?'

'They are films of the Guru and his work, mostly in America, rather well done. The customs in Sri Lanka might make them contraband, they are sometimes a bit funny about that sort of thing.'

Of course I agreed. They were quite bulky but did not show, and nobody strip-searched me. All the same it was extremely uncomfortable having to wear a pullover on the boat to Sri Lanka, in all that heat.

# 19

# Sri Lanka

Sri Lanka is the most beautiful country I know. Certainly the lushest, with its thirty-foot palm trees, its gigantic pineapples, its dozen different kinds of bananas. Those bananas! Red ones, green ones, savoury ones, big and small ones. After Sri Lanka I could not look at an ordinary banana for three years. Then there was another fruit called a tambali, like an outsize green coconut; it could be bought from a vendor very cheaply, already cracked open to expose the juicy delicious pulp. I have never seen one of these anywhere else.

Like Venetia, Julian West had found an old embassy for her mission; the former Chinese one, in Skelton Road, Colombo. There was a good big satsang hall. She had furnished it entirely with cushions; it was softer, tamer than Venetia's set-up, but it did very well. Julian bustled around in her sari, organizing meetings and satsang sessions, getting posters done, telephoning all over the world. The Sri Lankans were an inquisitive people; they were round us like flies round a jampot every evening from 7.00 pm when we opened to callers. A man came in and gave us yoga lessons; I set up a small barber's shop in the building and cut everyone's hair.

But it all seemed rather cushioned, part of the Sri Lanka of the rich. When I went outside I discovered the real world and its crying need. With Julian's full approval, I started doing social service. First I went round the Colombo hospitals cutting the patients' hair for no money; most of my 'customers' were children and teenagers. They only got a basin cut, but it saved them or the hospital two rupees a time, which was useful because the hospitals got no Government help. My customers were infested with lice, which got into my own hair; I always knew I would come out of the hospital full of hoppers. I didn't mind them, I'd seen enough of them in the trade. A strong solution of carbolic soon killed them off.

After a bit I began to feel that cutting hair in the hospitals was not enough; I must throw myself wholeheartedly into serving others. I felt degraded by my addiction, and determined to atone for it. Perhaps a period of really hard self-sacrifice might finally give me release. I made my own enquiries, and discovered an orphanage for handicapped children at Prittipura, a couple of miles from Colombo.

Dr Brian ran it; he had been a Church of England clergyman but had renounced his orders, become a Roman Catholic and founded this orphanage. He was gaunt and tanned, with fine features and white hair in a quiff, dressed in a shirt, khaki shorts and sandals. He was a saint in the Western, activist mode, as different again from Mahatma Charanand and from Oki Sensei as they were different from each other. His orphanage had begun in one Nissen hut, but by the time I arrived it had grown to hold 100 children. They suffered from all manner of deformities: brain damage, growth abnormalities, spastic and total paralysis. Most did not stay beyond the age of thirteen, when they were moved to a Buddhist mission nearby. Dr Brian had about five women helpers, who lived in or came daily. He had married one of them, a sweet woman who still spoke little English; they had three children of their own and lived in a small circular house by the orphanage. He at once accepted my offer to help.

'We can always use another pair of hands,' he said.

'When do I start?'

'Now's as good a time as any,' he said. 'You can take over this dormitory.'

It housed fifteen boys and girls on ugly cots covered with red vinyl; a ceiling fan rotated sluggishly. A big vase of frangipani stood on a table in the middle of the room, its fragrance only partly masking the stench of urine and excrement. In one corner was a tap over a rectangular concrete bath. All my children were completely bedridden. One character was about five feet long, frozen solid. He had no neck – his head seemed to be stuck straight on to his body – but he had a beautiful face which was always smiling. Quite unable to move, he beamed with happiness. I put food and water into his mouth every day at the same time; then an hour or two later, also always at the same time, he would defecate. Another had a great distended belly and little stick legs; he was only about three feet long, though he was already fourteen. He had a weird, rather Japanese face and pointed teeth that stuck out. Another little fellow was an extreme hunchback; he could move a little, but only on all fours, his spine was so deformed.

In the end I came to love my fifteen friends, but at the end of my first day with them I lay face down on my bed and wept. This passed; I soon got used to the job, taking courage from my companions, though still appalled at what can be inflicted on innocent little people. It was always an effort to enter my ward in the morning and face the smell. Each child had to have his or her nappy removed, then be carried to the bath and scrubbed under the tap with a cloth combined with coconut husk which resembled a pot scrubber. Some of them took this passively, but others used to kick or bite. Then it was back to bed and a clean nappy. The next task was to take the bucket with the dirty nappies on to a raft moored to the bank of a small lake nearby; with one of the others, I would punt this raft into the middle of the lake and scrub the nappies with a yellow bar of soap. A hundred yards from us was a man on stilts fishing for the orphanage. There was a natural cycle; we washed the remains of the fish back into the lake, nourishing the algae and water-plants which fed the next generation of fish.

About three hundred yards away from Dr Brian's home was the Intercontinental Hotel with its swimming-pool, air-conditioning and atmosphere of high-tech luxury. The management of the hotel was good to us and so were some of the guests, who were often aircrew from British Airways (then BOAC). I went there quite often for a bottle of cool water from the fridge, which tasted like champagne after the stale water of the orphanage; they never charged me for this. Also, I could go any time I liked to the marvellous weekly entertainment the Intercontinental provided for its guests, with firewalkers and devil-dancers. The hotel guests came and bought things at our little craft shop, and some of them could be persuaded to see a bit more. They grew pale at some of the sights, but we got some good donations in cash and in kind. One couple, a pilot and a stewardess, brought a supply of Johnsons baby powder and nappy pins, exactly what we needed. Another visitor took a picture of me with some of my friends and sent it with a letter to my mother.

There were many Buddhist temples nearby with which we were on visiting terms; I made friends with some of the *bikus* and *bikunis* (Buddhist monks and nuns) and encouraged them to come to the orphanage. Although I was still vomiting, I began to feel that I was growing in spirit, so much so that I even thought I might stay on and make my life in Sri Lanka. I talked to Dr Brian about this.

'They won't give you more than one extension to your visa, which will give you two years at the very most,' he said. 'The only way to get permanent residence would be if you became a *bikuni*.'

This would have been a mockery unless I conquered the bulimia, and there was no sign of this. In any case I did not feel ready to have my head shaved and put on the orange robe; I still had some living to do. A fortune teller who used to come every Friday encouraged me to think in this way; he told me I must be free to dance. So, with only a limited time in Sri Lanka, I decided not to spend all of it in Dr Brian's orphanage. I would still do social service, but also see more of the country.

Dr Brian let me stay, even when I stopped working for him full time. Through him I met a woman MP who introduced me to the Peace Corps; I used often to work for them at weekends, and this took me all round the island. Sometimes we were helping to set up a new farming co-operative; in these cases we dealt with comparatively educated, westernized people. At other times we gave assistance to an existing village where the people were much more primitive. Our team dug a new well for one such village where the people specialized in making drums using animal skins. This job made them into untouchables. One of my colleagues decided he wanted his hair cut; as usual I had brought my scissors along, so before we started work I obliged. The villagers gathered round, and the head man said he wanted his hair cut too. I did this, then everybody else wanted the same. The others had to do the digging without me that day, which suited me; I preferred cutting hair, when it came down to it. At the end of the day I had barbered all the adult population of the village, leaving a great mound of black hair.

Once or twice I helped my friend the woman MP to conduct a sort of census, but after a bit I became rather unhappy about this.

'Those shacks up there,' she said, 'that'll be some Tamil tea workers. Could you just find out how many there are, and their ages? They are more likely to tell you than me, and they're sure to talk a bit of English.'

The people had fine features, but were darker than most Sinhalese; grave and unsmiling but scrupulously polite. They told me all I asked.

I said to the MP, 'Why should they tell me more than they tell you?'

'Oh, they're quite a different race from us, you know,' she said. 'They come originally from India. They wouldn't like a Sinhalese asking questions, so they might easily not tell me the truth.'

'Why, particularly?'

'Well, this isn't a Tamil area, and they know it; their area is in the North of our country, and in the East round Trincomalee.'

'Don't you want them here?'

She answered rather too rapidly. 'Oh, it's nothing like that, it's just that we want to know where they are, and how many.'

It wasn't my imagination; this lady, so charming, self-confident and direct, was suddenly avoiding my eyes. There's something wrong, I thought, without quite knowing why; and I'd rather she did her own snooping. Now the racial troubles of Sri Lanka have led to fighting and killing; my friend's wish to check up on the Tamils was the cloud no bigger than a man's hand that announces the storm. I avoided doing this job again without disclosing my scruples to her. We remained friends.

As a matter of fact she was very kind to me; she even got me into hospital with a view to treating my bulimia. This was a failure. A psychiatrist interviewed me in depth, then told me that my trouble was that I ought to have been born a man, I was a male spirit in a female body. This, if true, gave no hope of a remedy in this life, and in any case it seemed nonsensical. I discharged myself.

One day in July Dr Brian said to me:

'It's the feast of Parera over in Kandy next week. We try to send a party from here; I should like you to take them. It will save someone else from going, and I think the ceremony will interest you.'

'It certainly will,' I said, for this is when the great tooth of the Buddha is taken from its casket in the Temple of the Tooth in Kandy and shown to the people. So nine of the older and more active boys and girls were chosen, Dr Brian gave me a little money, and we set off.

On arrival I had to find somewhere for us to sleep, and it was soon clear that this would be difficult, especially as the money I had was nothing like enough for a hotel or guest house. All the temples seemed to be full. Perhaps they really were, for after all it was a festival time; but it could be that some people were put off by my poor charges. I was used to their deformities and twitchings, their spastic efforts at smiling or talking, but to outsiders they must have been hard to take, and there were a lot of them. In the end I took them all to Kandy College; I had made friends with the principal on one of my journeys into the interior. He had given me his address and invited me to call on him some time. He won't have bargained for my turning up with nine grotesques, on the eve of the Festival of the Tooth; all the same he was kind.

'You must sleep somewhere,' he said. 'I have no spare beds, or bedclothes either; the best I can do is the floor of a classroom.'

'That will do fine,' I said, 'and I can't thank you enough.'

That done, we had time to appreciate the splendour of Kandy by its calm lake. We watched the procession of priests and horn-blowers and magnificently caparisoned elephants. I loved it, and my little friends were agape with wonder. At last we returned to our classroom at Kandy College and lay on the floor. It was hard, but in the tropical night we needed no covering. My nine charges were asleep as soon as they hit the deck.

I knew that in an hour or two, under the moon, the priests would

return the Tooth to its casket. I looked at the children; they were sound
asleep, good for eight hours. I got up, left them there, locked the door,
and emerged into the hot and scented night. I discreetly elbowed my
way to the privileged terrace where the priests were; no-one stopped me.
There, by the light of flaring torches, I saw it all. There was a flourish of
trumpets, a crescendo of drums. Reverently the tooth was shown one last
time to the people, reverently it was laid in its gorgeous casket,
reverently it was conveyed back into the pink temple. Silent as a cat I
slipped back to the college. None of the children had stirred.

I went up to Nuwara Eliya quite often. It took three hours in an old
red bus, packed with cheerful people. On the way we stopped off for *chai*
and sesame seed balls. The bus transported me from one splendour to
another, from the luxuriant and stifling tropics to a soft, temperate hill
landscape with magical views. Little Scotland, they called it, with its
oaks and lakes. People wore more clothes, different ones too: army
jackets and stetson hats. The architecture was sturdier, more European.
I found an orphanage there where they let me help part-time for a few
weeks, just for my keep; Paynter House, a home for Eurasian children.
Many of them were far more Euro than Asian, with ginger hair and blue
eyes. Besides their ordinary lessons they learned farming. It was very
English; there were eggs for breakfast, and toast and marmalade.

I also went to Trincomalee, on the east side of the island. There is
every possible place of worship there, all thronged: temples, churches,
mosques. One can shop around for spirituality in Trincomalee as if
shopping for fashion in Paris. The Annie Besant Lodge, headquarters of
the Theosophical Society, held services of divine healing every Sunday.
These seemed to work, especially against mental illness and diabolic
possession, which was apparently rather prevalent. Then there were the
fortune tellers; there must be more of them to the acre in Trincomalee
than anywhere in the world. As a rule they were part-timers. A bank
clerk or railway official would come home from work, put on robes and
see clients for a small fee in cash or in kind. He might prophesy on a
sword, or pass on messages from one of the Hindu gods, Lord Ganesh or
Lord Ram. Some went in for astrology or palmistry. They were not, on
the whole, con-men; they really did solve people's problems. A house-
girl might be suspected of stealing a couple of pounds of sugar; her
mistress went to a fortune teller, and quite often he was able to expose
the culprit.

Also in Trincomalee I found the Sivananda orphanage; I remembered the name from the ashram I had visited at Rishikesh. It was
run by a marvellous old lady in her late seventies whom we called

Reverend Mataji or Mother. She was a Tamil of high caste and good family. She had only about three teeth left, her face was heavily wrinkled and had never been beautiful with its pug-like features, but there was something fine and strong about it; her brown eyes were arresting. The scent of aromatic oil of rami ambla hung about her, she wore soft orange robes. Her hair was still thick and long; by rights it should have been white, but it was iron grey. She liked braiding or plaiting it, running it through her fingers; not, I am sure, out of vanity, but as a meditation. Though utterly selfless, she was hard; she reminded me of my grandmother, Mary Taylor, and in a way also of Oki Sensei. She was severe with the children, and they were in awe of her; they probably didn't love her much at the time, though I hope some of them may remember her now that they are grown-up, and love her in retrospect. She gave them a good education, and made them learn skills: weaving, cooking, growing and picking rice in the orphanage's paddy field. When I went to offer my services she took me on at once; in the East people don't ask for credentials as they do in the West. So I was soon installed in a cell, sleeping on a wooden board with my clothes for a pillow. Three or four ragged children slept with me.

The Sivananda orphanage took in children of all classes – most were from poor families, but there were one or two Brahmins – and all religions. Someone would come to the gate with a child, perhaps a single parent. Whoever was there simply wrote out a note saying the child had been accepted, giving its name and the name of the person who had brought it. This was taken to the police station for stamping, and that was it. I received two children in this way.

Religion was a vital part of life there. We were up at 5.30 every morning, sweeping the terraces and paths. Then morning prayers were held in the temple with *badgens* (chants) to Krishna, Lord Ram, Ganesh, Haneman, Ganapatti, and the late founder, Sri Sivananda. I felt nothing could go wrong with a day that started like this.

Again one of my jobs was washing the children. This time the problem was the water supply. I had to lower a bucket down a deep well; it seemed an age before there was a distant splash, and I could begin raising the full bucket. However, this was a problem I was able to remedy when the Reverend Mataji shrewdly started using me for public relations. Asking for things and getting them is something I have always been quite good at, and people still liked to oblige a white person. When milk powder was scarce and there was a danger we might not get all our ration, I was the one whom Mataji sent up the road to the welfare office with the coupons, taking three or four children to add poignancy to my appeal. I was never short-changed. Then I went over to Colombo and visited the Lions Club, a charitable group that often gave to Dr Brian's.

'Come for some things for Prittipura?' asked the secretary.

'Not this time,' I said. 'But I'm still on the scrounge. Have you ever heard of the Sivananda orphanage in Trincomalee?'

'Can't say I have, it's outside our area.'

'That's where I'm working now. It gets very little help from anyone, donations of anything would be most welcome.' I went on to describe it.

My request was granted. Next *poya* or full moon, instead of giving to Prittipura the Lions voted to pay for a new well to be dug at the Sivananda orphanage. I did not feel bad about depriving Dr Brian just this once, he had quite a lot of help and Mataji's need was greater.

Her children were not handicapped like those at Dr Brian's; nevertheless they were often very pathetic. One little boy missed his mother dreadfully. I longed to hug him but had to hold myself back, otherwise he would become dependent on me, only to suffer another deprivation when I left. For I knew I should leave, if only because of my visa, though the Reverend Mataji wanted me to stay permanently. She gave me one task that was a real honour; painting the inside of the temple. It was to be a terracotta colour, with the most sacred areas white. The job took me all day, and then we had a talk.

'You are happy here,' she said. It was a statement of fact, not a question.

'Yes, Reverend Mataji, I am very happy.'

'You are good at what you do, and I think you enjoy it.'

'You are all very good to me.'

'I am getting old, one day I shall not be here.'

'Surely you are good for many years yet.'

'That is as providence will decide, but I shall not live for ever. You could take this place over, after I am gone.'

This was a surprise. 'Do you think so, Reverend Mother?'

'Of course you would have to become a renunciate, a *sannyasin*, but that would not be beyond your strength, and the life would suit you.'

Her high opinion was a compliment. The trouble was that I knew I could not live up to it. It was impossible to prepare myself for renunciation, let alone for succeeding Mataji, without conquering my sickness. With all her shrewdness, Mataji had not seen into my inner torment. 'I am not ready for that,' I said.

She looked hard at me. 'Think about it.'

Certainly I should think about it, wistfully, as something that I should have loved but could not attain. The bulimia was too strong for me. Mataji never again made the proposition directly, but often singled me out for a talk on other things. Once I said I should like to meet the yoga master Swami Satchikananda, attached to the Sivananda ashram in Kandy.

'That can easily be arranged,' said Mataji. 'My sister and I discovered him when he was a hermit in the woods outside Kandy, we brought him to the ashram there.'

'Really?' I was impressed. Satchikananda had a great reputation, especially among my American friends.

'To tell the truth, he's still a bit of a young pup,' she said.

I was taken aback. 'Swami Satchikananda?'

'Oh yes. He can do some hathayoga, and he has a knack of teaching it, but that does not make a man a saint. There's a lot that he neglects.'

'People I've met respect him.'

'Americans, I expect. Anyone can impress Americans.'

'I've heard his foundation there is pretty good.'

'You know how that came about? This American came here, found him, thought he was the cat's whiskers, took him out to the States where he did too well for his own good. To me he's a young pup. But I'll take you to meet him, since you're interested.'

I thought, if this wasn't Mataji I might think her just a tiny bit jealous. She did take me along to Kandy and introduce me to Swami Satchikananda; he gave me some of the best yoga lessons I have ever had. Mataji's sister was in Kandy too, a softer, more intellectual version of herself; she was librarian at the ashram, from which Mataji had taken herself off to run the orphanage at Trincomalee. The two sisters had worked together as *sannyasin* for half a century, since the 1920s.

I went back to Julian West's mission, which had prospered. An Indian mahatma was in residence, and the mission had acquired great satsang wagons, like floats, and organized processions in the streets. I didn't stay long, though, for Christmas was approaching, and I was not feeling festive. My illness was as bad as ever; my time in Sri Lanka had not done me a blind bit of good in the way that really mattered. I arranged to spend ten days in retreat in a Buddhist temple, Bawana Vipasan.

There were fourteen of us lay women in the cloister where I was; we mostly wore white, in contrast to the orange robes of the priests. In another part of the temple grounds there were men in retreat; I didn't see much of them. At first I was the only Westerner, later a Dutch girl came and a Theravada Buddhist lady from Hampstead. The Hampstead lady was particularly devout; I once tried to talk to her, but she had not come all this way for cosy chats. Every day, as part of the routine, each of us had an interview with a *biku*; this was enough conversation for her.

We were taught to do everything 'mindfully'. Every action had three stages; intention, attention, action. We had to be aware of all three, which meant doing everything in slow motion. When eating, for example, we were supposed to feel the food with the hand (all food was eaten with the fingers, of course), concentrate awareness on it, then deliberately place it in the mouth. For half an hour or more every day we paced round a courtyard; at each step we had first to intend it, then concentrate on the foot, then raise it deliberately and place it down, then move the body forward to the new balance point. One must not fidget, gesture or even smile; all attention had to focus on the walking. On and on it went. Once I rebelled. 'Damn it!' I said to myself. All my companions suddenly seemed so *boring*. I span round, pirouetted like Isadora Duncan, ran a few paces; it must have looked insane. There was no trouble about this, even the lady *bikuni* had a little smile for me.

It's rather wicked to say so, but the *bikunis* were a bit like a friendly version of the prison screws. One seemed to like me, and some imp in me told me to try and get beneath her austerity and aloofness and reach her as a person. This was a very unrealized thing for me to do, but I did it, and we had some agreeable talks.

I found a little spare room where I could practise hathayoga. Every day, sometimes more than once, I did an intense workout in this place, all the poses and variations I knew as well as the breathing exercises. Probably this was against the rules, but nobody ever disturbed me.

But for my bulimia I should have liked the eating arrangements. There was a light breakfast, then a main meal at 11.00 am, then nothing more for the rest of the day. The early lunch was vegetarian, but delicious and varied, with up to eight courses. I ate in the slow way we were supposed to, doing more than justice to it all; then, alas! I went and lost it, all that daily banquet that had been prepared with such reverence. After the high, the hunger, coming and going in waves all day; for in Bawana Vipasan there was no access to the kitchen, no sneaking out for a bite.

After my retreat I returned to Dr Brian. I was cleansed in a way, but dreadfully disappointed at not having shifted my bulimia. This depression took away my self-image, for a time I stopped bothering about how I looked. I kept clean like the native women, but that was all I did.

Once I went to Anuradhapura, which was the Buddhist capital of Sri

Lanka before Kandy. In ancient times it housed millions; it is smaller now, but surrounded by grandiose ruins. Today pilgrims go to Anuradhapura to see the sacred Bo tree. This tree, a kind of fig, was grown from a cutting of the very tree near Benares where the Buddha preached his first sermon. The Indian Princess Sanghamitra planted the cutting about 250 BC, which makes it more than 2200 years old. It is in a compound surrounded by golden railings; rags are tied to its branches as the equivalent of Christian *ex-votos*, denoting prayers and vows. I was there during Poya, the feast of the full moon, when they spend three nights in prayer and meditation listening to readings of the *sutras*. Pilgrims kept coming with food and other offerings, and it was moving to see the people curled up on the hard ground, blissed out on the peace of the Buddha.

My two years were not up, but I was now making plans to leave Sri Lanka to take advantage of an invitation from the Reverend Mataji. Every year she went to the shrine of Ramana Maharish, known as the Silent Saint. He was not her guru, but she had known him while he was alive and revered his memory. She sent me a message from his ashram asking me to join her, and there was no way I was going to miss this. I made a last visit to Nuwara Eliya, where I distributed some woollen clothes to the children of the poor Tamil plantation workers in their Nissen huts, said all my goodbyes, and set off for Madras.

# 20

# South India

The ashram of the Silent Saint was at the foot of Mount Aranchalla, not far from Madras. They showed me to a bed in a dormitory shared with some other English seekers, then I went to look for the Reverend Mataji. I found her reclining in a small clay hut, playing with the thick tress of her hair. Her eyes sparkled like black pools in sunlight; I felt a wave of happiness just at the sight of her.

'I'm so glad to see you, Mary dear,' she said. She always called me Mary. 'Sit down, make yourself at home.'

'This is a beautiful place,' I said.

'There are good vibrations,' she agreed. 'I think you will like it here. Tomorrow I will guide you to the top of Aranchalla and the saint's cave, where he attained *samadhi* when he was still in his body.'

'What, climb all that way?' For the mountain was at least a thousand feet high; it was visible from where we were.

'Bless you, no; I'm too old for that lark. I'll just show you where to start, then go round the path at the bottom, that's more my cup of tea at my age. Wait for me when you get down.'

So next day we parted where the path to the summit began, and Mataji started off round the mountain at a brisk pace, murmuring her mantras. I climbed to the top and saw the cave; it was spotlessly kept, with a little altar and an image of the saint. Then I turned and looked to the horizon over the south Indian plain, took a few deep breaths, drank in the purity of that solitary place under the hot sky. I descended, and soon Mataji came into sight, still saying her mantras. She had not rested once in the two hours since I had left her to go up the mountain.

In a day or two she decided to move to Madras; I went with her and helped with the luggage. We installed ourselves in the Sanga Hall where there were continuous ceremonies, ringing of bells, chanting, incense; I immersed myself in the fervour of the rituals, sinking into anonymity, forgetting my I. But I was not always worshipping. There was a dear little old man who taught me a technique of foot massage; I had massaged feet at Oki Sensei's, and this allowed me to combine two methods. Mataji also introduced me to several interesting people, including Queen Frederica of Greece and her daughter. They seemed sincere seekers.

The time came for Mataji to go back to her orphanage.

'I'm not looking forward to the journey,' she admitted. 'To tell the truth, I'm getting a bit old for that train and boat.'

I dreaded the thought of the old lady undergoing those long hot hours and having to cope with her luggage.

'You ought to fly,' I said.

'Oh, I couldn't do that, my dear, it would cost too much.'

For once I had money; all the time I had been in Sri Lanka my expenditure had amounted to about five pounds for a succession of Bata men's casual shoes in canvas, each pair bought when its predecessor fell to pieces, plus the cost of my eating habit which in that country was not great. I had earned little, but spent even less, and my family had sent subsidies.

'I'll pay,' I said.

'That's very good of you.' She was really pleased and relieved. 'I am most grateful, I am longing to get back to my children. But in that case there is another thing I must ask you to do, Mary dear. I've got some statues for the altar of the temple; they'll never accept them on the plane. Could you send them to me at the orphanage?'

They were life-size plaster busts of four Hindu gods; Krishna, Hannama, Ganesha and Siva.

'Of course,' I said. 'Anything for you and the children. Don't worry about it, I'll see you get them.'

I went with her to the airport, where we said a profound farewell; both of us felt more than we expressed.

I decided to leave Sanga Hall the next day, which meant doing something about those busts immediately. That evening a young American came in; he was planning to go by boat to Sri Lanka the following day. I told him of Mataji and the Trincomalee orphanage.

'It sounds great,' he said.

'If you could manage to take her these four busts,' I suggested, 'she'd be really grateful to you; she'd put you up, show you round, you could have no better introduction to Trincomalee.'

'No problem,' he said. 'I'll be glad to do it.'

So that was solved. I got out my crumpled notebook to see where I

should go next, and decided on the Tibetan refugee camp at Chittore to
the west of Madras. It was the time of the Tibetan New Year and I felt
the celebrations would be worth watching. The refugee camp had been
set up some fifteen years previously when the Dalai Lama had left Tibet,
to house about three thousand lamas and others who had left at the same
time. It was strangely insensitive of the Indian Goverment to choose
Madras State for these people. The climate was tropical, the countryside
was parched and absolutely flat; in every way it was the opposite of the
Himalayas. Having little choice, they had accepted, and made a
surprisingly good go of it under the leadership of some of their oldest and
highest lamas.

When I got to the camp I found some offices; no-one stopped me, so I
entered. I walked in on a group of Tibetans having a discussion; they
welcomed me with their eyes, so I joined them. By and by one of them
turned to me.

'I think you are a new visitor here?'

'I have just arrived.'

'You are welcome. Perhaps you would like to see round.'

So I set off to explore this new little world, feeling like Alice down the
rabbit-hole, for it was quite unlike anything on the outside, a dream
world two miles round. I met a large group of Tibetans dressed in
everything from the strictest traditional dress with its stand-up collar to
blue jeans and leather jacket. I accosted one of them, who answered in
good English:

'That's the Red Hat camp, and that over there is the Yellow Hat
camp.'

'Why are they called that?'

'They are the areas of the Red Hat Lamas and the Yellow Hat
Lamas.'

Each had its temple, shops and sleeping quarters. There were schools
for the children, and weaving sheds where cloths and carpets were made
which sold well, all over the world – well enough for some of the younger
Tibetans to be able to afford large loud motor-bikes and Western
clothes.

It was evening, and I was directed to the Red Hat temple where a
New Year service was proceeding under gigantic statues of Buddha, one
sitting and one reclining, each of which had at least a hundred burning
candles attached to it. It was warm-hearted and cheerful, with little
formality. Those who were not actually taking part in the chanting
seemed to pay no attention to the ceremony; as the hours wore on, I
realized that this was because only the exceptionally devout would

follow a service that was so interminably long. When I arrived, the congregation was busy eating; a group invited me to join them. We sat round, monks and laymen, women and children, dogs and cats, and partook of goat stew from a big tin bath, throwing the bones to the animals who might or might not be interested. Then I was given a big mug of hot tea with a lump of butter on the top, rapidly melting. It is surprising how quickly one can accept pools of grease floating on one's tea, especially under the stern gaze of a tough-looking monk.

What could I do in return for their hospitality? Perhaps some of them might like a foot massage. One of the monks accepted this, and proffered his foot. This gave me another shock. I had not looked at the Tibetans' feet, which were black underneath, seemingly because of some sort of thin plimsoll. However the monk took nothing off, and when I looked closely at his foot I saw that it was bare, that what I had assumed to be footwear was a covering of impacted dirt. Naturally I did the massage without showing surprise.

Tibetans are Mahayana Buddhists, and their ceremonies differed from the Theravada services I had seen in Sri Lanka. For one thing they were much noisier. After long chants and wails, a long line of men each with an enormous horn about five feet long gave a series of blasts in unison. Then came clashing cymbals and clanging bells.

The hours passed, and it was dawn. Suddenly I realized that I had been in the temple all night, and fatigue caught up with me. A kindly fat lama offered me a mattress in the hut he shared with his young scribe and factotum, as thin as the lama was stout. I sank down and knew no more for two or three hours.

I was awakened by itching; the whole place was alive with fleas. My hosts were quite used to this, but I had not itched so badly since my days in the Tunis jail. It became clear, too, that there were no proper washing arrangements. Most people in India and Sri Lanka are obsessively clean, but the Tibetans practically never wash; they seem to regard dirt as sacred protection. The young scribe was no different in this from his master, though he was much more Westernized, owning, for instance, a big black Kawasaki on which he liked to zoom around when he was not carefully copying centuries-old texts under the meticulous eye of the old man.

Despite the fleas I stayed a week in that place, giving English lessons in the little school. I was more successful with the Tibetan children than with the keen Japanese businessmen, and both the pupils and I had fun. A lot of the time I was answering questions about the Queen, or about London and other parts of England. I didn't know the answers to all their questions, but I was better at this than at formal language teaching.

The settlement was economically self-sufficient; it made most of its money out of selling hand-woven carpets in traditional Tibetan designs of dragons and gods and demons. The weavers repeated a mantra as they worked. They and their families lived in neat family units, going about their daily lives in the same way as if they were still high up in the mountains. It must have been cruel for mountain people to be sentenced to life on that burning tropical plain, yet they seemed to accept it without repining. They ranged from ancient to modern; a young man with a Beatles haircut in a leather jacket would be doing tricks on his motor-bike, and nearby a woman in traditional costume, plates crossed on her head, would be turning an enormous prayer-wheel.

The time came when I had to go; for one thing I was longing for a decent wash. I said goodbye to the lama, then came on his young apprentice as he was revving up his motorcycle.

'I'll give you a lift to the gate,' he said, so I jumped on with my bag.

Suddenly I remembered that he had admired my shirt, a thick Indian one of a rich burgundy colour, bought in Hardwar. When I alighted from the bike at the gate, I pulled it over my head and threw it to him, shouting:

'Remember me to the Buddha!'

He caught it, we laughed at each other, and then he zoomed away, back into the settlement. I travelled to Pondicherry, and spent a month in an ashram there with Swami Gitananda who offered instruction in hathayoga, Indian massage and numerology. Numerology didn't appeal to me; my arithmetic was not up to it. So I perfected my shoulder stands while Beryl Jones pondered the significance of the two Es in her name and Andy Watts worked out what it meant to have no Es but two Ts. This apparently made her a leader and him only a follower.

The best part of this month for me was the massage course. I felt that I reached a professional standard, and got the idea that this was going to be my future occupation. I considered going southwest to Kerala State where I could have gone to a health farm to learn a special form of massage done with the feet, which is a development of Kathakali dancing. The masseur holds on to two ropes attached to the ceiling above the patient, who is immersed in oil, and runs back and forth across the patient's body. I could have become the only person in the West to do Kathakali massage, but I felt there would be little opportunity to practise the art. Setting up the equipment would be quite a business; it would mean talking a health farm into investing the money not only in ropes and pulleys but in skilful publicity, and I wondered if the phlegmatic English would really take to it. In any case my money was again getting low. It was November and I had been away more than three years if you didn't count the short time I was in London after Japan.

I went to Bangalore, where I booked a place on an aircraft leaving in two days' time. Those two days I spent in another Buddhist temple. The great thing about the East is that once you have truly committed yourself to spiritual search, you can always find shelter. You don't need to look around for some seedy lodging-house, there will always be an almshouse in a Hindu or Buddhist temple. The temple I found in Bangalore was run by a Buddhist priest who had been converted from Hinduism and was full of *shakti* – spiritually, or rather spiritual energy. He had the perfect balance between Buddhist phlegm and Hindu enthusiasm. Many of his young pupils were Tibetans, and there were also people from other Buddhist countries and a number of Western seekers.

Getting on the plane for Heathrow was a real wrench; I wondered if I would ever again walk the soil of Mother India. I still wonder this.

When I landed in England in November, I felt still more depressed; it seemed as if the sun had gone in for good. I telephoned the Divine Light ashram, spoke to Sister Sandy whom I'd met that first day with Mahatmaji. Yes, she said, they would fit me in somehow. The people on the bus and the Underground seemed grey, strained; they chewed gum, twisted their faces about. Some were Asians; they were no better than the rest, the drabness of London seemed to have got into them. As for me, I could feel a throbbing in the centre of my forehead over the 'third eye'. In a day or two this became a boil, exactly in the place where Hindu women paint their red spot or *kikka*. For all I know it may have been a psychosomatic protest against leaving the East. Even the premies in the ashram seemed tense, there was no joy in them.

I holed up with an Arab girl called Belkis and her mother, who was a practising Muslim, thus keeping a sort of Eastern connection. Belkis was a trained seamstress, following her profession by day and giving satsang in the evenings. She helped me replenish my depleted wardrobe with two Gipsy skirts in dirndl style and two Liberty print garments, a dress in navy blue with white spots and a skirt in a hot poppy red with a green pattern; she charged me very little for this, and it cheered me up. But what was I to do? I felt I couldn't face England, any part of England. At home I should be in everybody's way and constantly shamed by my bulimia, and London seemed to have exactly nothing to offer. Sod England, I said to myself, damp home of the grey and twitching. I still had about thirty pounds.

Where to go? Suddenly, on hardly more than a whim, I thought of Cadaques. The rocks might be rough and the thorns sharp on the gorse, but that was better than stained and littered pavements. The people were not open exactly, but at least they didn't twitch all the time. It will be empty of tourists, I said to myself, but I shan't mind, I shall seek solitude in the hills under the pale winter sun. Perhaps with fasting and meditation I can even cure myself; at least I can become acclimatized again to Europe and to normal life. So I went to Victoria coach station and boarded what we always called the 'magic bus' which in twenty-four hours or so takes one to Figueras, the market town near Cadaques.

# 21

# The Strength of
# the Hills

Cadaques had a Christmas crib on the Rambla; this made my arrival feel like a true homecoming. There is nothing quite like the sight of a crib for someone who has been brought up a Christian. Then I saw something that cheered me up even more; the twins, sitting in a café and looking more than ever like a pair of beautiful wood carvings. They greeted me with love, but coolly, as was their way; no shriek of surprise, no questions. Here I was, and that was that. They had a pretty girl with them, she had bright blue eyes in a face as dark as theirs and turned out to be their younger sister Sally.

'Tony Smart's in town,' said John.

'Do I know him?'

'You soon will; he's English, and he's putting on an English pantomime in the theatre at the back of the Hostal.'

'A pantomime in Cadaques? You're joking. Who's in it?'

'Everyone, just about,' said Denis.

Sally asked me where I was staying.

'Nowhere at the moment. I've got to get moving on that.'

'You might come in with me,' she said. 'I'm staying free at a flat in this new apartment block in return for doing some cleaning work; I don't think they'd mind if you moved in, and we could share the work.'

In this way I got myself housed for six weeks in a spanking new flat done up in whitewash with a black iron chimney, very avant-garde, that tapered like a witch's hat. The place had hardly any furniture, but it was centrally heated. This was crucial because I was there during the very coldest part of the winter, from just before Christmas to early February. Outside the Tramontana whistled and roared, fresh from the Pyrenean ice; inside it was warm. There were no wages, though, so without any money coming in I had to be economical; most of my eating was done at soup and salad parties. There was a surprising amount of social life, to

185

which the twins introduced me. When there wasn't a party I mostly ate bread and jam.

Tony Smart's Christmas pantomime was a *tour de force*. He had the help of the Hostal's Australian owner, Bob Cordukes, who was keen to see a real English pantomime, and lent his little theatre for it; but it was Tony who wrote the words and played the lead, Tony who scrounged props from the village people, Tony who mobilized the denizens of the cafés, including the winos and deadbeats, and turned them overnight into actors. Having arrived too late to be recruited, I was only in the audience, but I thought it an astonishing feat.

At the end of our time in the flat, Sally returned to England. If I'd had any common sense I should have done the same, for by now I had no money left at all. However, we were into February and the weather was a little warmer; the almond blossom was out. The twins were staying in the house of the same German count who had first brought us all to Cadaques. They didn't feel able to move me in there, but the Count had an olive grove to the north of the village where on previous visits the twins and I had done some clearing work; they were vaguely responsible for looking after it.

'Why don't you stay in the shepherd's hut?' said John. 'We shall be moving there, but only in a couple of months when it gets warmer.'

'It'll be cold for you,' said Denis, 'quite a challenge to keep warm.'

But I tend to accept challenges, and anyway there seemed nowhere else I could stay without any money, so I moved into the shepherd's hut. A good number of these dry-stone structures are dotted about the hills round Cadaques, some ruined now but many still perfect. Nobody knows when they were first built, or indeed whether they were built for shepherds, but they are old. As a rule they are square or oblong outside, but inside they are circular, the walls rising to a dome which sticks out from the square base. The dome is perhaps nine or ten feet high in the centre and the internal circular base about ten feet across. The entrance is no more than three feet high; one must crawl to get in. There is always a big flat stone at the apex of the dome which can be removed to let in light or let out smoke. So when I left the centrally heated apartment, I moved into this hut with a discarded eiderdown and an old duvet, decorating the floor with a piece of Persian carpet I found on a beach.

It suited me. I had come to Cadaques not for the village or the people or the café life, but for the hills, for solitude among the rocks in the pure air. My friends and relations tell me it was foolhardy to live absolutely alone, half an hour's walk from Cadaques and quite a way even from the nearest dirt track. All I can say is that I got away with it, and I don't really think I ran much risk. There is no dangerous wild-life; one hears of adders and wild boars, but never sees them, and they are shy creatures anyway. I had no possessions that would interest a burglar. Some people with my history might have been afraid of being attacked and raped, but oddly enough the thought never crossed my mind. The only real danger was from the men who came at weekends to shoot partridges and rabbits. They did not expect anyone to be there, so it was dangerous to be near their line of fire. I was never hit, but was startled once or twice by pellets rattling down.

At first I spent most of my time collecting wood to burn. Every day I worked at gathering a huge pile of brushwood and dead branches of olive, cork or pine, often lacerating my hands and forearms. I had no axe but became quite good at breaking it without, sometimes using the stone terrace walls to get a purchase. Then as the sun began to go down I removed the ceiling stone, piled all the wood in the hut and lit it. Soon there was a blazing fire; I undressed and sat there naked and cross-legged, sweating as in a sauna, unfolding in the heat. The fire burned high for an hour or so, then after another hour the embers began to cool. I dressed again, crept out, scrambled up to the roof and replaced the ceiling stone. I then slept like a baby till dawn.

I drank water from the stream which flows nearby; this meant climbing down boulders and filling at one of the pools some rather unsuitable vessel such as a wine bottle left by a weekend sportsman. The water was pure and sweet; in the middle of the week I consumed little else, and never went near the village. Then on Friday evenings I knew the weekend activity would be beginning, and felt very hungry; I went down to pick at the leftovers in the restaurants, and did the same on Saturday and Sunday. But my real day for bingeing was Monday, because of the weekly market. The food thrown out would have fed thirty people. There were slightly bruised apples, oranges with a little mildew, bunches of grapes with some that had gone brown; there were loaves of bread; there were bananas, avocados, tomatoes, carrots and aubergines, second rate perhaps but perfectly edible. I loaded a selection into an empty crate, hoisted it on to my head, and loped up towards the hills, getting surprised looks from the locals. They were accustomed to their own grandmothers going around with loads on their heads, but it was not something foreigners did.

As soon as I was well clear of the village I stopped for my first binge, repeating this twice or three times on the half-hour walk to my hut. By the time I reached it I was usually in pain, and this grew more and more acute, often forcing me to lie down for a couple of hours until my poor stomach had settled. Often it would blow out with wind until I seemed five months pregnant. I trembled violently. To ease the pain I used certain yoga techniques, especially rolling on the ground from side to side with knees pressed hard into my body. But with this pain there came an intense joy. Pain usually confuses and gets in the way of perception; not in this case. I felt I could perceive with utter clarity. It was as if I was travelling at speed, yet instead of a blurred landscape I could see every detail of it as it flashed by, every vein on every leaf. The whole experience was bitter-sweet, agony and ecstasy in the same moment.

Then came the remorse and the fear; remorse at my addiction, fear at what might become of me. After the crisis I exercised like a maniac, usually starting then and there with a violent ballet workout to Fauré's *Requiem* or Mahler's *Death in Venice*, for I had a small cassette machine and some tapes, rather frowned on by the twins who felt it dishonoured the mountain to play any but natural music. When the weather got warmer, I took to swimming a mile or so in the sea. I would then dance all night in the Hostal or a nightclub. The exercise gave me a high; it also eased my conscience and my terrors. I could tell myself that what I was doing could not be too bad if I remained so fit. Except that I never really fooled myself for an instant.

On Tuesdays I stayed in the hills, eating and vomiting what was left of my Monday store; sometimes there would be a little for Wednesday, sometimes not. On Thursdays I rarely ate anything, and on Fridays also I fasted until the evening when, 'empty, swept and garnished' like the man in the bible from whom the devil has been temporarily expelled, I went down to the village, ripe for repossession.

These midweek days were glorious. As I recovered and calmed down and gathered my wood I enjoyed the silver-skinned olive trees and the sudden flowering all over the mountains of the white cistus flowers. I no longer missed the garish colours of Sri Lanka; my eyes became attuned to the greens and greys and browns of the Catalonian mountains and I could love the humbler, smaller flowers that adorned them.

In this way for a time I lived on absolutely no money at all, but it could not last. I needed little things: soap, candles, rope-soled *alpargatas*. The wild lavender came into flower, and coming across a patch of it I drank in the fragrance. Suddenly I had an idea. Lavender bags! Such an English speciality. Nobody had ever seen one in Cadaques; they would be a novelty for the tourists and weekend visitors. So I gathered stacks of the wild lavender heads which are squat and fat, on a much smaller plant than garden lavender, and set them in the sun to dry. Then I ripped off the bottom tier of the blue and white Liberty print dress that

Belkis had made for me at the London ashram, cut it into pieces with my hairdressing scissors, covered the pieces with piles of lavender and sewed them into bags with needle and thread.

In a few hours I had three dozen of them in different shapes: square, round, oblong, oval, triangular. Then I thought, how shall I present them? I had found a round waiter's bar tray on the rubbish heap, dented and rusty, and taken it with the vague idea that it might come in useful. It was all I had, but it was not good enough. Cover it in fabric, I thought. My Buddhist literature was wrapped in half a yard of gold brocade; sorry, Lord Buddha, I must borrow this for a bit. Wrapped in it, suddenly the tray looked quite good. It was Friday evening, so I put the lavender bags in a holdall, picked up the brocade-covered tray, and set off for the cafés. I wore my red and green skirt and a black three-quarter sleeved leotard. The leotard was one of two which I wore all the time, one to wash and one to wear; it substituted for bra and knickers. A red kerchief brightened up my top half. I had as usual fasted for a couple of days so felt well and balanced.

Outside the Café Maritim on the sea side of the Rambla, I arranged the bags on the tray, then suddenly thought, lipstick! I had a stub on me, and a bit of broken mirror. Down with the tray, a quick application. I made my entrance with the tray, heads turned. I strode to the most tipsy-looking customer, and offered him a bag for 100 pesetas (50p), crunching it in my hand to increase the aroma. He bought it. In less than half an hour and in that one crowded café the whole lot went. I had 3,600 pesetas; £18, but worth at least twice as much then as now. I felt really rich, and even stood myself a coffee to celebrate, the first I had paid for since moving into the hut.

My first few batches of lavender bags were not much good, because wild lavender has less scent than the domestic kind, and loses it more quickly. When I discovered this I invested in a bottle of strong lavender water – Lavanda Puig, for the record: I can recommend it – and sprinkled some over the contents of the bags. I thought of new sales gimmicks, too. If I saw a likely-looking customer leaning on the bar, I took an oblong lavender bag and turned it into an elbow-rest for him; he usually bought it. Or on a Sunday afternoon I would catch a well-heeled Barcelona couple getting ready to motor away, string one of my bags over their car mirror and tell them it kept mosquitoes away; the Trades Descriptions Act was not a worry. In the end, at the cost of a couple of skirts and some remnants of cloth given me by a kind friend, I amassed about £300, after paying for all my little needs. People began calling me 'Lady Lavender'. Australian Bob had sold the Hostal to a shrewd

Italian called Marzi, who offered to go into partnership with me, employ pickers, hire a sewing machine, invent a trade mark. I refused, for this would have made a game into a business and spoilt the fun.

The person I did team up with was Tony Smart. After putting on the Christmas pantomime he had holed up in a disused *finca* in the hills, and created a set of papier-mâché puppets and a black-curtained puppet stage; with the coming of summer he began performing on the Rambla. It was similar to the traditional English Punch and Judy show, though he performed other playlets as well, all in Catalan. Tony was a man of magical charm who made things happen by making people love him; he also had every artistic talent one can think of. A year or so later he was to be drowned in a stupid accident at sea, so we shall never know if he would ever have become successful. He had weaknesses; he cared not at all for his body, in his early thirties he already had a beer-belly. One day he asked me if I'd like a part in a film.

'Of course,' I said. 'What is it?'

'The Walrus and the Carpenter; you know, from *Alice*. You're just the person I want for the Eldest Oyster.'

'What do I have to do?'

'Only shake your heavy head,' he said. 'You're the clever one, the others get eaten.'

The film was apparently going to be bought by some Canadian, but I don't think anything came of it. Tony was the Walrus, the Carpenter was a hugely tall German by the name of Hubert. John Myers was Tweedledum; Denis, as Tweedledee, had to intone the poem. There were a couple of other Oysters besides myself. We had our heads plastered in seaweed and were fixed into flat papier-mâché shells from which protruded our heads and bare arms and legs. We went with a cameraman to a quiet beach to the north-east of Cadaques; shooting took all afternoon, though the film can't have been more than ten minutes long. Tony was a perfectionist; at one moment it even looked as if we might have to pack up and resume next day. But when the sun was dangerously close to sinking, Tony said, 'There we are, that's it. Now we'll eat.'

He set up a barbecue and pulled out of his bag a kilo of sprats, together with long loaves of bread, a dozen bottles of red wine and some mineral water. I helped gather brushwood for the fire, mostly wild rosemary because it smells good, broke it into manageable pieces as I was so good at doing after daily practice, then watched as Tony grilled the sprats. He did it neatly, expertly; not one sprat was either carbonized or underdone.

I also came in on his puppet shows. Sometimes I helped manipulate the puppets, sometimes I was detailed off to advertise the show by doing a bit of tumbling. I dressed in a green leotard with matching tights and a red sash, and painted my face white with freckles and clown's red cheeks; in imitation of Miss Lily of the Palais de Merveilles my hair was plaited round wire to make it stand up like antennae. A few cartwheels, then I sank backwards on to my hands to do a crab-walk on hands and feet, back towards the ground and stomach high in the air. Every few minutes I stopped and took the hat round the audience. Between playlets the twins played strange Eastern music on their flutes, to which I danced. Our performances only lasted about 20 minutes; at the end we packed up our gear and went to a back-street café to share out the spoils. The others celebrated with a cremat, sweet coffee laced with spirit that the waiter lit with a match so that blue fire flickered over it. However, a plain coffee was enough for me. Later I danced until about 4.00 am at the Paradiso, the disco which went on longest. My feet cooled off as I ascended the track to my hut, dripping with sweat and floating on the exercise high.

Meanwhile I had changed huts because the twins had come to reclaim their summer dwelling. My new one was a couple of hundred yards lower down; it was better in some ways, for it had a smoother floor and was in a slightly different, paler stone with a hint of yellow in the grey which I liked. I decorated it rather nicely; besides my Persian carpet on the floor I now had a red velvet curtain to hang inside the doorway and made a duvet cover from an old curtain of satin brocade in yellow and green with a little pink. These were given me by my Belgian friend Sophie, a tall and beautiful middle-aged lady who gave me bundles of old clothes and furnishings rather than throw them away. I changed my decor from time to time; I had plenty to choose from, and the fabrics faded and rotted rather quickly in the exposed conditions.

Water became a problem. The stream dried up for the summer, so I had to go to a well belonging to a deserted *finca* about half an hour's walk away. No longer could I depend on the occasional discarded wine bottle; I secured two big proper water-bottles that held a day's supply between them. Someone must have still used this well, for it was kept in repair, but I was never disturbed as I sent the bucket on its rope rickety-racketing down the echoing depths; there was a far splash, then the slow wind up. I stripped, emptied the bucket on myself, shouting in pure delight at the ice-cold drenching in the strong sun. It gave me a wonderful feeling of freshness, because I was always salty from swimming in the sea and sweaty from climbing the hill path. Then came another bucketful for a proper wash with soap, then a third to fill my bottles. How I loved the solitary walk home – even in the summer the dirt road was little used – holding my two bottles, wearing a toga that was still damp but drying by the minute in the evening sun. Not far off the track was a magnificent mulberry tree lying on its side; when the fruit was ripe I made a detour to plunder it, as in Formentera all those years before. I never tired of the surreal cloud-shapes over the dun hills which themselves resembled animals – an elephant, a centipede, a sugar mouse. I was a queen as I returned to my newly-furnished hut in the gathering dusk. I left the ceiling stone off, and lay for hours gazing at the stars which crept across the opening. When the moon was full I went outside and saw every twig, every leaf, every stone as clear as in the day, but as if reproduced in silver by a supreme craftsman. All around the herbs exhaled their fragrance into the quiet air.

This was high summer, July, when the village became over-stuffed with tourists and cars parked or queueing, full of lobster-red families petulant at losing the swimming time their travel agent had sold them, honking sometimes and shouting at each other in various languages. I avoided the village except to sell lavender bags and collect things to eat; the dancing places were too crowded.

On one of my trips into town I found the twins with Catherine Guinness, a friend from the old days in London. She used to come to their studio and had been interested in the Divine Light Mission.

'Catherine!'

'Shoe! We were just talking about you, John says you're living in a stone hut.'

'That's it, round the back of the Montaña Negra near the count's olive grove. Where are you?'

'With my family at San Sebastian, you know, the white house on the mountain under the balls.'

She meant the Pani, the 1800-foot mountain which sports the two giant white balls of the Air Force radar station and dominates the south side of the village just as my Montaña Negra, the other side of the road, carries the television aerial and dominates the west side. It clicked, of course. The Guinness house was that white oblong near the top where Alexander Mosley had been staying a few years back. The conversation moved on to other things. Another time Catherine introduced me to her brother Jasper, and while their family were there the two of them were part of the scene.

'Dad hardly ever comes into the village,' Catherine told me once. 'He calls it "the behavioural sink".'

'Behavioural sink?'

'Yes, he's into animal behaviour, he uses expressions like that. He says we all go down to the village and misbehave, and I suppose we do in a way.' She intercepted a passing waiter. '*Otro cuba libre, por favor.* Anyone else like one?'

After the drinks question had been settled, I said to Catherine: 'I suppose he's fairly square, at his age, your father.'

'In a way; more of a tease, really.'

In September the crowds gradually dispersed, and the village recovered its sanity. One could watch the weekly *sardana* dancing without needing to jostle through a crowd; and again the English staged their cricket match. I tried my hand at picking and shelling almonds, there were plenty of these going begging in the hills, but a whole day's hard work didn't produce more than a pound or so, so I gave this up.

The life suited me; there seemed no reason to move, so I stayed. Autumn wore on and gave way to winter. Again I managed to find free accommodation in the town for the coldest part. This time it was the top floor of what was then the Hotel del Mar, now a private house; it is situated right on the beach so that when there was a strong east wind the building was lashed by the spray. The hotel was shut up for the winter and, as in the previous year, I paid for my accommodation by doing some cleaning.

In the spring I moved again into my stone hut, throwing away my furnishings and putting in new ones from the lavish store Sophie had given me. Lavender bags still sold at first, but the time came when the market was saturated. For a time I took to washing cars, which was all right until water began to be short; but in the summer I became seriously unpopular when I used people's taps. In any case I was developing another source of income, and a better one. Fanny was a friend of mine – a tall, lithe, still attractive lady who had retired from a career as a dancer and regularly visited Cadaques with the painter who was her long-standing partner. She had the use of a big room, and started giving lessons there; the place became a dance studio. I went a lot, naturally. After one workout, as I was putting on my boots, I noticed the girl next to me was nursing her feet.

'I'll give those a rub, if you like,' I said. '*Masaje.*' I rubbed my own foot to show what I was talking about.

'*Por favor,*' she said, and let me take a foot. I used what the Madras swami had taught me, varied a bit by what I had picked up at Oki Sensei's. The girl was really grateful, and after that I made a habit of helping dance pupils with their aching feet.

Then Fanny asked me to do her back. Again I worked from memory, but as I got into it I thought less and less about technique and let myself be led by my feeling. Massage is a strange thing, all sorts of influences can pass both ways, from client to masseuse, from masseuse to client. One must open oneself to the client, which means taking on the tensions that are present; this can drag one down. Fanny had no tensions; easily and naturally, her pain dissolved under my hands.

I didn't need to be told I had done a good job, so it didn't surprise me when she said, 'Shoe! That was marvellous, I've never had a massage like it. Could you do it next week as well? I'll pay you of course.'

From then on I was in the massage business. Every weekend I had four or five regular clients, with quite a lot of casuals in the tourist season; I used sunflower oil with a little lavender water to give a scent to it and because lavender was my trademark.

It was also at Fanny's that I first met someone who was to become my constant companion. Marianne.

She was an Australian of Dutch extraction, a beautiful dancer, ballet trained and slim as a reed, with almost no bust. To myself I called her Fey, because she was, or Pinocchio, because of her funny little pointed nose. Her light brown hair was fine and reached her waist. There she was one afternoon in Fanny's studio, up for the weekend from Barcelona where she worked at odd jobs and studied ballet. At the end of the class we chatted a bit.

'You live here, then?'

'Yes, in a stone hut on the hillside; I'm going back there now.'

'Is it very far?'

'Half an hour or so, perhaps a bit more.'

'I'd like to come too, for the walk.'

'That would be nice,' I said, meaning it, for I liked this girl at first sight and admired her dancing.

She was the best kind of company on a mountain walk; silent, receptive, someone to whom the scenery spoke profoundly. The stream was now flowing again, though still thin as a hairpin between the pools. At the sight of it Marianne changed, becoming – there is no other word for it – skittish. Skittish, that is, in her own special, Marianne fashion. Without speaking or smiling, with total elegance, she slid down the smooth face of a boulder to the edge of a waist-high pool; she took all her clothes off and bounded in, dipping her face and shoulders in the water, splashing herself with an air of ceremony, almost like a self-baptism. Still dripping, she did ballet exercises. She was a water-sprite, a naiad; she belonged to the hills and the stream.

She left then, but came back to Cadaques the following weekend, found her own stone hut not far from mine and installed herself. We were not always together, she wandered around a good deal more than I did. For days at a time she followed the shepherds whose migrant flocks graze the hills in autumn, collecting piles of wool which she intended to spin. She returned from the first of these expeditions covered with dust, her beautiful hair matted. Careless of her appearance, she came to look really wild. Washing bored her, except her hands and face. This was a difference between us, because I always kept clean.

Marianne and I often danced together at the Hostal, turning the bar into that different kind of bar at which dancers exercise, spinning round the pillars, doing splits or pirouettes between the tables as the drinkers stared in surprise. Lady Lavender and the Sheep Girl; it was quite an act. Marzi, the owner, put up with our antics, on and off, for the best part of two years. Marianne, at least, was worth watching, despite being dressed like a tramp. She could have been one of Martha Graham's girls. As for me, if my dancing wasn't quite up to hers at least I looked smarter. Then again, when the mood took me and there was a decent group I would sing at the microphone, anything I knew that the group could play; jazz songs, folk, whatever was going. Marianne carried on dancing, serious, introverted; yes, fey.

It was never very clear what Marianne lived on; savings, presumably, from dancing jobs in Barcelona or before that in Amsterdam. After a bit she began to give dance classes to local children. At one point the school thought of taking her on as dance teacher, but they had second thoughts, probably because she looked so wild. She ate like a bird, becoming thinner and thinner. She was a classic case of anorexia. What a pair we were! An anorectic and a bulimic, pretending to be super-healthy nature girls. At one time Marianne became so undernourished that she lost her memory.

In July I found a good new client; Frau Margarethe Peddinghaus, the white-haired widow of a German industrialist. She had a house halfway up Mount Pani. Her living-room was full of graceful frescoes of deer painted by herself; she was a fine artist. She also had a soft heart for animals, giving open house to a shifting population of stray dogs. Marianne used to help her caretaker work in the garden; that was how Frau Peddinghaus came to hear of me. She liked my massage so much that she commissioned me daily for her whole four weeks holiday. She was kind to me, letting me use her bathroom; a small thing to her, perhaps, but at that time an enormous luxury for me.

The view from her house was panoramic. To the left, the whole village lay spread out below like a model around the bay from the Rocamar Hotel at the base of the Pani round to the Caials peninsula, to the right were undulating folds of ground with the sea and the horizon beyond. Behind the house rose the Pani. The white building surrounded by trees, below the summit, was no longer just an oblong patch but definitely a house, with a roof and windows. One window was rather curious, it looked like the top segment of a big circle, or the mouth in a Halloween pumpkin. The Guinness house, where Catherine's family came for the summer; I had never seen it so close.

# 22

# Dancing for Dali

Tini Duchamp, widow of Marcel Duchamp, was playing chess in the Bar Meliton when a friend of mine introduced me as the village masseuse. She was old, but her black eyes sparkled and she had the sunny smile of a baby. Her hair was flaxen; well done, I thought, you're not one to give in to a little thing like age. Before Duchamp she had been married to Matisse, which meant she married two of the greatest artists of her time, one after the other.

She became one of my best clients when she was in the village, and once she actually arranged for me to go to her house near Fontainebleau to help her recover after a car accident. I wasn't a good guest; my food addiction was going through a bad phase and life in the mountains had made me careless and a bit uncivilized. Once I left a sheepskin rug too near the hearth in my room and it caught fire, covering everything with greasy black soot; if Tini's Moroccan servant had not seen smoke the house would have burnt down. I was apologetic, of course, and dear Tini forgave me, but I now realize with remorse that I took it far too lightly. As soon as I knew no-one was hurt it seemed scarcely to matter. I was at that time such a wild creature that I saw people's possessions as having no more value than Sophie's discarded curtains in my stone hut.

Tini knew masses of people, from John Lennon to Madame Mitterand. She took me everywhere; I particularly remember the opening of the Centre Pompidou or Beaubourg, that odd structure covered with multi-coloured tubing like a factory turned inside out. We also went to visit a friend of hers called Nathalie who lived in an exquisite 18th Century château in Fontainebleau that had belonged to Madame de Pompadour. She had masses of paintings, Rubens's as well as Picassos and Dalis. One Dali was in a room given over to her dogs, which was not an insult to it because the dogs were very important to her. There were a lot of cats as well; Tini told me she had four people to look after the after the animals. Perhaps this included the horses, because she liked riding; when she felt like it she would ride her thoroughbred mare into the library where the walls were lined with leather-bound books. Nathalie and her son came to dine with us and I gave the son a haircut.

Over the years, the twins had become friends of Salvador Dali; he was fond of them and sometimes called them his sons. Once John had turned up with a front tooth missing, and Dali had given him 10,000 pesetas to get it fixed; I think he felt this was like paying for the repair of a great work of art. Again they took me to see him. A character I knew from the bars met us on the stairs, carrying a tray with empty champagne glasses.

'*Que tal*, Lady Lavender?' he greeted me, all smiles. Evidently he was one of Dali's manservants. I greeted him back, pleased to be recognized. John mentioned to Dali that I sometimes entertained in the village. He looked at me hard.

'*Il faut que vous reveniez tous Dimanche, quand viendront les musiciens, et que cette demoiselle chante,*' he said to John in his Catalan French, then to me, in strange, slow English: 'Soondayee, you com heerr and seeng to oos, Dali invites you. Therre weel be museeciáns.'

'Certainly I'll come,' I said, and of course I determined to give of my best, for to me Dali was up there with Picasso and Matisse and Modigliani, the last of the great masters.

I gave them folk songs mostly, 'Scarborough Fair', 'Early Morning Rain' and so on. Dali must have approved, because we often went on Sundays after that to perform for him. Marianne came along sometimes and we danced together, as in the Hostal. Dali always had a few friends there; the one I remember best is Antonio Pitxot, a fine painter specializing in human figures put together from stones on the same lines as Arcimboldo's vegetable people. Then there was Amanda Lear, the tall deep-voiced blonde; partly through Dali, Amanda made it to stardom. Dali was said always to like blondes, and Amanda was a great favourite. But then he liked me too, though I was not a blonde; once or twice he crowned me with a garland of tuberoses, and occasionally he let me and the twins visit him when he was working, which was a rare privilege. I remember him modelling a figure in red wax, shaping it as we talked; I picked up a handful too, and made a woman's torso like one of those Victorian dress models with a wooden plug instead of a head.

I don't know if he would have liked me so much if he had known of some of the things I did on my visits. When I excused myself, the lavatory was not my main goal; I made a detour via the kitchen. If there was nobody there I raided the fridge near the door, snatching a handful of whatever was there; smoked salmon usually, caviare once or twice, dressed crab, listening desperately for footsteps.

My thirty-third birthday came around on 26 June, 1977, and Dali said he would give a party for me.

'Come at four o'clock,' he said. 'There will be one hundred invited.'

At the time my bulimia was in one of its worst phases, completely out of control. I had a terrible morning on my birthday; I suppose I allowed myself to indulge more than usual, and the high summer was always a bad time with too many kind people offering me a puff-pastry *palmera* in the shape of a palm leaf, or a doughnut or three. That was how it was at breakfast time on my birthday; after a crafty chunder I went and bought myself a big tin of cooked pigs' trotters. These I ate, sicked up, ate again and sicked up a second time, an action that marked my lowest point of degradation. I did get a surge of energy from it, but when this had passed I was scared witless. If people knew how bad I was they would lock me up; yes, in a way I ought to be locked up, yet if I was it would kill me. In the meantime I must now be cleansed, cleansed inside and out. Swiftly I strode to my sweet-water well, lowered the bucket, drew it up, drank a quart of water. I did the same again, then finally dropped exhausted there in the sun. Then came the pains, gastric pains, cramps in the lower bowel. When they had subsided a bit, I walked up and over to a special vantage point with a panoramic view where the rock face emerged from reddish earth partially shaded by a group of pines overlooking a bay. I lay shivering, my teeth chattering as if with a high fever, on the pine needles among the cones. But I fed on the clean scent of the place, soothed by the humming of insects, and gradually my shuddering subsided.

I was all dressed up in my silk toga for the party and I thought, it'll be time to start off in a couple of hours, I'll be back to normal by then. But I wasn't. The pains went, but they were followed by a terrible depression. I said to myself, if I go to that party I shall binge again, there will be more humiliation, more pain. These trees, these rocks, this shimmering sea below and this startling dark blue summer sky above, these are my real friends and healers; I dare not trust myself among my own kind. They'll notice my absence for a minute or two, then forget about me and have their usual good time on Dali's pink champagne. I'll apologize to Dali when I see him next. Another wave of depression; I lay face down on the rock and sobbed. I slept a little in the shade of a pine; in the evening, full of an empty calm, I returned to my hut.

For some days I stayed there, living on water and blackberries; these, in Spain, ripen in late July. The twins came up to see me. John said, 'Where were you? Why didn't you come to the party?'

'We were worried about you,' said Denis. 'Everybody was. Are you all right?'

'I was ill, stomach trouble. I'm all right now, but it was bad. Look, could you make it all right with Dali?'

'Of course, he'll understand.'

'I hope so,' I said. 'I was dreadfully disappointed to miss it, tell him that. I'd have come if I hadn't felt really rotten.'

About a month later I went to an art exhibition. There are several galleries dotted around Cadaques, and on Saturday evenings in the season they give *vernissages*, offering acid wine with ice in it and showing pictures that are mostly bad. For if there are eight galleries in Cadaques and each gives four exhibitions every summer, that makes thirty-two artists. True, some top names do exhibit in Cadaques, as well as some good unknowns. But thirty-two exhibitions every summer in a Costa Brava village is too many for even half of them to be interesting. Anyway the smart set of Cadaques, such as it is, goes round each *vernissage*, praising the picture as long as the artist is within earshot, then going back to exaggerated greetings and kissings of each other. It is as if none of them have met for at least a year, despite all having been at the same party the night before.

This particular gallery I went to was run by a friend, which is why I turned up, nicely washed and made up and with my hair shining. It was a hot night and I wore a sleeveless white cheesecloth number. It was one of a pile of cast-offs someone had given me, but fresh looking, quite elegant, with lace fastening up the front and panels of crochet work; it set off my deep tan. I had not eaten all day; I should most likely binge later, but for the time I was feeling well and happy, ready for an evening's dancing. The exhibition was terrible; posters of pop stars in pink and green that could have been by Warhol on an off day. I got myself a mineral water and wandered round, pretending for form's sake to have a look before reparing to the Hostal.

I came face to face with a man in blue denim with a shock of grey hair like Mahler or Beethoven; he was a bit tubby and had bright blue eyes.

'You're Shoe, aren't you? I'm Jonathan Guinness, Catherine's father.'

His voice seemed affected, over-refined, yet I liked it. We shook hands and struck up a conversation. He walked about the mountains a lot, he said, and sometimes he'd spotted me; in the village as well.

'I know you so well by sight I feel as if we were old friends,' he said.

The pictures were pretty awful, we agreed. He knew I knew so-and-so. We talked about the Guru Maharaj Ji because Catherine had been interested; he'd been to a Divine Light gathering to see what it was like. The Guru had been expected but had not turned up. I sheered off the subject, sensing that he had found the experience a turn-off, that underneath his politeness he disapproved. I did not want to bring this to the surface.

For I liked talking to this man, under the scrutiny of those pale eyes. He didn't stare, in fact his eyes darted about so much that he might have been bored with me and trying to escape. Yet I knew – how? – that on the contrary he was trying to avoid being caught staring. I had this overwhelming sense of being admired, more than ever in my life, and I am a sucker for admiration. He said nothing to indicate that he liked me, he made nothing remotely resembling a pass, yet I felt that this man wanted me as I'd never been wanted before. I soaked myself in his admiration as if it was a scented bath. I didn't want to move, I couldn't move. There was no reason to move anyway, I was perfectly safe. Jonathan simply appreciated the way I looked, and I was never one to mind that. In fact his admiration excited me. I felt myself radiating attraction. I was more than safe, I was in control! Oh, I didn't want this meeting to end. The small talk ran out; I began talking about myself. I even told him I'd been in prison.

'Holloway?' he said. 'My mother was in Holloway.'

I suppose I wasn't as surprised as some people would have been. 'How long for?'

'Three and a half years. I used to visit her in the school holidays.'

The idea of three and a half years terrified me. 'What on earth did she do?'

'Nothing against the law; she was a political prisoner. They locked her up for being the wife of the fascist leader, Sir Oswald Mosley.'

None of this meant much to me. He added, 'Tell you what, I'll send you her autobiography, it'll interest you as an old Holloway inmate.'

Soon after that we left, he with one group and I with another. It was over. What was over? A chat with the father of friends of mine, well into middle age, rather portly, not in the least alternative; married, as well. Yet without saying a word out of place, without touching me, without even staring, this man had in a ten minute conversation made me feel like the goddess Venus.

It didn't last, of course. Later that night I ate some scraps, then cowered in a back street and was squalidly sick. A ginger alley-cat turned its head, alerted by the sound of my retching. Suddenly I thought, that might have been Jonathan Guinness watching me, even now he might come round the corner. I thought, if he knew of my habits his admiration would turn to contempt. He must not know; he must always think of me as this triumphant beauty. I must never let him get close.

For a day or two I thought about this incident, then it dropped out of my mind. After all, what reason did I have to think it meant anything? Perhaps Jonathan was like that with everyone; perhaps he hadn't really been like it at all and my imagination had become over-heated. If cross-examined I should not have been able to recall a word, even a gesture, that meant more than ordinary pleasant politeness. Again the summer visitors left and the place settled down.

Then a few weeks later John Myers joined me at a table in the Casino. 'Parcel for you,' he said , and put down what was obviously a book.

Something from Mother, I thought; but no, it was from London. I tore it open. On the back of the dust-cover there was a picture of Holloway, I'd know that place anywhere. *A Life of Contrasts*, Diana Mosley; it was Jonathan's mother's book. A letter fell out, in small rather ugly writing. I put it away, saving it for the trip I was taking later in a friend's dinghy.

It was not long, and the little awkward scrawl was quite easy when I got used to it, but I took an hour to read it. As when we talked in the gallery, I never wanted it to end. Though agreeable and entertaining, it was in no way a love letter. That made no difference. In the gallery I had thought Jonathan fancied me, but I might have imagined it. Now I had two material objects, a book and a letter, to prove that I was still in his mind.

I took a whole afternoon to answer. At the time I was living in the garden shed of a Rumanian artist, Sandu Babeanu, next door to Dali. I sat in Sandu's garden with ballpoint and paper writing draft after draft. Would Jonathan think my handwriting unformed, would he laugh at my spelling? Oh, my awful spelling! I was so uncertain of it that I spelt the same word several ways on the same sheet so that at least once it might be correct. At times I thought of scrapping the lot, not replying; but no, I wanted to reply, to communicate. Painfully at last I made a fair copy and sent it.

An answer came back, and a correspondence was under way.

# 23

# Love at a Distance

January came round, and one day I went to Figueras to do a bit of shopping, calling as I usually did at a little kiosk that sold snacks and souvenirs. It was just outside the station, and was often open when everything else was shut; a good place to binge on doughnuts. I was quite friendly with Rafel, the stocky Catalan who ran it. Pinned to a cardboard sheet at the back of the kiosk were some tiny red enamel hearts, little Sacred Heart badges such as people had often worn in Spain a generation before to show they were good Catholics.

The little hearts were so much out of fashion that I think Rafel had forgotten all about them. The board was half hidden behind another displaying cheap cigarette lighters. To make Rafel understand what I wanted I had to point to my chest and the board, several times.

'Heart,' I said stupidly, my Spanish not being up to it.

'*Ah, si,*' he said, '*corazon, corazon sagrado,*' and got the board out. There were about ten left.

I was with a friend who also found them charming, and between us we cleaned him out. One badge was a double one, two hearts with a little chain between them and the word *ENCADENADOS*. Chained. I thought, I'll give this to Jonathan when he's here for Saint Sebastian's day next week.

When the day came the twins and I walked up to the house on the Pani with its chapel, and there was Jonathan outside it, greeting us in worn corduroy trousers and a navy blue fisherman's coat. He was like a bear. I thought, I wish you weren't so overweight. But he gave me a great hug and kissed me on both cheeks, as everyone does in Cadaques. He asked us to lunch, so when the time came we went through into the dark dining-room with its tiled floor. A stuffed eagle in full flight hung in the middle of the ceiling and there was a long table against the wall with chicken, salad, beans, giant potato crisps. An open fire was throwing smoke into the room. I saw little of Jonathan during lunch, but afterwards I found him behind the house and pinned the double heart badge on him, and some single ones for luck. His eyes sparkled, but I bounded away before he could do more than thank me.

He went back to England, and I wrote to him. The letter I sent seems to be lost, but I still have one which I wrote and didn't send, in which I come clean about my daily vomiting. That is why I didn't send it; I wanted to tell him, but didn't dare.

When Jonathan came in the summer we met from time to time in the village, but I saw his family more than him because he mostly kept out of it, walking by himself or writing. I, too, stayed away most of the time, coming in mainly to massage. When we did meet he would kiss me socially and we would have a little chat; that was all.

Then in early October I got a letter from him. He was coming to Cadaques by himself; he hoped we should meet. Oh no, I thought. What shall I do? Will he want to get closer to me? It looks as if he will. With half my mind I hoped for this, but I also dreaded it, for I knew I should have to refuse any serious advances he might make. This was not so much because of his wife; I didn't know her except by sight so she wasn't real to me. It was because of my illness. I was terrified of seeing his admiration turn to disgust, for it seemed obvious that if we had an affair he was certain to find out about it and be turned off me. At the same time, I knew that if he made no advances I should feel rather let down. I remember, too, a certain curiosity; how, exactly, was he going to break through his politeness and admit to those feelings I knew he had?

He arrived on the day he said he would, I could see the lights on in his house after dark. The moment of decision? Not necessarily. I thought of a way of meeting him, yet evading the issue. Next morning I said to Marianne, 'Come up to San Sebastian with me, I want to offer Jonathan a foot massage.'

She looked at me; I was dressed in a Catalan-made tartan kilt with a white lace blouse, dinky as a Dagenham girl piper. I even wore white socks and black lacquered shoes. It was not an outfit I'd normally wear to walk up the Pani. Oh, she read me like a book.

So I armed myself with some towels and we set off up the mountain. Jonathan's cook, Josefa, greeted us politely, but I was glad I was not on my own; I should have felt embarrassed. She fetched him out; he was surprised, openly delighted. I made him lie on the stone table and roll up his trousers, then set to work on his feet. Funny little feet they were, too small for a man his height, but I liked them. The Japanese would have said they had a spiritual arch, they believe that flat feet signify materialism, that the higher the arch the greater the spirituality. As I worked we talked about the mountains. He said he always walked up and down between his house and the village when he could spare the time; walking about the mountains was what he liked doing most in Cadaques. I said I agreed. But we kept to generalities; there was no suggestion we might go for a walk together.

This came in a note I received the next day. Would I come for a picnic in two days' time? He'd bring sandwiches. I said yes, but again arranged for a chaperon when the time came. This time it was Denis. If Jonathan was disappointed, he didn't show it. We all went up to the olive grove. Denis turned aside to relieve himself. Taking advantage of this I said to Jonathan, 'Like to see my hut, where I live in the summer?'

'I'd love to,' he said, and we scampered down to the lower terrace. I wasn't going inside with him, of course: none of that. But I thought, really I owe him a minute alone with me, as long as we remain visible. So I climbed up on to the roof.

'Come up here and see the view.'

It was the same view as from below, since ten feet makes no difference, but up he climbed. Perhaps he held my helping hand a second or two longer than strictly necessary, but it was not so long as to make any particular point.

'Here's the roof stone,' I explained, picking it up. 'You take it off when you want light, put it back to keep out the rain.'

He tried it. 'Takes a bit of lifting.'

'Oh, you get used to it.'

Denis appeared, saving the situation or perhaps spoiling it; at any rate the sacred interlude was over. We all walked together down the stream, stopping to drink a solemn toast to each other and to the mountains, in pure water from the stream. I had brought three wine glasses for this little ceremony.

A couple of days later I gave Jonathan a one-woman performance in Fanny's studio. A one-woman performance for a one-man audience; he sat on a chair while I got up on the little stage and, without accompaniment, belted out Elvis Presley numbers and the occasional Marlene Dietrich.

'But you're brilliant,' he said, between each number. 'Do me another,' and when my range had run out he made me do some of them again. How can I convey the thin, pure joy I drew from this one person's solitary appreciation? If the applause of a mass audience is like brass band music, this resembled a solo violin playing a Bach *partita*. What a delicate pleasure to get in response to a performance of 'Hound Dog'.

Jonathan went back to England, but said he was returning in six weeks, just for the weekend. He left me in a dream state. I spent some time in Fanny's studio by myself, listening to Fauré's Requiem and thinking about him. His admiration, expressed in every medium but words, had dissolved defences that no frontal assault would ever have breached; the gates were open, he had only to walk through.

But I had been celibate for years; it was quite an effort to remember my last little one-night stand. There hadn't been much lovemaking in my life after Rob Roy; a little, but not much, and not serious. I must prepare myself. Would it be enjoyable for me or for Jonathan? Would it be disappointing, even unpleasant? It was reassuring to feel this steady, golden glow of Jonathan's admiration; there seemed nothing aggressive in it but it was all-pervasive, like an atmosphere.

I asked him to a small party on the Sunday evening, the last of his weekend visit, with the twins and a few other friends; if our encounter went wrong somehow we could then lick our wounds at leisure and apart, perhaps to try again, perhaps not. But I didn't wait till the evening to see him. On the morning of that day I walked up to San Sebastian, alone this time.

'It's such a lovely day,' I said, 'let's go for a walk.'

We started down the mountain together, then agreed to sit for a while and look at the view. But he looked more at me than at the view, and finally I guided him to a stone hut I had often slept in, out towards the sea. This time we went inside.

We met again at the party. Herrdien, a big jolly German artist with a beard, played the guitar and sang; I thought, this is the best playing I have ever heard, and the best voice. Jonathan glittered with happiness.

He saw me home to the room I occupied in the village; I had avoided eating, so as not to have to vomit. It was very late before he went up to his house. As he dressed, I put on my night attire. I had made this from a cream silk shawl by cutting out the centre so that it fell back and front like a herald's tabard; I tied it round me with a sash. It looked odd I suppose, but the silk felt superb against the skin.

'I like your rags,' he said.

'Rags indeed! It's a beautiful silk toga.'

A kiss on the forehead, and he was gone. He left the next morning, as planned; we said a loving goodbye on the Rambla.

That Christmas I went home to Lancashire; Ronnie killed the fatted calf, and also gave me enough money to keep me going for a bit. But early in the new year I went south, staying for a time with some people in Kent; Jonathan came for the day. From there my friend Patrick Villiers-

Stewart invited me to spend some time in Dromana, the great house in the south of Ireland where he lived with his mother. It was cold and damp after the dry warmth of Cadaques. I kept warm by helping with the housework; that place had never been so vigorously swept in its long life. I was in pain from my illness, and eventually it got so bad that I went into hospital for a stomach probe and some treatment. This reduced the pain, but the addiction which caused it was still there. Back at Dromana, I became depressed, though Patrick and his mother were both angels. It became clear that nothing much had changed. True, I had a relationship going with Jonathan, but it was only an occasional one; worse, to my mind it was based on a lie. Jonathan still didn't know about my bulimia, and I felt that I must conceal it from him at all costs. This was out of pride; he had put me on a pedestal and I dreaded falling off it. I succeeded in this; he never did find out the full truth till long after I was cured. This fixed idea that my addiction was so disgusting that it must put anyone off may itself have been part of the illness.

I felt that Jonathan had fallen for a façade, an exterior; and I looked in the mirror to check that at least my appearance was still all right. What I saw worried me; I seemed to be losing my looks. The wrinkles on my forehead seemed like ditches, the pouches under my eyes like flabby balloons. This was not a complete illusion; vomiting floods the lymphatic system with water so bulimia can cause pouches under the eyes. My false teeth weren't very good, either. I decided to create a new me by having plastic surgery and purchasing a better set of false teeth.

At least the teeth were a success; I am still wearing them. The plastic surgery put me through a hard time, and I was lucky it was not a permanent disaster. It was my persuasive powers that did for me. I convinced the local GP that I needed plastic surgery for my peace of mind, and he gave me a certificate to this effect which I took to a hospital in Cork. The trouble was that nobody in this downtown burns unit had ever thought of cosmetic surgery; the surgeon there was just the man for third degree burns and skin grafts, but a lady's vanity was not the sort of problem he came across. He thought I was off my head and pleaded with me to change my mind, especially as I was only thirty-four. But I had my piece of paper and in the end the surgeon had to comply.

'Very well,' he said, 'I'll do a dermabrasal on your forehead to get rid of the lines, and remove the pouches under your eyes. I still think you're wrong, but I'll do it.'

There were some pretty terrible sights among those awaiting surgery in that burns unit; raw and ruined faces, victims from Breughel or Bosch. They depressed me, but I didn't connect them with myself; I expected the new me to emerge, perfect, straight off the operating table. On the morning of the operation I was dressed in the surgical shroud, all ready for the anaesthetic, and as I was about to go under I suddenly thought of the word *dermabrasal*. I thought, braising is what you do to steak. My God! They are going to burn me! But it was too late to back out.

When I came round it felt as if someone had poured a kettle of boiling water over my forehead, the pain was fearful. I needed a lot of painkillers at first. Then I looked in the mirror. Horrors! My face was all puffed out and swollen with only the nose protruding. Also they had crudely shaved a lot off the front of my hair, there was a red scar along the hairline and other angry scars round my eyes where they had dealt with the pouches. I looked a freak.

'When will my face get back to normal?' I asked the surgeon. 'Or will it?'

'You'll be fine in four months or so,' he said.

Four months. It sank in; four *months*! Why hadn't the silly clot told me this when he was trying to talk me out of having the operation? I kept this thought to myself; there was no point in putting the man's back up, what was done was done. Well, one thing was sure; I wasn't going anywhere near Jonathan until properly healed. But what could I do? I went back to Dromana for a bit, but I was sensitive. I thought, I can't stay here, it's not fair to expect them to put up with someone looking like this.

There was an advertisement in a magazine for a health farm, Joyce's Mill, giving an address in the West. It cost £60 a week, which seemed reasonable. True, I only had £75 in the world, but this would be enough for one week. After that I'd have to see; but I did after all know a bit about massage, and perhaps once there, among the massage conscious, I might find an opening to pass my four months' purdah. I booked in on the telephone for one week, and made my way there by bus.

Joyce's Mill wasn't Champneys by a long chalk. It had no elaborate equipment or anything fancy, not even so much as an exercise bicycle; but there was a decent-sized recreation and exercise room with mattresses to work out on, a sauna, and above all the incomparable Irish countryside for walking and jogging. Essentially it was a one-woman operation; Margot owned and ran it with one assistant, Noreen, and a couple of domestics. There was only room for eight clients at the most; when I went there were three others besides myself.

I immediately made friends with Margot and soon started massaging the other clients, making myself quite useful. All the same, as the days passed I began to wonder about the future. Then on the Friday, the day before I was to leave, Providence took a hand. Margot said to me:

'There's been a disaster. Noreen's crashed her car, she's not badly hurt but she's shaken up; the doctor says she can't come to work for a fortnight.'

'How awful.'

'I might have managed, only we've Easter coming up and we'll be having a full house. I was wondering would you consider staying on for a bit? Just for your keep and full use of the facilities? I wish I could afford to pay you something, but you know how it is, we're on a shoestring here.'

That was a bit mean of her, but I didn't care. I was saved. In the end I stayed for three months.

I learned a good deal about running a small health farm; how to work a sauna, for instance, and particularly how to deal with clients. The morning was devoted to hathayoga and keep-fit, in the afternoon we went on long brisk walks. Most of the guests were out of condition, of course, but every now and then there would be a formidably fit girl trying to get even fitter. One of these taught me speedwalking, how to walk twelve miles in an afternoon. She had walked to Rome, she told me. Her technique put Croagh Patrick within easy range; I climbed it several times with some of the more active guests and once on Good Friday, when I put a photograph of Jonathan under a stone at the summit.

The local Church of Ireland vicar used to come to the health farm; he suffered from headaches and found that a sauna helped. I gave him a cranial massage which he said worked like magic, and he began visiting three times a week. He had a big round bald head like a marble boulder. He talked a lot as I worked, at first mostly about the problems of his parishioners; there weren't many of them, but they had problems. Then he talked about himself.

'The happiest time in my life was when I had a church in Simla,' he said.

'I understand that,' I said. 'I was a long time in the East, India and Sri Lanka. I felt a real spirituality there.'

That started him off. It turned out that under the clergyman's suit and dog-collar there lurked a passion for the Hindu religion. He had read and pondered the Mahabharata and the Vedic Hymns, and talked to many scholars. It wasn't that he had lost his Christian faith, but he'd looked over the wall and loved what he saw. I felt the same, of course, but for someone in Holy Orders it must have sometimes been difficult. He didn't allude to this in any direct way but talked round the problem, opening up to me almost as if I were his father confessor. He became more and more hooked on my cranial massage – almost it seemed as a substitute for prayer.

'There, how's that?' I'd ask at the end of his session.

'Terrific,' he said, 'you really have the touch, I've never known a touch like it.'

One day he put on an Indian evening for us. He showed a film about Mother Theresa and brought along a pile of saris and shawls from Assam in which we all dressed up.

Not long after Easter Margot got a letter from Mr O'Grady, a well-to-do Dublin solicitor, with a twenty-eight day booking for himself and his wife. They were overweight, he said, and his doctor had advised a health farm. Margot was immensely impressed, it wasn't often she got a four week booking.

When they turned up it was clear why they had decided to come for so long. They waddled in looking like a pair of little Michelin men; he was 5 foot 4 and twenty stone, she was 5 foot 2 and eighteen. As they registered I sniffed a bit; had someone broken wind? Then I forgot about it. Later they were sitting in the big airy recreation room surrounded by diet and exercise charts, and Margot said to me:

'Can you smell anything strange?'

I sniffed. 'Yes,' I said, 'definitely.'

The smell followed the O'Gradys up to their room and hung about the landing. By the time I got out of bed next morning the whole of the first floor smelt of sweaty socks. It got worse and worse. Margot got a supply of Airwicks and put three in the recreation room, but they didn't seem to work. The vicar stopped coming for his head massage. Then a couple who had been booked in for a week left after two days.

Margot said, 'They didn't give a reason, but I think we know why they went.'

'Yes,' I said, 'I think we do.'

'At this rate we'll lose everyone except the O'Gradys,' she said. 'Can you think of anything?'

'Perhaps I can,' I said. 'It'll be easier for me than for you. Give me a couple of track suits, about their sizes.'

Armed with these, I knocked at the O'Gradys' door, taking a deep in-breath as I did so in order to avoid having to take one in their room.

'Come in.'

'I've brought you these,' I said. 'You'll find if you take your clothes off and put them on, you'll feel more sporty, more flexible, more ready for action.'

'Good idea,' said Mr O'Grady, and I left them to it. By and by they came down in the grey track suits and I darted up to their room with a couple of plastic sacks. I shoved in all their clothes and took the sacks down to Margot in Reception.

'These are their clothes,' I gasped, puffed from holding my breath.

'Well done,' she said, locking the sacks in a wall cupboard.

This made matters better, but it was not enough. The O'Gradys did keep-fit classes, after a fashion. They could get their hands above their heads, but when asked to touch their toes they put their arms just below the chest and leaned forward, like a pair of skittles. As they exercised and became warm, the smell filled the room. It was their bodies, and there was nothing for it but to wash them.

I told them, 'There's a new technique just over from America, I'll give it you if you like. The All-American Scrubdown.'

'And what's that?' said Mr O'Grady.

'The patient gets in a hot bath and I scrub him hard with a special loofah. I'm trained in it, got my diploma last year. It breaks down the cells in the fatty tissue and gets the circulation going.'

'Why don't we try it, dear?' said Mrs O'Grady.

'It really works,' I said, willing him to agree. 'And it's on the house of course, no extra charge.'

'Sounds good,' he said, and I was on.

She was first, and what a sight she was. She was only about fifty-eight, but she could have been eighty-eight the way she got into that bath. I scrubbed her with the loofah all over as she stood there. She had quite a thin face and small bones, but gross arms and thighs and an immense swelling stomach with two great aprons of fat which I had to lift one after the other to wash away the accumulated grime underneath. There was a hard yellow crud attaching to her ankles and feet like dried Cheddar, which I had to get off with a knife. Then it was his turn; for decency's sake he wore a pair of red trunks. He was gross too, but being naturally big-boned he carried it better than she did. Again there was this yellow stuff I had to take the knife to. Neither of them can have had a bath for twenty years.

The All-American Scrubdown became a daily ritual, and I massaged them as well. This really took it out of me. One after the other I'd help them on to the massage table where they lay like great white mountains. Even fairly fat people usually lose their paunches when they lie on their backs; not the O'Gradys. I pushed and kneaded till the sweat ran down me. Turning them over was quite an operation, too, as neither of them could do it themselves; I had to live up to my 'Strongest Woman' billing.

Every morning the O'Gradys hired a taxi and went to Mass. On their

return they would sit motionless for twenty minutes in the recreation
room, eyes closed, muttering something, with what looked like bus
tickets on their heads. Mrs O'Grady's ticket fell off one day and she
asked me to put it back on. It said 'Hail Mary, full of grace . . .'
Obviously they were repenting of something, and I soon found out what.
The hotel in the local town where I went for my binges was quite a good
one; I would gorge on its slap-up selection of vegetables, sautéed carrots,
leeks, steamed cauliflowers, onion rings in batter, all marvellously
presented. It was a magnificent feast when one was on 600 calories a day.
One day I went in and there were the O'Gradys sitting at a table for
four, each tucking in to a huge mixed grill with a heap of chips and a pile
of white bread and butter. A large slice of Black Forest gateau awaited
each of them as well, and a generous plate of creme caramel.

'Couldn't keep it up,' he said. 'You won't split on us now.'

'Of course not; I shouldn't be here myself.'

'Come and join us then.'

So we sat and sinned together. Mr O'Grady ordered me another
round of onion rings, and at the end paid my bill. As they moved slowly
towards the restaurant door, I slipped out and into the Ladies to be sick,
then caught them up as they waddled towards the hotel entrance. An
empty taxi was about to draw away so I nipped out and got it for us,
eased the O'Gradys into the back and sat down in front.

'Oh, you're a dote,' said Mrs O'Grady; this was her own special
compliment, I've never heard anyone else use it.

But I thought, I am worse than you two, though you don't know it.
There's a sort of honesty about the way you hold on to the food you
devour. By rights I ought to be as gross as you. You only pig out; I pig
out and spew as well. We binged together in the hotel fairly often after
that. Margot never knew, but she must have thought it odd that after
four weeks on 600 calories a day all the weight the O'Gradys lost was one
stone, each. They never gave me a tip despite all the work I'd put into
them; but then they had paid for some of my binges.

I left Joyce's Mill in early June and went to a rock festival, where I got
talking to a young couple, Patrick and Liz. I mentioned Cadaques, and
they asked me if I knew Jonathan. 'He's my uncle,' said Patrick, and
they took me home to the cottage where they lived in the grounds of
Leixlip Castle, belonging to Jonathan's brother Desmond. Jonathan
was quite surprised to get a letter from me there. I stayed a few weeks,
exercising on the wide lawns which made a perfect natural gymnasium,
and massaging the feet of Desmond's cook.

Five hundred boat people had arrived in Ireland, Chinese refugees from Vietnam; I decided to spend a day seeing what I might do to help. I hitched the thirty-five miles to where they were housed.

Mr Sharples of the Salvation Army was organizing the reception. He was dry and determined, spoke fluent Cantonese, and knew exactly what he wanted for the refugees and what he didn't.

'We don't want offers of turf cutting jobs on the Aran Islands,' he said. 'We've got artists here, skilled people, makers of prize pasta, an acupuncturist, a champion duck roaster, and they expect them to cut turf.'

He showed me their kitchen which was a marvel of gleaming pots with curtains of draped spaghetti and edible seaweed in neat piles.

'What can you do?' asked Mr Sharples.

'I'm trained in oriental foot massage,' I said.

So I spent the afternoon massaging the feet of alert old men in grey Chinese tunics with rows of gold teeth, and felt I was back in the East.

Then I went to an alternative community called Atlantis in Donegal, where I watched a clash of cultures. A Krishna Consciousness wagon arrived, and the poor little Hare Krishna men with their prudish ways and abstemiousness were assaulted by large Cockney women who had gone there to get rid of their inhibitions. The women's treatment had been all too successful, or perhaps it had never been necessary in the first place; for half way through the evening some of them snatched the robes off the Krishna men and tried to take their pink loincloths as well. Aghast at this threat to their virginity, the Hare Krishna party left in the middle of the night.

By now I felt I looked all right, so I went back to London where I stayed with a succession of friends, seeing Jonathan from time to time. He noticed no difference in my appearance; the plastic surgery had no net effect at all as far as he was concerned. I didn't mention it to him. Entirely through word of mouth, I gathered a good massage clientele including some quite prominent people. And at last I began to cure my bulimia. Meeting Jonathan had given me a motive; now I found a method.

# 24

# Towards a Cure

It happened at a party I was taken to in a big garden in Kew in south-west London. On the right of the garden the hostess was dealing out tea and cucumber sandwiches to a group of straight people, in the middle a game of croquet was in progress, and on the left there was a motley crew of alternatives and fruit-eating Rastafarians, friends of Charlyte, the son of the house, who had the top floor flat. They were gathered round a tin bath full of all kinds of fruit which they were ripping up and devouring, without implements. They had cucumbers, avocados, mangoes, bananas, pineapples, you name it; also a supply of coriander powder which some of them liked to put on the fruit as an extra flavour. I stayed with the cucumber sandwiches long enough to gross out, but after coming out of the downstairs lavatory I felt directed to the fruitarians, who seemed like my kind of people.

I talked to Charlyte and his middle-aged friend Jim.

'Do you really eat nothing else but fruit?' I asked.

'Too right, man,' said Jim. 'Like we don't, you know, pull things out of the ground.'

'No roots, then? No potatoes or carrots or swedes?'

'You got it,' said Jim. 'Nothing but what can drop to the ground. We'll cut a cucumber or pick an apple, but we won't pull things out of mother earth. Like we respect, you know, life.'

'And everything is raw, is it?'

'Right.'

'How long have you been keeping to this?'

'Twelve years,' said Jim.

'And you're how old? Forty or so?'

'Just turned fifty,' he said.

He was slim, fit, bright-eyed; his skin was clear and smooth. The only sign that he was even as much as forty was his greying hair, which he

wore lank and unkempt. He worked as a hospital porter; this impressed
me because it meant that he was a person who held down a serious job,
not an alternative bum. I delved into the tin bath and came up with half
a cucumber; I should have liked a dollop of Thousand Island Dressing,
but made do with the coriander powder. I went on to a banana, then a
mango and a guava and a papaya; then I saw a homely ordinary apple,
looking up at me like an old friend, so I ate that. I went to be sick again,
then came back and ate some more with the alternatives. I talked to a
sweet young girl, big-eyed and dark, who explained a bit of the theory.

'Cooking destroys most of the vitamins, and by losing the juice you
lose some of the minerals as well,' she said. 'So who needs to cook?'

After all, in Cadaques I had been half way there, with my crates of
discarded fruit out of the market; without actually committing myself I
was already pretty well a vegetarian. But I noticed the difference
between spewing up the cucumber sandwiches, neatly cut and crustless
though they were, and vomiting the fruit. My first go was quite heavy
and nasty, the second was light, almost pleasant.

I told Jim of my illness, how I got high through being sick. He said:

'No problem, man; get into this style of eating and you'll be high all
day, every day. It don't matter vomiting a bit at first; the righteousness
of this good food will take care of you.'

The dark girl put in, 'You've got bulimia, right? My father's got a
cure for it, I'll send you his pamphlet; you might take one of his courses
in hypnotherapy.'

'Thanks,' I said, and gave her my address; but it turned out that her
father was a Harley Street specialist who charged the earth, hundreds of
pounds for a course. I read his pamphlet but that was all.

'Abide by the rules of nature, like us,' said Jim. '*Nature* will save you.'
He wandered off to wash his hands with the juice of a lime. Charlyte told
me he and Jim even used limes, with hot water, to wash their clothes.
Soap was taboo.

'Come and see my plants,' said Charlyte. 'I save all the seeds of what I
eat, and see if they will sprout.' His attic was a jungle paradise with its
wonderful little avocado and papaya plants and sprouting mango
stones. The air was sweeter than honey. Charlyte was as gentle as a
butterfly; he worked in a nature reserve for the local council. He had not
combed his pale brown hair for three years; his matted ringlets were
wound on the top of his head in the form of a cone. This looked a bit odd,
but he was obviously totally healthy, his body weight normal. I
commented on this.

'On a fruit diet you need to get enough starch, oil and protein,' he said. 'Bananas give you starch, avocados give you oil and protein; I eat a lot of both.'

I returned to play a little croquet, after which I made friends with a paraplegic chap in a wheelchair. He was only in his twenties and a car crash had left him unable to move legs or arms. He chatted me up exactly as a normal young man chats up a girl, he was in his way the bravest man I have ever met. It seemed more worthwhile to stay and talk to him than to gravitate to the food and have yet another binge. It struck me how lucky I was to have all my faculties; I took the address of the hospital where he lived, and wrote to him a few times.

The next day was Monday; I sauntered off to the greengrocer and gave him a large order. I didn't stick entirely to Jim's principles, for I bought some carrots and celery. I had it all packed in a box, then stopped off at a hardware shop and bought a grater. From then on for a year I ate nothing but raw fruit and vegetables, being careful to include plenty of bananas and avocados as Charlyte had advised. I also added sunflower oil and soya sauce.

I continued to vomit. At first I had no real intention of stopping, and the habit had become so ingrained that at first I couldn't. All the same it became less painful, less distasteful; I brought up less acid. After a couple of weeks I felt really fresh and clean; I also found it less necessary to drink great quantities of water to flush myself out. More important, I stopped being afraid of what I was eating, afraid that it would make me put on weight; in the complex of reasons for vomiting this fear usually figured. After a while a great ease came to me and I realized that I didn't *need* to be sick. I began to feel a glimmering of real hope.

I still over-indulged. Some days I would put away five pounds of apples, five of carrots, three or four grapefruit, bunch after bunch of grapes, six avocados and so on, after which I would have a tremendous vomit. I ate a crate of oranges a week, 200 of them. But I felt well and poised; I neither lost nor gained an ounce of weight. My motto was 'have grater, will travel'; I stayed with various people, and the only item in their larder that interested me was the fruit and vegetable shelf. My eyes cleared, my face looked less battered, well-being suffused me. One day soon, I felt, I should find I was no longer vomiting.

Not long after the party I went to the Festival of Mind, Body and Spirit at Olympia. This was made for me, with its array of healers, palmists, astrologers, whole earth people, martial arts experts and yogis. Rachel Pinney had a stall there for non-competitive games; the very idea of a non-competitive game made Jonathan laugh. All the same he went along to the Festival, on a different day from me, and took quite a lot in; though unfortunately he found a stall dedicated to the Japanese board game, Go, and seems to have wasted most of his morning playing with the man in charge. When I went I was given a bundle of tickets by a swami in orange robes from the Sivananda Yoga Vedanta centre, which then had its London base just off Regent's Park; each ticket gave the right to a free class. I knew the name from the centre I had found in Rishikesh, and Reverend Mataji's orphanage.

Jonathan and I went along to an open class; Jonathan ought to have done a beginner's course first, because he had never received any instruction in yoga at all. He got away with it because he had practised a little by himself from books and was able to do a headstand. The class was taken by Swami Padma; a tall, lanky South African with cropped hair and a fringe beard who taught beautifully and was clearly a spiritual person. The whole place felt spiritual, with a spirituality that was so sure of itself that it needed no pretension. Afterwards we sat round on cushions drinking camomile tea. We both became members of the centre then and there.

The people impressed me deeply because they were utterly uncorrupted. There was no charlatanry, no exploitation; a lesson only cost £1.50, and even this was excused to the poor and unemployed. Many of the same people still run the new centre in Chepstow Villas. The system seems to me to be a good one. Lessons are given according to a format. Individual teachers have their different habits and preferences within the format, so there is in practice a good deal of variation giving a wide perspective on the art, but there is a basic structure and discipline. The class is positioned in lines along the walls of the room, each person staying in his place; there is no breaking off and gathering round the teacher for a demonstration, and nobody feels like talking. Other schools of yoga sometimes teach no breath control until pupils are advanced; the Sivananda centre teaches simple forms of it to beginners, always at the start of the class. I believe this is right, both because breath control – *pranayama* – is such an important part of yoga, and because the practice of it puts a person into a mental condition of calm and receptivity, making him do the postures better. From then on, Jonathan and I went often to the Sivananda centre, sometimes together and sometimes singly.

I went off to a Divine Light Mission festival in Kisemi, Florida, which is near Disneyland. It lasted a week, with three thousand of us living in a temporary town of tents and marquees. I met many friends I had known in the early days, and spent a lot of time around the healing tents, exchanging tips with the masseurs. A husband and wife team of chiropractitioners, Barry O'Shea and his wife, became friends of mine, and I stayed with them for a while in Boston after the festival. They soon had me massaging the occasional client, and in that wonderful open American way they introduced me to all their friends. One of them, Gretchen Pattison, was an expert in colonic irrigation and cross-grain muscle massage, a severe technique which can be quite painful but adds tone to muscles and helps lymphatic drainage. She invited me up to her log cabin in Vermont and taught me both techniques, letting me sit in while she worked and also allowing me to practise on her.

Gretchen was a born again Christian, and like many healers she was attracted to the charismatic movement. I told her all about my addiction, and one day she took me to Father Vanzetti's all-day healing service in a Roman Catholic church in Boston, hoping to rid me of my devil.

There was a choir and a nine piece band, all dressed in little red hats and red and white uniforms, akin to those in a Kentucky Fried Chicken place. They played rock hymns while the church filled with cripples in wheelchairs or with crutches or support collars, blind people with their guide dogs, big black ladies heavily laden with gold chains and crucifixes. When the church was full, Father Vanzetti appeared with his mother. He was a bald, stocky man of Italian appearance with a sensuous mouth and great liquid brown eyes; one liked him at first sight, he exuded compassion and kindness. He took the microphone.

'Stand up, please.'

We stood.

'Now offer your spirits to the Lord! Cry for help and eternal salvation! Call out to the Lord to save one and all!'

We did this; it was a hubbub. He then directed a lady at the back of the church to walk up the aisle. I was near the front but turned to watch; the woman hobbled with the help of crutches.

'Drop your crutches,' said Father Vanzetti. She obeyed, and continued without them.

Father Vanzetti praised the Lord, the band struck up again and the congregation sang. The priest talked of the Lord's mercy, of his prophecies and his gift of intercession.

'Is there anyone here with cancer? I'm calling you. In the name of the Lord Jesus, Son of God, come up, brother, right up here to me, let me heal you, Son, come home to the Lord.' A man came up and received his blessing.

It went on for hours; blacks, whites, children, people of all ages went up to be healed. One couple stricken with arthritis were asked to waltz down the aisle, which they did with apparent ease. A man was told to throw away his neck collar; a limping boy was made to run down the aisle into the arms of the Lord. After each cure Father Vanzetti would thank the Lord, then we would sing.

Then he called out, 'Is there a rape victim here? Up at the front, there's a girl, a foreigner, who has been raped. Come forward and be healed.'

Without hesitation I walked up, it seemed right to do so, for I knew he meant me.

'Where's your home town, dear? Tell them all.'

'Oldham, England,' I said into the mike.

'Come home to your Saviour! You've suffered, but the Lord will heal you.'

With that he laid his arms on my shoulders, and the choir started to sing. I fainted at his feet, slain in the spirit, coming round in my own time in a state of euphoria.

'Let us pray for Shoe's soul, ladies and gentlemen; let us unite in love and thank, yes thank the Lord for the miracle of healing! Go back to your seat now and rejoice.'

I floated off, full of hope and joy, full of awe.

Another hour passed with the congregation approaching a state of mass ecstasy. People flopped to the floor, slain in the spirit, all over the church. Often it was the black women, who were also the keenest to wail 'Save me, Lord, save me!' as they writhed and waved their arms. Such was the mighty power being invoked that Friday.

Suddenly the priest called for a woman living with stomach pains, living in sickness; a woman who'd been in prison. I knew it was my turn again, though I waited to see if anyone else raised a hand. Then I rose.

'Come up again, child, the Lord wants to heal and forgive you. Shoe, lay your head at His feet and ask for mercy and forgiveness. Repent! He'll cleanse you of your sickness, heal you of your sins. Come home, child.'

With that he placed his hand on my head, and again I collapsed like a stringless puppet. I basked in the golden glow from the effulgent altar piece, the voices of the choir, the aura of Father Vanzetti, the soft red carpet under my body.

'Sisters from the church bring you round,' called Father Vanzetti. 'All laud and praise be to Him.'

'Honey,' cried a soul-sister, 'this is your special day; join hands and praise Him today.' I did so.

We left the church at five in the afternoon; the service had taken seven hours. I was in a daze as we drove home; on arrival I went straight to bed. I had felt in touch with the angelic hosts. I left Gretchen for England soon afterwards, full of gratitude; she had given me much.

All this time I had kept up my fruitarian diet, and whether because of that or the healing service, I found I was suddenly vomiting less. One fine day, I didn't do it at all. I returned to the habit next day, but despite setbacks I improved steadily from then on. I stayed with friends and had joyful times with Jonathan; my massage clientele was expanding.

One day in November something happened to me that I had almost forgotten about; I started a period, my first for five years.

The Sivananda centre was organizing a teacher training course in its ashram on Paradise Island in the Bahamas, to start on 1 February.

'Why don't you go on that,' Jonathan said, 'and get a diploma, a qualification? I'll pay for it.' So I booked in.

For Christmas I went off to Cadaques on the bus, and on the journey I felt nausea, nothing to do with bulimia. I thought, I'm getting travel sickness in my old age. When I arrived the odd feeling of being on board a rolling ship didn't leave me; I was definitely queasy. I slunk off to the olive grove and spent Christmas Eve and Christmas Day by myself, eating a crate of oranges and drinking spring water, reading *Autobiography of a Yogi* and *The Nazarene*; for I had caught from Jonathan the habit of reading. I didn't feel up to striding about the mountains; I longed instead for a nest, a haven, everything that was soft and feminine. If I'd had wings at that moment I'd have flown home to Mother.

Days passed in this odd, passive state. I moved to a cave and went to bed in the afternoon, as soon as it got dark. Then as soon as I settled down I usually felt the need to relieve myself; this was happening all day, it was quite a nuisance. My breasts felt uncomfortable as well; they seemed to be getting bigger, firmer. Vaguely I worried about cancer. I was not sorry to get on the bus back to London, but this time I felt seriously sick and kept having to stop the bus to go to the lavatory.

In London I had arranged to stay on the floor of a dear friend, a middle-aged premie, who despite her reverence for the Guru remained a typical cosy Cockney. When I arrived I said, 'Gosh, I'm glad to see the back of that bus; I've been feeling really travel-sick.'

'Travel-sick? That's not like you, the amount of travelling you do. Let's have a look at you.'

She cocked her head on one side, like a mother bird.

'I'll tell you what's up with you,' she finally pronounced. 'You're pregnant.'

'Pregnant? What are you talking about?'

'Course you are, Shoe, look at your face. There's a baby written all over it. I've had three, dear, and I'm a gran as well; you can't tell me nothing about babies. Come on, you sit down and I'll make us a cuppa.'

Shocked, I collapsed into a chair. Could it be true? This continuous nausea, quite unlike the sickness of bulimia which was the affair of a minute or two: this unusual state of mind: and heavens, yes, this firming of the breasts. Had I menstruated lately? No, come to think of it, not for nearly two months. I'd only had one period since resuming after five years, so missing it was not something I noticed. Mr Steptoe, all those years ago when he saw me after the rape, had thought I'd not conceive easily. But he could be wrong.

Suddenly I was convinced. I knew that there was a little being inside me that would grow to be a baby, a child, a person; a friend, a partner. A golden girl; I knew she was a girl, and felt her giving off light like a torch in a scarlet cavern.

I had already planned to take a cottage in Zennor, at the tip of Cornwall, from the family of my friend Anne Fleming who had put me on the plane to Japan and shared my elephant ride in India; now I was glad to be going, I needed quiet and solitude while I was digesting this possibility and finding if it was true. The long train journey passed in a dream; I hoped against hope that my friend's hunch was right. The house at Zennor was a good place for contemplation; damp and mild, among green fields with granite outcrops above a bracken-covered slope that led straight down to the Atlantic Ocean.

Soon after arriving I saw a doctor, who confirmed that I was having a child. Again I felt a surge of joy, but this time there was a worry as well. This might lose me Jonathan's friendship. We had been two free beings, floating in and out of each other's lives on equal terms. Our affair had been joyful, but utterly lighthearted. Perhaps that was all he wanted. One thing was sure, I wasn't having an abortion. I should carry this child to term and look after it, whatever he said or didn't say. I'd never depend on him, never ask him for anything. Nor would I ever reveal who the father was, he could rest assured of that.

At all events he must be told, and at once. I rang him at his office.

'Shoe! Good to hear your voice. Where are you?'

'In Cornwall.'

'Cornwall? Why there?'

'Never mind that. I've got something to tell you.'

His voice became less happy, responding to my unusually brisk manner.

'What's that?'

'I'm having a child. I'm pregnant.'

'Good heavens!'

'If you want me to have an abortion, forget it. I'm having this child whether you like it or not.'

He said something as I was talking, but I paid no attention to him, I was going to have my say. 'This child will be the companion of my old age, we'll be a team, she and I – I know she's a girl. You need never see us and don't worry, I shan't ever give you away.'

'Now look,' he said. 'Of course I'll see you and the child, support you in every way.' And he added something quite unexpected.

'It's an honour, you know that? I feel it an honour to be the father of your child. Naturally I'm not breaking up my marriage or changing my arrangements, we'll have to think a bit about the practical side of things. But I, too, wouldn't want you to have an abortion.'

We discussed the yoga course in the Bahamas, and agreed that I should still go. Pregnant women certainly did yoga, there was a special class for them at the Sivananda centre. I went back to London and talked to the swamis, and they confirmed that I would be quite all right.

'There can be no better place for a pregnancy,' said Swami Padma.

How right he was. I left a grey English February on my cheap flight by Courier Services, and arrived at the tropical sun of Nassau. A short trip in a motor-boat over the sparkling blue sea took us from there to Paradise Island. Sandwiched between the Mediterranean Club and Richard Harris's house, the Sivananda Ashram had tents and octagonal wooden chalets, an open air meditation sanctuary, spaces for hathayoga classes about the size of tennis courts, all set among trees and flowers. There was a long house for when it rained and a communal dining-room under a canopy. All the staff had taken Indian names. Gopala grew the vegetables, Bharata ran the motor-boat. The diet was vegetarian, free of garlic or dairy products. I chose a green-topped tent for us; us, for to me the child and I were already two people. Everyone was given white Indian trousers and loose shirts in sunshine yellow, ideal for my coming expansion round the waist. We rose at 6.00 am and had three two-hour hathayoga sessions a day with lectures and singing in the evening; we also shared in the domestic work of the centre.

At first I was still nibbling and spewing, though the grip of the disease had weakened. Now I told myself, this child needs to grow in peace, not be buffered with these spasms of vomiting. As she becomes conscious they will become as frightening as an Atlantic storm. She might be injured, even battered to death. It was my vomiting or my baby; a choice. Up to now my sickness had only hurt me. Now there was somebody else, a little helpless pink person inside me, more precious than anything I had ever known. For myself alone I was too weak to overcome my bulimia, though Father Vanzetti and the fruit diet had both helped to make it less severe. Love for my child gave me the strength, at last, to stop making myself vomit. It was not a cure; if I do not watch my diet I am sick to this day. But it gave me control.

# 25

# Three Births

Nobody loves massage more than an American alternative unless it's a Canadian one, so in my free time I set up shop as a masseuse. I rigged up a portable table in my tent space, lit a cedarwood joss-stick, and worked away in the sweltering heat. Considering my pregnant condition I probably over-did it, being a typically strenuous Leo, but I earned some dollars to stuff under my pillow. I had someone to save for now. I also got around the island a bit. One afternoon, with another girl, I took a stroll out of the camp and we were invited next door to visit Richard Harris's house. It was another world; film people in smart bathing suits and sunglasses with long cool cocktails sprawled in deckchairs round a luxury pool. My pregnancy earned me a few curious questions. On the other side of our ashram, the rock band at the Club Méditerranée thumped a lullaby every night. These neighbours only served to remind me what an oasis of purity was the four acres of the Sivananda Centre.

When the two-month course ended I was given my diploma, with a respectable grade, but I was in no hurry to leave. I signed up as resident masseuse, in return for a proportion of my earnings. My clients were a kind and generous lot. They offered me three different arrangements for the birth in the United States. I could have given birth holding a sunflower in a birthing commune, or listening to special music in another; someone even promised to pay all my expenses in a high-technology New York clinic. All the same I decided to return to England, and so as not to be debarred from travelling by air I flew back towards the end of my seventh month.

I installed myself in a basement room at the Sivananda Centre in Albany Street, London. I thought, here I am aged thirty-seven, and after seventeen years of travelling and searching I at last have a place of my own. The traces of mildew on the walls showed that the room was damp most of the year, but in the hot summer of 1981 its cool was ideal. I had it painted candy pink and peppermint green; there was no furniture, so I grouped boxes together, draped them with fabric and made them into tables; I also acquired a couple of bean-bags. The window looked out on to a wall; I had this painted white and hung flower baskets from black wrought iron poles. Jonathan used to come often, and we walked in Regent's Park which was out the back, enjoying the rose gardens and the beds with begonias and delphiniums, listening to the band.

I took a train to the Elephant Fair on Lord Eliot's estate near St Germans in Cornwall; all the alternatives in England seemed to be gathered there. I was huge by now and not very active, but there was a lot to see: conjuring acts, village dancing, acid rock sessions, a kite display, palmists, yoga demonstrations. I settled in the debate tent and listened to Dora Russell, John Michell, Rupert Sheldrake and others. They talked about all sorts of things: Neanderthal man, fertility rites, the superiority of the old measurements over the metric system. I then went to stay in Devon with Dr Michael Ash, who had given up a Harley Street practice to do alternative medicine. I was suffering from oedema, swollen wrists and ankles. Dr Ash put me up in his summer house for two days and directed me in a water purification course, fifteen pints a day. This was completely successful.

Despite my size I still taught yoga classes twice a week; but I stopped this when a student fell out of a head stand and I could not move fast enough to catch him. One baking day I took train and taxi to Hove and sat, enormous in a bikini, on the hot sand among the multitudes. A man came up to me, shook my hand and asked if I was a Russian. Then I ran into the sea and splashed about like a great whale. This was a last burst of high energy before the onset of labour next day.

It had been an ideal pregnancy; I wish I could say the same of the birth. On the evening of Sunday 30 August I started mild contractions so I thought, time to go into the Middlesex hospital. I brought my sandalwood worry beads and a cassette machine to play Indian chants; I planned to sing along with these to help ease the birth. But I had another think coming. Directly I delivered myself to the hospital it was as if I became a piece of equipment carried on a conveyor belt for processing. It was Bank Holiday weekend, and I am sure it was this that made them so determined to hurry everything up.

At seven in the evening I was strapped down to an alien-looking machine for monitoring, and my arm attached to a saline drip feed. I was only $1\frac{1}{2}$ centimetres dilated at that stage, but the night nurse decided to rupture the membrane. I can see her now, hoisting herself on to the bed to get a purchase and hacking away at something that was not yet ready to burst, finally rupturing it by main force. They gave me an injection to hasten the contractions, then gas and air, then a doctor in a white coat came and prescribed an epidural. Nobody smiled or chatted; I was a job to them, not a person. Two nurses were sitting outside the delivery room, knitting; one or other of them peeped at me between rows. Another walked briskly in, read the monitoring machine, then disappeared without glancing in my direction. Each time there was a contraction I sounded a chant into my abdomen; the knitters giggled, but they were embarrassed, not amused, clearly thinking I was off my head.

The final humiliation came at 6 am, eleven hours after I had got on to that bed. The dilation was still only 7 centimetres, whereas 12 centimetres are necessary if the baby is to come through; and my child's heart had begun to peter out. Someone handed me a paper agreeing to an emergency Caesarian section; I signed. By now my friend Clio had arrived, a trainee nurse at the hospital and a fine yogini. I entrusted her with my pearl pendant and teeth, telling everyone present that she was to be the guardian of the baby if I did not survive. Clang went the emergency bell, and I was whisked down the corridor on a trolley. Next moment, as it seemed, I was looking at a little pink creature with a mouth like a tearose, and the long night was forgotten. The Venus de Milo, I said to myself, and I took her into my arms. Eventually I registered her as Diana Gloria Isolde Rose Dimilo Taylor; I hope having so many names will not be a bore for her.

Clio had assured me that aftercare at the Middlesex was the best in London. It was good, I think, but it needed to be. As soon as I got mobile I started nosing around, hobbling at first like a bent peasant in a Japanese rice paddy. I looked at the notes displayed over the cots. There were many Caesarians, and of the rest not one seemed to have escaped without episiotomy and high forceps delivery. Well, one lives and learns.

While in hospital I had received a notice to quit my room at the Sivananda centre as the centre itself was having to leave the premises In any case I should not have wanted to stay with a baby in a damp basement as winter approached. A kind friend gave me accommodation in her house in Fulham while she was away, in exchange for looking after her two Burmese cats; graceful creatures who eyed Diana with a cold stare as if to say, we are the ones who should be getting all this attention. I spent a lot of time in my friend's lovely brass bed feeding Diana, from the breast of course, and listening to classical music; but there was also a lot of washing, of Diana herself and her nappies. I dressed her in white Victorian lace for when Jonathan came; she was the sweetest little thing

I had ever seen. We had her christened at St Peter's, Fulham; among friends who came was Rachel Pinney. Cosima Fry, Lord Londonderry's daughter, was chief godmother and gave a little party in her house; she was a dear friend, regularly visiting me and bringing exotic cheeses; normally I am not a believer in dairy products, but when breast feeding I make an exception.

When my Fulham arrangement came to an end I moved with Diana first to Cornwall, then to Hay-on-Wye. This is a great centre of the book trade; whoever suggested it to me felt that I might find massage clients among all those intellectuals. Before I went, one of my closest friends said:

'But that's where my aunt lives, Penelope Betjeman, wife of Sir John. She sometimes lets out part of her house and I don't think she's got a tenant at the moment. You and she would get on.'

I installed myself in a small bed and breakfast place in the village, and asked the landlady where Lady Betjeman lived.

'Oh, it's way up in the hills,' she said. 'Can't say as I've ever been there, The New House they call it.'

I hired a mini and drove up there, following a map; from my landlady I had the impression that it was at the back of beyond, but really it was only two or three miles, though the road was steep. It wasn't a new house at all but quite an old one, with an extension and some outbuildings. Across the road was a tatty pine forest. The place looked suitable. I didn't call in then and there, but got hold of the ex-directory number and telephoned. A self-confident, rather cockney voice answered. I told her I was a friend of her niece who had thought she might have some rooms to let.

'I'll need to meet you,' she said, 'can you find me?'

'Certainly, I passed your house earlier today.'

'Very well then, my dear: two o'clock tomorrow.'

I turned up with Diana. The door was opened by this rather short, chunky old lady with grey hair in a page-boy cut and bright brown eyes in a weather-beaten face. Her manner was bossy and downright, yet she had charm and one could sense a great underlying kindness. Her voice had a sort of comic harshness to it that made everything she said sound amusing.

'I don't believe it!' she cried. As I was to discover, this was one of her catch-phrases. 'You've got a baba; you didn't tell me that.'

'She's not much trouble.'

Penelope considered for a bit; Diana gave a winning smile. Naturally I had her looking her best. 'All right, I'll take you. You can have the whole extension.' This consisted of a big living-room with cooking area, two bedrooms and a bathroom; it had its own staircase.

Penelope was one of the great teachers in my life, for she had so many sides. She was a deeply religious Catholic, yet as an expert on Indian art she had absorbed, partly I think without knowing it, a great deal of Hindu philosophy. She was a countrywoman who didn't a bit mind being alone, yet she had so many friends from London and Oxford and elsewhere that at times she seemed the most social person on earth. She tried to find me a husband.

'I'll take you to tea with the Hugheses,' she said. 'The son's very eligible.'

They were a dear old couple in their eighties who owned a thousand acres or more. Mrs Hughes gave us a lovely old-fashioned English tea with scones and Welsh cakes. We ate by the light of candles as there was no electric light, and all the water came from a well – there were buckets and bowls of it all over the floor. The son came in, aged about fifty, tongue-tied and shaped like a turnip. Neither of us fancied the other.

Penelope did have electric light, but it came from an engine which also pumped up the water and turned itself off at night. The house was heated by wood stoves which were efficient but used a lot of fuel; life revolved around keeping them fed. Penelope had permission to gather unusable branches from the Forestry Commission wood across the road. Every day she and I and Diana and Sambo, her black pekinese, set out on the flat cart drawn by Bracken the pony, and collected wood which then had to be sawn into logs and stacked in her outhouse. I was a tenant, not an employee, but she had me working hard for her, never flagging or complaining but rarely getting a compliment. This did not worry me in the least; I knew perfectly well that she appreciated what I did, but she was a no-nonsense character like Oki Sensei or one of the Himalayan *sadhus* who were her friends. I soon mastered the art of chain-sawing, though I remember Penelope exclaiming:

'*Do* be careful of Baba's head!'

Penelope rode a lot, and sometimes put me on the end of a lunging rein. She also taught me how to make bonfires, real professional ones that burned for two or three days. We walked the lanes together; I shocked her by knowing very few wild flowers by name. She scolded me for this, and from then on our walks became lessons in natural history. She liked my hathayoga, though, and encouraged me to teach it to her guests. She also found massage clients for me, horsewomen mainly and fellow Roman Catholics she knew from church. Where we differed was in diet. She ate little meat, but was far too fond of sugar in every form. I used sometimes to tell her that her sweet tooth was making her overweight. She in turn never understood how I could exist on mainly raw foods without meat and with hardly any bread; nor of course did she realize that if I had eaten in her way I should have been sick, and might have gone back to my bulimia. Penelope was a good cook, and at first used to offer me some of what she made; but when it was fudge, or egg custard, I turned it down. The only thing she could always get me to accept was her sorrel soup. In this matter, though in no other, it was my influence that prevailed. She gave up sweets and had dried fruits instead; raisins, coconut or dried pineapple.

As winter approached she buried potatoes and carrots in clamps, and prayed to St Swithin that we should be snow-bound for at least a few days. Being cut off was her great joy, because it tested her Girl Guide resourcefulness. The road was steep, so it happened quite often. The year I was there St Swithin was generous; we were marooned for nearly a fortnight. Penelope was glad of the thermalactic underwear I had given her though at first she had rather turned up her nose at it, preferring her pashmina silk long combinations and vest even though they were in holes. We did a lot of tobogganing, scrambling out into the forest with 'Baba' looking like a tiny Abominable Snowman.

She had a plan to retire on a plot of land in Llandridnod Wells near a convent. Somehow this didn't ring true to me; I found it impossible to imagine her as a frail old person in a protected environment. Sure enough, it didn't happen. She died suddenly in the Himalayas a year or two later, leading a party on a hike, which was what she liked doing most in the world. I cried a lot when I heard this, but it was the best death one could have wished for her.

I left her after about a year, to go back to Cadaques. Jonathan was going there quite a lot in 1982 and 1983 to write his book *The House of Mitford*. I took a little beach house so that we could be together when he came. One day in May, 1983, we climbed the peak at the back of the Montaña Negra. In the sun and the breeze under the pale bell-tent of the sky it seemed unimportant that we had brought nothing with us.

As soon as I realized I was pregnant again, I wrote off to Dr Michel Odent, the gynaecologist who practises natural birth in his clinic at Pithiviers not far from Paris. I had cut out an article about him in a magazine and kept it, just in case; for I was resolved never again to undergo a high-technology birth. The fact that my thirty-ninth birthday was approaching didn't worry me in the least; nor did my Caesarian scar. I was convinced I could pull it off the natural way, and in any case Dr Odent had all the facilities available, the article assured me.

Weeks went by, and months, and there was no reply. More direct methods were needed. In October, with Jonathan's help, I rented a house next door to Tini Duchamp in Villiers-sous-Grez; her daughter Jacky Monnier also lives in the village, and Jacky and I motored over to Pithiviers.

Dr Odent was delighted to accept me. He gave me a thorough examination.

'There should be no problem,' he said. 'The scar has healed perfectly; we often deliver babies naturally after a Caesarian. Also for mothers a lot older than you.'

'I wrote to you,' I said, 'and you didn't answer.'

'Come here,' he said, and led me into an adjoining office where there was an enormous pile of unopened letters. 'I expect your letter is among those. Nobody's got the time to answer them, we are too busy delivering babies.'

During that waiting time at Villiers I massaged Tini every other day and we renewed our friendship. I think she found me saner than when I had stayed with her before, in the grip of my bulimia. Three times a week I drove my Volkswagen camper to the Pithiviers clinic to take part in sessions of singing and yoga; sometimes we danced, I remember dancing with Dr Odent to the theme tune from Dr Zhivago. All this was part of his preparatory treatment.

The contractions started on the morning of 14 February 1984, and I motored over to the clinic, which was by now a familiar place. Sister Sharon, a trainee from Boston, Massachusetts, devoted her entire day to me. She brought her lunch and cassette player into the environmental labour room and simply stayed around. There was no bed in it, just some orange iron and plastic chairs stacked up against modernistic murals of odd-looking women giving birth to peculiar babies. At regular intervals a French midwife popped in to check on my progress. I wore no clothes; this felt right. Sharon talked to me, sometimes we danced, but she offered me no drugs; no pity either when the contractions became excruciatingly painful.

What patience that girl had! The labour went on for sixteen hours. About half an hour before the birth I did weaken, but Sister Sharon cried, 'Throw your shoulders back, take some deep breaths and soldier on.'

It was exactly right. If at that moment she had softened and comforted me I should have collapsed and pleaded for pain killers, which were in fact readily available. After a bit the midwife came in, examined me, and with her little finger simply popped the bulging membrane; fleetingly I remembered the struggle this had been for the nurse at the Middlesex. These things, it seems, are so easy when the moment has come.

No trolley was needed this time. I walked to the delivery room, which was like a bachelor girl's pad with brightly coloured floor cushions, a bed on a dais; there was also a wooden birthing chair. The walls were painted in primary colours, the lights were low. Two midwives held me, one by each arm. I felt the baby's head trying to emerge; one hard push and out she rocketed.

'Tiger!' I shouted, as Aster emerged. It is still one of her nicknames.

Ten minutes later, as I lay with my baby, a girl appeared clad only in a tee-shirt, a Scots lass who had flown in the day before from Edinburgh. She proceeded to have her baby there in front of me. I wondered why she was wearing her tee-shirt; some sort of modesty? I moved to my own bedroom which I shared with a charming Malay, and fell into a profound sleep.

Dr Odent had been away, but he came back next day and we all had a picnic on biscuits and fruit juice. I asked the Scots girl why she had been wearing a tee-shirt.

'It's my judo club tee-shirt,' she said. 'I wore it for luck.' It transpired that she was a black belt.

Diana, Aster and I went to live in Cornwall, in a little house rented from Anne Fleming's mother. While living there, I gave birth to my son Thomas on 10 January, 1986. This gave rise to a battle of wits between me and the authorities, which in the end I won on points, though only just. Until ten days before delivery I assumed I should have a natural delivery in the Bolitho Clinic at Penzance; but when I went to see the resident obstetrician he squashed that idea after one look at my notes, before even examining me.

'You're forty-one,' he said, 'and you've had a Caesarian. All sorts of things could go wrong, I'm not taking responsibility. You must go to Truro.'

Truro, where the high-tech hospital was. The Royal Middlesex all over again.

'But I've had a natural birth in France, *after* the Caesarian! Nothing went wrong then, why should it go wrong now?'

'You were lucky,' he said, 'and your luck might not hold. You are a high-risk patient.' I could not budge him. It was a terrible feeling. As a single parent one must be able to trust one's doctors, count on them as friends. Oh, this man meant well, but I'd been through both sorts of birth, and my experience told me that he was sending me to be butchered. I went to my own doctor who supported the obstetrician; he even made out that I was wasting everyone's time by my complaints.

Then I became angry. They were not going to have their will; at any rate I would not go unprotected into this ordeal. Time wasn't on my side; I felt the baby's head engage, it would not be long now. I got on the telephone, talked to people, and finally unearthed Sister Goldstone, a retired Queen's Midwife, loved by all her patients. She agreed to come out of retirement for my delivery. Goldie proved a Godsend.

She was already with me when the ambulance arrived, and accompanied me to the high-tech hospital. The labour was going much faster this time; I was so far dilated that on arrival they ushered me into a side room. The hospital midwife I was allocated busied herself with moving all sorts of machines into the room; I was happy for her to get on with this futile pursuit as Goldie and I proceeded with the real business of the hour on the floor in a corner. At last the hospital midwife got the saline drip fixed up to her satisfaction, then she turned to me and said she'd like to rupture my membrane. I refused to let her do this, but agreed to get on to the bed when she said she knew nothing about delivering on the floor. I seized the bed-head rail and hung on it like an ape, just in time to watch my son, nine pounds of him, slither into Goldie's expert hands. The other midwife immediately injected my leg for a smash and grab placenta delivery; let her have it, I thought. It was lucky that the whole thing had only taken two hours, otherwise there would have been more problems. Oh, I had to have two stitches. They dressed me in bottle green and wheeled me into the operating theatre to have this done.

'Are these necessary?' I asked the male nurse.

'Not really, Madam, but I'd better do them, now you've been sent to me.' So he did.

I looked around. Everyone in that theatre looked rigid, stiff; there was no joy. One might as well have given birth in a morgue. But on the whole I'd had my way, and I also had my son.

There is not much more to say. All my life I have never had much idea of what the future might hold, and I still haven't. For now, my life is tranquil. Mostly it is occupied with the children, but I run what amounts to a mobile massage service, and also cut a few people's hair. Lately I have begun dressing up to do vaudeville and Old Time Music Hall acts at amateur benefit concerts to raise money for cancer victims, handicapped children, disabled riders. I swim, I ride, I practise a lot of yoga. When Jonathan comes we walk the coastal paths together.

What have I picked up in my odd life? Some skills, some knowledge of people, some experience of beauty and of spirituality, a great deal of awareness of what to avoid. I have felt God's goodness and power manifested in a number of different beliefs, and can state from my direct experience that He is not, as we are told, a jealous God. I am glad the Church in whose faith I was brought up no longer insists that He is. I have also learnt something else, after being imprisoned, degraded and disgustingly addicted; namely that it is always possible to bounce back. If I have passed this confidence on to even one of my readers, it will have been worth while allowing Jonathan to write this book.